全国高职高专医药院校“十三五”规划教材

供临床医学、护理、助产、中医、药学、医学相关技术各专业使用

# 医护职业英语


主　编　江晓东　冉凌云　邬文婷

副主编　郑雪茜　余仕湖　庞　凌

编　委　(以姓氏笔画为序)

王炎峰　冉凌云　邬文婷　刘　军

江晓东　余仕湖　陈琰晗　庞　凌

郑雪茜　贾雪宁


U0913195


華中科技大學出版社

http://www.hustp.com

中国·武汉

# 内容简介

本书是全国高职高专医药院校“十三五”规划教材之一。全书分为10个单元。每单元包括提高学生相关信息收集能力的医学图表、提高学生医护职业场景会话能力的情景对话及提高浅显医护英语文章阅读能力的医学相关文章。

本书根据教育部高教司颁布的《高职高专教育英语课程教学基本要求（试行）》的相关内容，参考全国医护英语水平考试（METS）大纲的部分要求，针对职业院校医药类学生的具体情况进行编写。本书体现“实用为主”“够用为度”的思路，力图使教学内容与学生职业场景相结合。

本书供医药类普通专科、高职专科、成人专科临床医学、中医、药学、护理、医学相关技术各专业学生学习，亦可供有初步英语基础的医护人员在职自主学习。

**图书在版编目(CIP)数据**

医护职业英语/江晓东，冉凌云，邬文婷主编. —武汉：华中科技大学出版社，2016.8
ISBN 978-7-5680-2094-7

Ⅰ.①医… Ⅱ.①江… ②冉… ③邬… Ⅲ.①医学-英语-医学院校-教材 Ⅳ.①H31

中国版本图书馆CIP数据核字(2016)第183887号

**医护职业英语** 江晓东 冉凌云 邬文婷 主编
Yihu Zhiye Yingyu

策划编辑：车 巍
责任编辑：刘 平
封面设计：原色设计
责任校对：李 琴
责任监印：周治超
出版发行：华中科技大学出版社（中国·武汉） 电话：(027)81321913
武汉市东湖新技术开发区华工科技园 邮编：430223
录 排：华中科技大学惠友文印中心
印 刷：武汉华工鑫宏印务有限公司
开 本：787mm×1092mm 1/16
印 张：16
字 数：386千字
版 次：2019年1月第1版第6次印刷
定 价：42.00元

本书若有印装质量问题，请向出版社营销中心调换
全国免费服务热线：400-6679-118 竭诚为您服务
版权所有 侵权必究

# 序言

XUYAN

为更新英语课堂教学的内容和方式，更好地为医护专业人才培养服务，我们组织有关教师和医护专业人员，根据《医护英语入门教程》在课堂教学中的使用反馈，对原教材进行了大量修改和补充，编写了该教程。本书按照《高职高专教育英语课程教学基本要求（试行）》的相关内容，参考全国医护英语水平考试（METS）大纲的部分要求，针对职业院校医药类学生的具体情况进行编写。其目的是通过情景会话、专业阅读训练，培养医药类学生在实际工作中综合应用英语的能力。

编者力图在本书编写过程中针对职业院校医药类各专业学生的英语基础学力和学习心理特点，以专门用途英语的相关理论为指导，把英语教学的新模式与医药科学的新知识、新进展、新观念有机整合，使本书内容新颖、充实，注重实用性和时代性，强化以学生发展为本的理念，适应课堂任务型教学和注重学生自主学习能力培养。

本书共10单元。医学图表部分旨在提高学生学习兴趣和培养学生从医学图表中获取重要信息的能力。情景对话部分以医疗服务流程中常见情景为题材，学习者可以根据这些对话，学会用英语准确流利地与患者或同事沟通。课文分为三部分：第一部分以医药领域新进展为主题，希望学生在英语阅读中积累医药核心词汇，同时了解医药领域的信息和资讯；第二部分是以医院为背景的英文故事，旨在培养学生英文阅读能力的同时提高其人文素养，使其体验患者和医护人员的情感世界；第三部分以常见人类疾病为主题，涉及这些疾病的概念、症状、治疗、预防等，通过这些短文的阅读，学习者能够熟悉和掌握高频医学词汇。课后练习含相关词汇练习、阅读理解练习和翻译练习。全书附录包括常见医学词汇的词干、前缀和后缀，医用拉丁语缩略语，医用英语缩写词，对话部分文本，课文翻译，课后参考答案，医护英语水平测试样题及其参考答案。

本教程编写工作分工如下：第一单元和 Appendix F 由余仕湖（重庆三峡医药高等专科学校）编写；第二单元和 Appendix G 由庞凌（重庆三峡医药高等专科学校）编写；第三单元由贾雪宁（重庆三峡医药高等专科学校）编写；第四单元由郑雪茜（重庆三峡医药高等专科学校）编写；第五单元由邬文婷（重庆三峡医药高等专科学校）编写；第六单元、第七单元和 Appendix D 由冉凌云（昆明医科大学护理学院）编写；Appendix A 由王炎峰（重庆医药高等专科学校）编写；Appendix C 由陈琰晗（重庆医科大学护理学院）编写；Appendix B 由刘军（河南信阳职业技术学院）编写；第八单元、第九单元、第十单元和 Appendix E 由江晓东

(重庆三峡医药高等专科学校)编写。

本书课文选材时,我们参阅了大量网上和报刊资料,对这些资料的作者和提供者表示衷心感谢。在本书编写过程中,我们还得到了昆明医科大学护理学院李保刚副教授、美国南卡罗来纳州英语教师 Temple Sterling 及昆明医科大学外语部的菲律宾教师 Maryknoll De Jesus 的大力帮助,重庆三峡医药高等专科学校教师 Stuart Dodson 和 Kayla Loving 对本书修订提出了宝贵建议,在此一并表示衷心感谢。

鉴于时间紧迫和编者能力有限,书中可能还存在错漏之处,敬请本教材使用者批评指正。

(特别提示:缩略语仅供阅读英文专业材料时参考,非临床使用标准;本教材所提供的信息也不能替代专业医护咨询或诊治。)

编　者

2016 年 6 月

# Content

# Unit One

## Learning Objectives

1. To seek and gather information about medical equipment, external human organs and CPR techniques from the pictures and charts.
2. To understand how to receive a patient in English.
3. To remember the commonly used medical terms and understand the texts.
4. To know how to write a birth certificate in English.

# Part One Pictures & Charts

## Ⅰ. Medical Instruments

**Direction: Label the pictures below using the words in the box.**

| | |
|---|---|
| stomach irrigator (洗胃机) | sputum aspirator (电动吸痰器) |
| simple respirator (简易呼吸器) | respirator (呼吸器) |

1

2

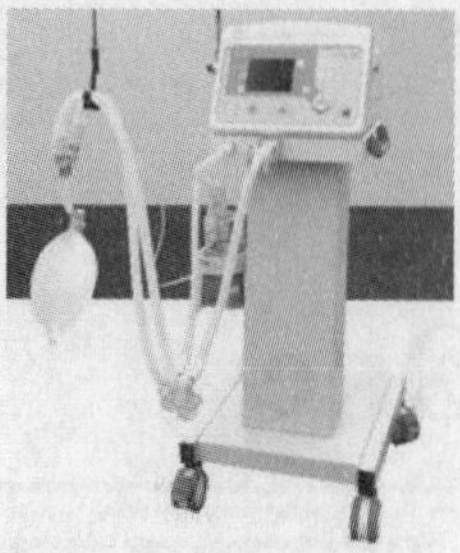

3

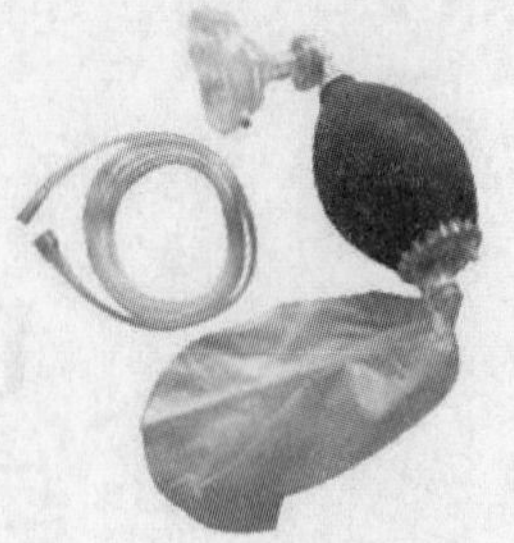

4

1. ______________________________
2. ______________________________
3. ______________________________
4. ______________________________

## New Words & Phrases

irrigator/ˈɪrɪgeɪtə/*n.* 灌溉车,灌注器

sputum/ˈspjuːtəm/*n.* 痰

aspirator/ˈæspɪreɪtə(r)/*n.* 吸液器,吸出器

respirator/ˈrespəreɪtə(r)/*n.* (人工)呼吸器

## Ⅱ. External Human Organs

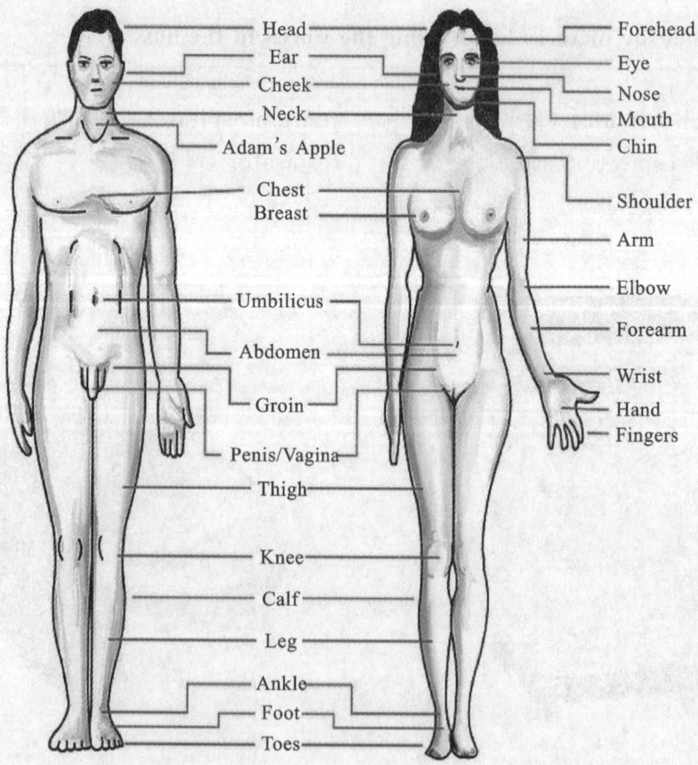

**Direction: Translate the following words into Chinese.**

1. umbilicus/ʌmˈbɪlɪkəs/ ______
2. abdomen/ˈæbdəmən/ ______
3. groin/grɔɪn/ ______
4. calf ______
5. ankle ______

## Ⅲ. First Aid: Cardiopulmonary Resuscitation (CPR)

Step One

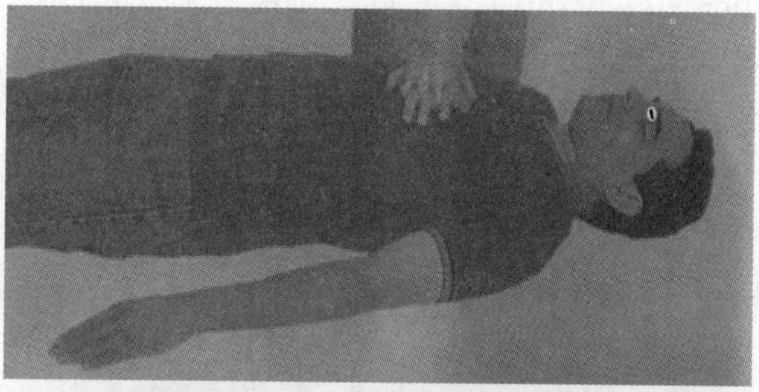

Step Two

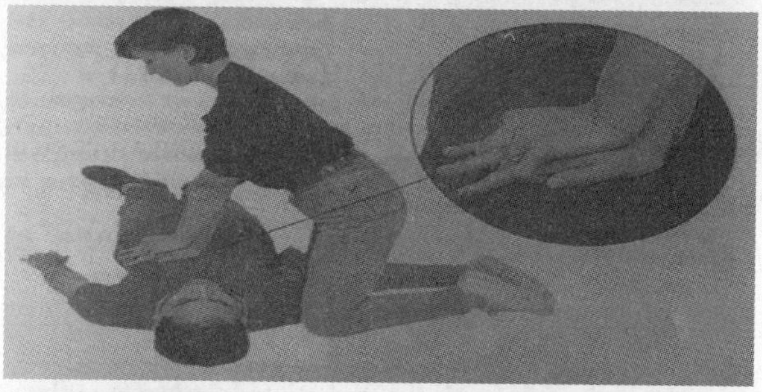

Step Three

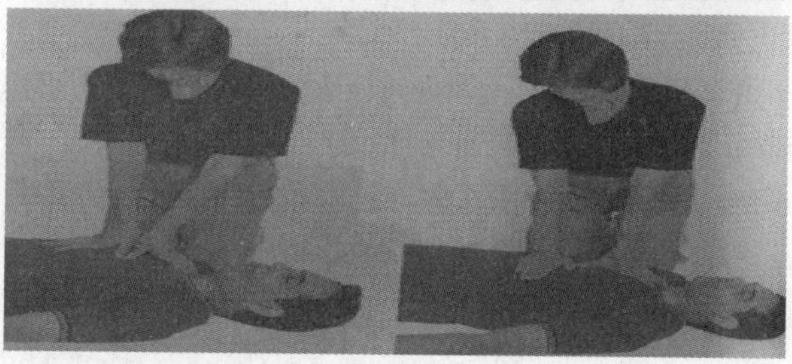

**Direction: Arrange the following steps in proper sequence based on the medical procedure.**

______ Continue CPR: Complete 15 compressions, give two effective breaths (EAR), continue compressions and breaths in ratio of 15:2 at a rate of 4 cycles per minute, check the pulse about every minute.

______ Keep the thumb of one hand in position and place the heel of the other hand on the top of the first hand, and interlock fingers of both hands.

______ Commence chest compressions: Position yourself vertically above the casualty's chest, with your arms straight, press down on the breastbone to depress it about 4-5 cm, release the pressure.

________ Position hands for CPR: Place the casualty on his/her back, find the groove at the neck between the collarbones, find the lower end of the breastbone by running fingers along the last rib to the centre of the body, extend the thumbs equal distances to meet in the middle of the breastbone.

## New Words & Phrases

cardiopulmonary/ˌkɑːdɪəʊˈpʌlmənəri/*adj*. 心肺的
resuscitation/rɪˌsʌsɪˈteɪʃn/*n*. 恢复知觉，苏醒
ratio/ˈreɪʃiəʊ/*n*. 比，比率
vertically/ˈvɜːtɪkli/*adv*. 垂直地，直立地
casualty/ˈkæʒuəlti/*n*. 受害者，死伤者

# Part Two Listening Comprehension

## Situation Dialogue: Receiving a Patient

**Task One Watch Episode One and fill in the missing words referring to the original text. Then check your writing against the original.**

Doctor: Good morning. I am Doctor Sterling. How can I help you?

Patient: Good morning, doctor. I am Emily. I have a ________ and ________ ________ since yesterday.

Doctor: Oh, did you take your temperature?

Patient: Yes, I did. The highest temperature was 39.8 ℃ at 11pm last night. I took one pill of aspirin and feel much better.

Doctor: Any other symptoms?

Patient: I have a ________ ________ and ________, too.

Doctor: OK, let me take your temperature first. Please keep this thermometer under your armpit for 5 minutes. Open your mouth and say "Ah", please. Your tonsils and larynx are red and swollen. Your temperature is 38.5 ℃. Your breathing sounds are normal and there is no problem with your lungs. You'd better take the ________ ________, OK? This paper is for the lab test.

Patient: Sure. I really hope I get better as soon as possible. See you later.

**Task Two Watch Episode Two and complete the answers according to the questions.**

1. What does the result of the blood test indicate?
   The result indicates that the patient has an ________ respiratory tract infection.
2. If fever persists, what should the patient do?
   The patient should ________ ________ if fever persists.

3. How many times a day should the patient take the medicine?
   The patient should take it ________ ________ a day.

# Part Three Reading Comprehension

## Ⅰ. Medical Horizon

### Influenza A Vaccine

Vaccines are available to protect against H1N1 influenza. These vaccines are made just like seasonal flu vaccines. They are expected to be safe and effective.

The vaccine is approved for people from 2 through 49 years of age who are not pregnant and do not have certain health conditions. You should not get it if you have a severe allergy to eggs, or to any other substance in the vaccine.

It should not be given to the following groups:

- children younger than 2 and adults 50 years and older,
- pregnant women,
- anyone with a weakened immune system,
- anyone with a long-term health problem such as heart, kidney, liver, or lung disease, and other blood disorders,
- children younger than 5 years with asthma or one or more episodes of wheezing during the past year,
- anyone with certain muscle or nerve disorders that can lead to breathing or swallowing problems,
- anyone in close contact with a person with a severely weakened immune system,
- children or adolescents on long-term aspirin treatment.

If you are moderately or severely ill, you might be advised to wait until you recover before getting the vaccine. If you have a mild cold or other illness, there is usually no need to wait.

The risks are expected to be similar to those from seasonal vaccine:

**Mild Problems (In children and adolescents 2 to 17 years of age)**

- runny nose, nasal congestion, or cough
- headache and muscle aches
- fever
- wheezing
- abdominal pain or occasional vomiting or diarrhea

**Mild Problems (In adults 18 to 49 years of age)**

- runny nose or nasal congestion

• cough, chills, tiredness/weakness
• sore throat
• headache

**Severe Problems**

• Life-threatening allergic reactions from vaccines are very rare. If they do occur, it is usually within a few minutes to a few hours after the vaccination.

## New Words & Phrases

influenza/ˌɪnflʊ'enzə/*n.* 流行性感冒
allergy/'ælədʒi/*n.* 过敏症，反感
allergic *adj.* 过敏的，对……极讨厌的
pregnant/'pregnənt/*adj.* 怀孕的，怀胎的
immune/ɪ'mjuːn/*adj.* 免疫的，有免疫力的
asthma/'æsmə/*n.* 气喘（病），哮喘
nasal/'neɪz(ə)l/*adj.* 鼻的
wheeze/wiːz/*v.* 发出气喘声　*vt.* 气喘地说　*n.* 喘鸣音
congestion/kən'dʒestʃən/*n.* 拥塞，挤满，充血
abdominal/æb'dɒmɪn(ə)l/*adj.* 腹部的
diarrhea/ˌdaɪə'riə/*n.* 腹泻
nasal congestion 鼻塞

## Exercises

**Task One　Choose the best answer to each of the following questions according to the text.**

1. What's the purpose of making these vaccines?
A. They are available to protect against seasonal influenza.
B. They are available to protect against H1N1 influenza.
C. They are available to protect against swine flu.
D. They are available to protect against cancer.

2. The vaccine is approved for people ________.
A. from 2 through 49 years of age who are pregnant
B. from 2 through 49 years of age who have certain health conditions
C. in any age
D. from 2 through 49 years of age who are not pregnant and do not have certain health conditions

3. The vaccine should not be given to ________.
A. anyone with a weakened immune system
B. children or adolescents on long-term aspirin treatment

C. anyone with a long-term health problem such as heart, kidney, liver, or lung disease, and other blood disorders

D. all of the above

4. Which are NOT the symptoms of a mild problem in children and adolescents 2 to 17 years of age?

A. Runny nose, nasal congestion, or cough.

B. Sore throat.

C. Headache and muscle aches.

D. Abdominal pain or occasional vomiting or diarrhea.

5. What are the mild problems in adults 18 to 49 years of age?

A. Runny nose or nasal congestion.

B. Cough, chills, tiredness/weakness.

C. Sore throat, headache.

D. All of the above.

**Task Two Fill in the blanks with the words given below. Make changes if necessary.**

**approve pregnant allergy wheeze expect**

1. It is unwise to smoke during ________.

2. He is ________ to cats.

3. The Council hasn't ________ the plans yet.

4. By the time he reached the top of the stairs he was panting and ________.

5. We fully ________ it to be a complete disaster.

# Ⅱ. Hospital Story

## Life and Death in Syria's Hospital

A father burst through the hospital doors, a blood-drenched son in his arms. A young man followed close behind, his face blown open in the latest air raids. In the hospital's reception area, a little girl cried as doctors stitched a foot torn open. A boy, 11, quietly passed away on his hospital bed, and his father wept. A nurse pushed through the crowd and blood splattered across her white uniform and headscarf.

This is an average day at this hospital in central Aleppo. Every day, about 70 to 100 patients pass through the doors here, 80 percent of which are civilians.

Volunteer medic Haleq, 24, was a veterinary student before the revolution began and now plays a key role. When fighting broke out in the streets of Aleppo, hundreds of doctors fled, leaving just a handful of trained professionals to deal with the medical crisis.

"These doctors made their fortune off the people, but when they were needed most, they left. Where is their humanity?" he asked.

Most patients arrive here on the back of pick-up trucks. Although torturous and potentially fatal, transporting patients this way cannot be avoided. Of the hospital's five ambulances, only one remains. The lone ambulance driver, Sadeen, who before was a wedding dress designer, said "Before I designed only for women. Now I work for all humanity." When an explosion rocked the street outside the hospital, civilians ran for cover. Several doctors raced toward the sound of the blast to look for survivors. Sadeen rushed to his van.

"My family has to flee the city. But I can't leave my post," said one of the nurses. Like many of the doctors, none of these women had prior experience in medicine. But now they are practically experts in the treatment of trauma patients.

Sitting outside on the curb, Haleq took a break from the madness. To his right, the body of a man and a boy were covered with a blue sheet, waiting to be identified. "In time, the death becomes normal," he said, surveying the scene. "Maybe we have lost our ability to feel... maybe."

## New Words & Phrases

drenched/drentʃd/*adj*. 湿透的，充满的
raid/reɪd/*n*. 袭击，突袭
stitch/stɪtʃ/*n*. 针脚，线迹　*v*. 缝，缝合
splatter/ˈsplætə/*v*. 飞溅
humanity/hjʊˈmænɪti/*n*. 人类，人道，仁慈
torturous/ˈtɔːtʃərəs/*adj*. 折磨人的，痛苦的
rock/rɒk/*n*. 岩石，摇滚乐，暗礁　*v*. 摇动，使摇晃
blast/blɑːst/*n*. 爆炸，冲击波　*v*. 爆炸
trauma/ˈtrɔːmə/*n*. 创伤，外伤
curb/kɜːb/*n*. 路边

**Task One　Translate the following sentences into Chinese.**

1. A nurse pushed through the crowd and blood splattered across her white uniform and headscarf.

2. "These doctors made their fortune off the people, but when they were needed most, they left. Where is their humanity?" he asked.

3. When an explosion rocked the street outside the hospital, civilians ran for cover. Several doctors raced toward the sound of the blast to look for survivors. Sadeen rushed to his van.

## Ⅲ. Human Diseases

### Common Cold

The common cold, also known as an upper respiratory tract infection, is a contagious illness that can be caused by a number of different types of viruses. Because of the great number of viruses that can cause a cold and because new cold viruses develop, the body never builds up resistance against all of them. For this reason, colds are a frequent and recurring problem.

Symptoms of a common cold include nasal stuffiness and drainage, sore throat, hoarseness, cough, and perhaps a fever and headache. Many people with a cold feel tired and achy. These symptoms typically last from 3 to 10 days.

Colds often get better within a few days to weeks, whether or not you take medication. However, a cold virus can pave the way for other infections to invade the body, including sinus or ear infections, and bronchitis. If you have asthma, chronic bronchitis, or emphysema, your symptoms may be worsened for many weeks even after your cold has gone away.

The common cold is spread mostly by hand-to-hand contact. For example, a person with a cold blows or touches his or her nose and then touches someone else who then becomes infected with the virus. Additionally, the cold virus can live on objects such as pens, books, and coffee cups and can be acquired from such objects. While common sense would suggest that coughing and sneezing spread the common cold, these are actually very poor mechanisms for spreading a cold.

Generally antibiotics are not useful for treating a cold. Antibiotics only work against illnesses caused by bacteria and colds are often caused by viruses. Not only do antibiotics not help, but they can also cause allergic reactions that may be fatal. Further, using antibiotics when they are not necessary has led to the growth of several strains of common bacteria that have become resistant to antibiotics. For these and other reasons, it is important to limit the use of antibiotics to situations in which they are necessary. Sometimes, an infection with bacteria can follow the cold virus. Bacterial complications that arise from common cold are treated with antibiotics.

Several treatments that can ease the symptoms associated with a common cold also exist. Decongestants and nasal sprays can help reduce symptoms. People with heart disease, poorly controlled high blood pressure, or other illness should contact their physician prior to using these medications. Additionally, over the counter nasal sprays should not be used for more than three days because the nose can become dependent on them and a worse stuffy nose will result when they are discontinued.

## New Words & Phrases

contagious/kən'teɪdʒəs/*adj*. 传染性的,会感染的

virus/'vaɪərəs/*n*. 病毒

recur/rɪ'kɜː(r)/*vi*. 复发

infection/ɪn'fekʃn/*n*. 传染,感染

bronchitis/brɒŋ'kaɪtɪs/*n*. 支气管炎

emphysema/ˌemfɪ'siːmə/*n*. 气肿,肺气肿

antibiotic/ˌæntibaɪ'ɒtɪk/*n*. 抗生素　*adj*. 抗生的

allergic/ə'lɜːdʒɪk/*adj*. 过敏的

complication/ˌkɒmplɪ'keɪʃn/*n*. 并发症

decongestant/diːkən'dʒestənt/*n*. 解充血药

spray/spreɪ/*n*. 喷雾剂

**Task One　Vocabulary Exercise**

**Direction: Match the words or phrases with similar meaning in the two columns.**

| A | B |
|---|---|
| 1. contagious | a. necessary for living |
| 2. organism | b. saliva |
| 3. complication | c. growth of bacteria |
| 4. vital | d. spreading by contact |
| 5. nausea | e. new development of illness |
| 6. culture | f. collection of pus formed in the body |
| 7. bacterial | g. difficulty in breathing |
| 8. abscess | h. living being |
| 9. sputum | i. feeling of sickness or disgust |
| 10. dyspnea | j. of bacteria |

# Part Four　Practical Writing

### Birth Certificate

**Direction: Read the following writing sample carefully. Design and finish an imitated writing task with the similar style.**

### 出 生 证 明

出生证明是一份重要文件,它包括以下内容:婴儿的性别、出生时间、出生地点、父母的姓名、婴儿的身高、婴儿的体重。

**【Sample】**

Birth Certificate

This is to certify that Wang Ming (male) was born on March 18,2008 in Shenyang, China,to Wang Dashang,father,and Li Yan,mother. Weight:3. 6 kg. Length:51 cm.

The People's Hospital of Shenyang

(sealed)

Signature:

(sealed)

Dated the 23rd day of April,2008

**【Assignment】**

请根据下列材料写一份出生证明。

姓名:刘阳　性别:女　体重:3.1 公斤　身高:48 厘米

出生日期:2008 年 5 月 1 日

出生地:上海第一人民医院

父亲姓名:刘宏伟　母亲姓名:江丽红

______________________________

______________________________

______________________________

______________________________

______________________________

# Part Five　Prefixes,Suffixes & Roots

**Direction:Learn the prefixes,suffixes or roots in the table by heart and then choose the best answers to finish the exercises.**

**Orientational System (方位系统)**

| 汉语/英语 | 常用词根 | 例　词 |
|---|---|---|
| 上 up | epi-;<br>super;<br>supra- | epiderm 表皮　epicytoma 上皮瘤;<br>superconductor 超导体;<br>supraaortic 上主动脉　supraclavicular 锁骨上的　supracapsulin (adrenalin,epinephrine)肾上腺素 |
| 下 down | infer(o)-;<br>infra-;<br>sub-;hypo- | inferolateral 下外侧的;<br>infraorbital 眶下的　infraauricular 耳下;<br>subaxillary 腋下的　subcutaneous (hypodermic)皮下的 |
| 左 left | leva-;<br>levo- | levamizole 左旋咪唑;<br>levocardiogram 左侧心电图 |

续表

| 汉语/英语 | 常用词根 | 例 词 |
|---|---|---|
| 右 right | dextr(o)- | dextrocardiogram 右侧心电图 dextrocular 惯用右眼的 dextrocardia (dexiocardia) 右位心 |
| 前 front | ante-; pre-; pro | antenatal 产前的; preoperative 术前的 precordium 心前区; prostatic 前列腺的 prophylaxis 预防法 |
| 后 behind | post; retr(o)- | postpartum 产后的 postoperative 术后的; retrobulbar 眼球后的 retrobronchial 支气管后的 |
| 内 inside | endo-; intra | endocardium 心内膜 endocrine 内分泌的; intravenous 静脉内的 intramuscular 肌肉内的 intrauterine 子宫内 |
| 外 outside | ect(o)-; exo-; extra | ectohormone 外激素;exocervix 外子宫颈; extraarticular 关节外的 extracorporeal 体外的 extracranial 颅外的 |
| 中心 center | centro- | centrocyte 中央细胞 centrokinesis 中枢性运动 |
| 中间 middle | medi(o)- | media 介质 mediocidin 中霉素 |
| 周围 around | circum-;peri- | circumcision 包皮环切术;periodontitis 牙周炎 |

1. The word meaning "of the area beneath the skin" is ________.

A. hypotension B. hypodermic C. hypothermia D. hypothyriod

2. On or of the outside is called ________.

A. extent B. extant C. extinct D. external

3. The equivalent to the word "endocardium"is the Chinese word ________.

A. 心内膜 B. 内分泌 C. 子宫颈内 D. 囊内的

4. The correct spelling for the word "中枢性运动" is ________.

A. centriole B. centrocyte C. centrokinesis D. centroplasm

5. The English term for "眼球后的" is ________.

A. retrocecal B. retrobulbar C. retrocavalureter D. retrocolic

6. What is the Chinese term for "levocardiogram"?

A. 左旋甲状腺素 B. 左位心 C. 左旋咪唑 D. 左侧心电图

7. The English term for"肘前的" is ________.

A. antecubital B. antebrachial C. antecubita D. anteflexion

8. The Chinese term for "circumanal" is ________.

A. 阑尾周围的 B. 包皮环切术 C. 肛门周围的 D. 眼周围的

9. The Chinese term for "dextrocular" is ________.

A. 右位心 B. 惯用右眼的 C. 右侧心电图 D. 右旋

10. What is the Chinese term for "supracapsulin"?

A. 锁骨上 B. 主动脉上的 C. 视交叉上的 D. 肾上腺素

# Unit Two

## Learning Objectives

1. To seek and gather information about medical equipment, internal human organs and first aid about choking from the pictures and charts.
2. To understand how to consult a doctor in English.
3. To remember the commonly used medical terms and understand the texts.
4. To know how to write a doctor's certificate in English.

# Part One　Pictures & Charts

## Ⅰ. Medical Instruments

**Direction: Label the pictures below using the words in the box.**

| | |
|---|---|
| digital blood pressure monitor（数字血压计） | blood pressure cuff（血压袖带） |
| pulse oximeter（脉搏血氧仪） | thermometer（体温计） |
| electric thermometer（电子体温计） | ID bracelet（身份识别腕带） |
| blood pressure monitor（血压计） | stethoscope（听诊器） |

1

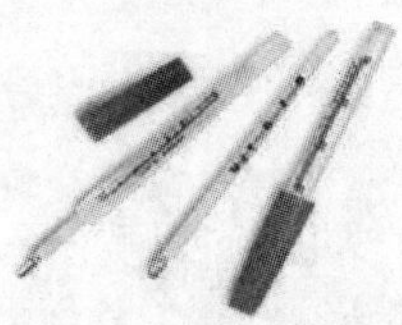

2

3

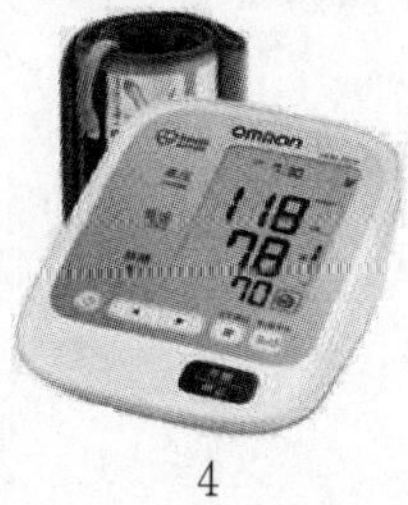

4

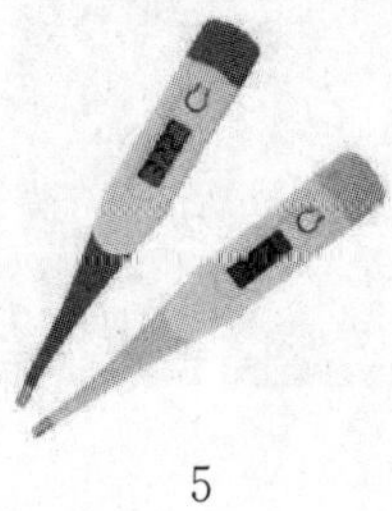

5

6

7

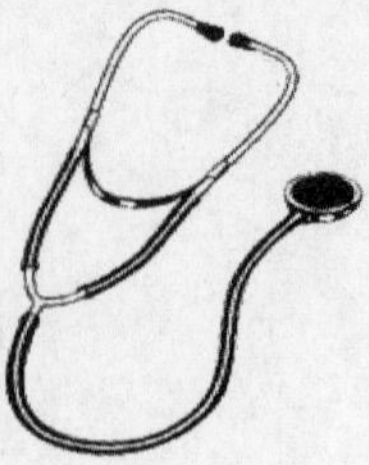

8

1. ______________________________
2. ______________________________
3. ______________________________
4. ______________________________
5. ______________________________
6. ______________________________
7. ______________________________
8. ______________________________

## New Words & Phrases

monitor/'mɒnɪtə(r)/*n.* 显示屏，屏幕
thermometer/θə'mɒmɪtə(r)/*n.* 温度计，体温表
oximeter/ɒk'sɪmɪtə/*n.* 血氧（定量）计
stethoscope/'steθəskəʊp/*n.* 听诊器

## Ⅱ. Internal Human Organs

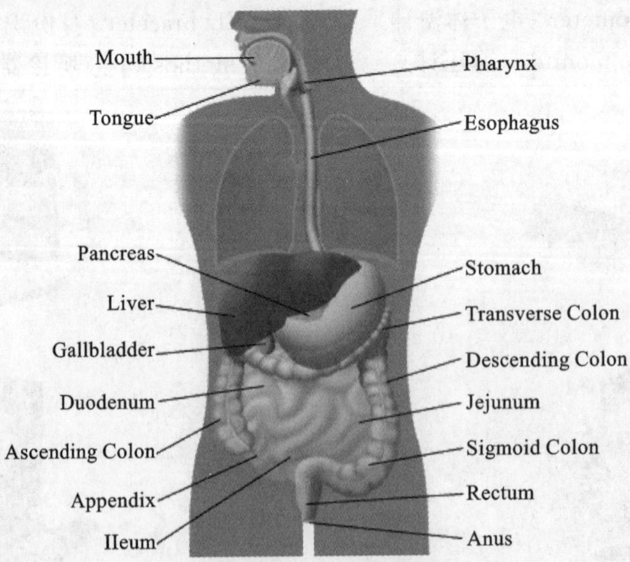

**Direction: Translate the following words into Chinese.**

1. pancreas/ˈpæŋkriəs/ ________
2. gallbladder/ˈgɔːlblædə/ ________
3. duodenum/ˌdjuːəˈdiːnəm/ ________
4. colon/ˈkəʊlən/ ________
5. appendix/əˈpendɪks/ ________
6. pharynx/ˈfærɪŋks/ ________
7. esophagus/ɪˈsɒfəgəs/ ________
8. jejunum/dʒɪˈdʒuːnəm/ ________

## Ⅲ. First Aid: Choking Adult

Method One

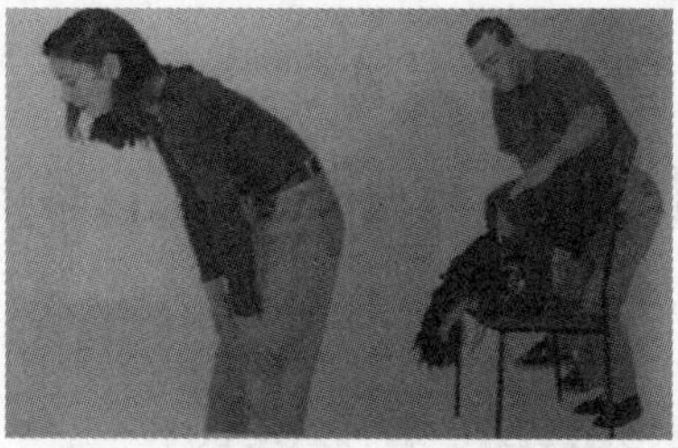

**Direction: Arrange the following steps in a proper sequence based on the medical procedure.**

Partial blockage:

________ If still unsuccessful, place the casualty on his/her side on the floor, and call 120 for an ambulance.

________ Ask the casualty to cough.

________ Encourage the casualty to relax and breathe deeply.

________ If unsuccessful, bend the casualty well forward and give 4 sharp blows between shoulder blades.

## New Words & Phrases

blockage/ˈblɒkɪdʒ/*n.* 堵塞物,[医](心理)阻滞

cough/kɒf/*n.* 咳,咳嗽 *vt.* /*vi.* 咳,咳嗽

blade/bleɪd/*n.* 叶片,桨叶

Method Two

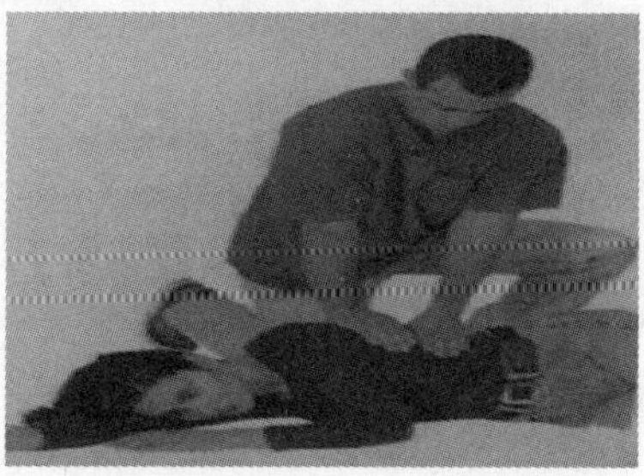

Total blockage:

________ Lie the casualty on his/her side on the floor.

________ If unsuccessful, give 4 quick downward lateral chest thrusts (place your hands on the side of his/her chest, below the casualty's armpit).

________ Give 4 sharp blows between shoulder blades.

________ If still unsuccessful, call 120 for an ambulance.

________ Repeat steps until help arrives or blockage clears

## New Words & Phrases

lateral/ˈlætərəl/*adj*. 侧面的，横向的

armpit/ˈɑːmpɪt/*n*. 腋窝，胳肢窝

# Part Two Listening Comprehension

## Situation Dialogue: Consulting a Doctor

**Task One Watch Episode One and fill in the missing words referring to the original text. Then check your writing against the original.**

Patient: This is the blood result of my ________ ________, and the other is the ________ ________.

Doctor: I see. I'd like to know your medical history first. Have you had any problems with your kidney or liver?

Patient: Yes. I was told I have IgA nephropathy 5 years ago because both my uric acid and creatinine were too high. My urine has been tea-colored for almost 5 years.

Doctor: Did you have a ________?

Patient: No. The doctor suggested the biopsy but I am really afraid of that. So they haven't been able to diagnose the IgA until now.

Doctor: What kind of symptom do you have now?

Patient: Oh, I have had a gout for a week, and my left foot is still ________ and ________.

**Task Two Watch Episode Two and complete the answers according to the questions.**

1. What is the patient taking for gout these days?

   The patient is taking a ________.

2. Why should the patient avoid the pain killers?

   Because the pain killers affect ________.

3. What's the doctor's suggestion?

   The doctor suggests trying some ________.

# Part Three Reading Comprehension

## Ⅰ. Medical Horizon

### OTC Drug Facts Label

Reading the drug product's labeling is important for taking care of yourself and your family, when you use an over-the-counter (OTC) medicine. The label tells you what the medicine is supposed to do, who should or shouldn't take it, and how to use it. The labeling of OTC medicines has always contained usage and safety information for consumers. In the Federal Register of March 1999, the Food and Drug Administration published the OTC Drug Facts Label regulation. The OTC labeling rule applies to more than 100,000 OTC drug products.

Before simplifying the OTC label, the FDA conducted extensive research on how consumers use OTC drug product labels. One major problem has been the readability of the labels, especially for older Americans, who purchase almost 30 percent of the OTC drugs sold in the United States. The FDA also found that consumers thought words like "indications", "precautions", and "contraindications" were confusing and not easily understood.

Finding information about inactive ingredients has also been a challenge for those who may be allergic to an ingredient in a drug product.

Patterned after the Nutrition Facts food label, the Drug Facts label uses simple language and an easy-to-read format to help people compare and select OTC medicines and follow dosage instructions. The following information must appear in this order:

- The product's active ingredients, including the amount in each dosage unit.
- The purpose of the product.
- The uses (indications) for the product.
- Specific warnings, including when the product should not be used under any circumstances, and when it is appropriate to consult with a doctor or pharmacist.
- Dosage instructions—when, how, and how often to take the product.
- The product's inactive ingredients, important information to help consumers avoid ingredients that may cause an allergic reaction.

Along with the standardized format, the label uses plain-speaking terms to describe the facts about each OTC drug.

If you read an OTC medicine label and still have questions about the product, talk to your doctor, pharmacist, or other health care professional.

## New Words & Phrases

Federal Register 联邦文件档

regulation/ˌregjʊ'leɪʃ(ə)n/*n.* 管理,规则

readability/ˌriːdə'bɪləti/*n.* 可读性,易读

purchase/'pɜːtʃəs/*v.* 购买

indication/ˌɪndɪ'keɪʃ(ə)n/*n.* 指示,迹象

precaution/prɪ'kɔːʃ(ə)n/*n.* 预防,警惕

dosage/'dəʊsɪdʒ/*n.* 剂量,用量

## Exercises

**Task One Choose the best answer to each of the following questions according to the text.**

1. What is the most important thing to do when taking an OTC drug?

A. Follow the doctor's advice. B. Read the drug product's label.

C. Listen to the opinions of others. D. Not Look at instructions.

2. What is the use of the label?

A. The label tells you what the medicine is supposed to do.

B. The label tells you who should or shouldn't take it.

C. The label tells you how to use it.

D. All of the above.

3. When was the OTC Drug Facts Label regulation published?

A. In 1998. B. In 1999. C. In 2002. D. In 2003.

4. How many drugs does the rule apply to?

A. 80,000. B. 90,000. C. 100,000. D. mone than 100,000.

5. What has FDA done before simplifying the OTC labels?

A. The FDA asked the doctor's opinions.

B. The FDA conducted researches.

C. The FDA did some questionnaire surveys.

D. The FDA conducted extensive research on how consumers use OTC drug product labels.

**Task Two Fill in the blanks with the words given below. Make changes if necessary.**

**content simplify comply dosage specific**

1. Some beaches had failed to ________ with environmental regulations.

2. I'm perfectly ________ with the way the campaign has gone.

3. Our aim is to ________ the complex social security system.

4. There are several ________ problems to be dealt with.

5. He was put on a high ________ of vitamin C.

# Ⅱ. Hospital Story

## An Ill Friend Means a Real Friend

Just three more days. Just three more trips. As I drove through traffic, I thought about waking up early to drive downtown, to wait in my doctor's office and receive radiation. I remembered the waiting room—the four wonderful women I had met there. We had developed something special—a bond that can only be built in those early morning hours waiting anxiously together.

One woman has cervical cancer—a disease that recently killed her mother. Another woman is from Bermuda, but is living with her sister so she can receive treatment at the hospital for cancer of the uterus. My third friend has advanced breast cancer. Although she must use a walker, and is in constant pain—she is always smiling. The fourth woman, though not a patient, I will miss most of all. Mary, the receptionist, has a way of making everyone feel at ease. Of making them feel cared for— of greeting everyone with her sweet voice.

When I first came to radiation I was nervous, anxious, and scared. But Mary could see the fear in my eyes. Her warm words and gentle smile dissolved those fears, and sparked in my heart a desire to confide in and bond to the other ladies in the waiting room. Mary had that effect on everyone. Instead of picking up a magazine, we shared our stories. Instead of staring vacantly, we communicated our fears and hopes. Instead of watching the clock, we bonded and made friendships to help us through.

It may sound strange to say this, but I feel privileged to have had this experience. I feel privileged to have experienced Mary's warm smile.

## New Words & Phrases

radiation/ˌreɪdiˈeɪʃən/*n.* 发光，发热，辐射

bond/bɔnd/*n.* 结合力，联结

cervical/ˈsɜːvɪkəl/*adj.* 子宫颈的，颈部的

treatment/ˈtriːtmənt/*n.* 治疗

receptionist/rɪˈsepʃənɪst/*n.* 接待员，传达员

spark/spɑːk/*v.* 点燃，鼓舞

confide/kənˈfaɪd/*v.* 透露，吐露

vacantly/ˈveɪkəntli/*ad.* 神情茫然地

privilege/ˈprɪvəlɪdʒ/*n.* 特权，优待

## Exercises

**Task One  Translate the following sentences into Chinese.**

1. We had developed something special—a bond that can only be built in those early morning hours waiting anxiously together.

2. When I first came to radiation I was nervous, anxious, and scared.

3. Her warm words and gentle smile dissolved those fears, and sparked in my heart a desire to confide in and bond to the other ladies in the waiting room.

# Ⅲ. Human Disease

### Life Process

The basic processes of life include organization, metabolism, responsiveness, movements, and reproduction. In humans, there are additional requirements such as growth, differentiation, respiration, digestion, and excretion. All of these processes are interrelated and function together to maintain individual life. Disease and death represent a disruption of the balance in these processes. The following is a brief description of the life process.

**Organization**

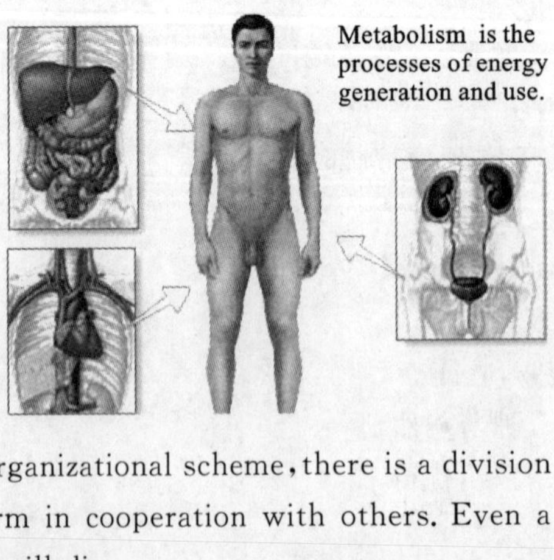


At all levels of the organizational scheme, there is a division of labor. Each component has its own job to perform in cooperation with others. Even a single cell, if it loses its integrity or organization, will die.

**Metabolism**

Metabolism includes all the chemical reactions that occur in the body. One phase of metabolism is catabolism in which complex substances are broken down into simpler building blocks and energy is released.

**Responsiveness**

Responsiveness or irritability is concerned with detecting changes in the internal or external environments and reacting to that change. It is the act of sensing a stimulus and responding to it.

**Movement**

There are many types of movement within the body. On the cellular level, molecules move from one place to another. Blood moves from one part of the body to another. The diaphragm moves with every breath.

**Reproduction**

Life is transmitted from one generation to the next through reproduction of the organism. In a broader sense, reproduction also refers to the formation of new cells for the replacement and repair of old cells as well as for growth.

**Growth**

Growth refers to an increase in size either through an increase in the number of cells or through an increase in the size of each individual cell. In order for growth to occur, anabolic processes must occur at a faster rate than catabolic processes.

**Differentiation**

Differentiation is a developmental process by which unspecialized cells change into specialized cells with distinctive structural and functional characteristics. Through differentiation, cells develop into tissues and organs.

**Respiration**

Respiration refers to all the processes involved in the exchange of oxygen and carbon dioxide between the cells and the external environment.

**Digestion**

Digestion is the process of breaking down complex ingested foods into simple molecules that can be absorbed into the blood and utilized by the body.

**Excretion**

Excretion is the process that removes the waste products of digestion and metabolism from the body. It gets rid of by-products that the body is unable to use, many of which are toxic and incompatible with life.

In addition to the processes described above, life depends on certain physical factors from the environment. These include water, oxygen, nutrients, heat, and pressure.

# New Words & Phrases

metabolism/mə'tæbəlɪzəm/*n.* 新陈代谢

respiration/ˌrespə'reɪʃn/*n.* 呼吸,呼吸作用

digestion/daɪ'dʒestʃən/*n.* 消化力,领悟

excretion/ɪk'skriːʃn/*n.* (动植物的)排泄,排泄物

interrelated/ˌɪntərɪ'leɪtd/*adj.* 相关的

disruption/dɪs'rʌpʃn/*n.* 中断,分裂

integrity/ɪn'tegrəti/*n.* 完整性

catabolism/kə'tæbəlɪzəm/*n.* [生物]异化作用,分解代谢

irritability/ˌɪrɪtə'bɪləti/*n.* 过敏性,兴奋性,易怒

stimulus/'stɪmjələs/*n.* 刺激物,刺激

cellular/'seljələ(r)/*adj.* 细胞的

molecule/'mɒlɪkjuːl/*n.* [化]分子

diaphragm/'daɪəfræm/*n.* 横隔膜

anabolic/ə'næbəlɪk/*adj.* [生化]合成代谢的

differentiation/ˌdɪfərenʃɪ'eɪʃn/*n.* 区别

distinctive/dɪ'stɪŋktɪv/*adj.* 与众不同的,有特色的

# Exercises

**Task One　Vocabulary Exercises**

**Direction: Fill in the blanks with the following words. Change the form if necessary.**

**excrete　component　toxic　malnutrition　fertilize**

**cellular　respiration　digest　irritable　mature**

1. Food is ________ in the stomach and bowels so that it can be used in the body.
2. Waste matter and sweat are ________ from human body.
3. The insecticide should be kept beyond children's reach because it is ________.
4. Many children in Africa are suffering from starvation because of ________.
5. ________ phone is also called mobile phone, or hand phone.
6. His body and character ________ during these years.
7. They failed to find the ________ sperm in the patient's body.
8. Artificial ________ is very crucial in first-aid.
9. Each ________ of human body has its own job to perform.
10. Some patients with mental illness tend to be ________.

# Part Four Practical Writing

## Doctor's Certificate

**Direction: Read the following writing sample carefully. Design and finish an imitated writing task with the similar style.**

### 诊 断 书

医生的诊断书包括：患者姓名、年龄、入院时间、入院原因、治疗方式和时间、出院时间、建议休息时间等。

**【Sample 1】**

### Doctor's Certificate

June 18th, 2012

This is to certify that the patient, Mr. Thomas, male, aged 41, was admitted into our hospital on June 9th, 2012 for suffering from acute appendicitis. After immediate operation and ten days of treatment, he has got complete recovery and will be discharge on June 19th, 2012. It is suggested that he rest for one week at home before returning to his work.

(Signature) Jack Hopkins
Surgeon-in-chief

**【Sample 2】**

### Doctor's Certificate

Feb 2nd, 2012

This is to certify that Ms. Zhou Xiumei has a high fever of 39℃ and a severe sore throat. We advise that she take a three-day rest, and, if necessary, come back for a check by that time.

(Signature) Dong Yuxi
Physician-in-chief

**【Assignment】**

请根据下面所给素材写一份医生诊断书。

张明，男，21 岁，在 2012 年 3 月 5 日因腹泻住院。经一周治疗已痊愈。将于 3 月 12 日出院。医生建议他在家休息一周再上学。

____________________________________________

____________________________________________

____________________________________________

____________________________________________

____________________________________________

# Part Five Prefixes, Suffixes & Roots

**Direction: Learn the prefixes, suffixes or roots in the table by heart and then choose the best answers to finish the exercises.**

**Respiratory System (呼吸系统)**

| 汉语/英语 | 常用词根 | 例词 |
|---|---|---|
| 呼吸 breath | -pnea;<br>pneum(o)-;<br>-spir(o) | tachypnea 呼吸过速 bradypnea 呼吸过缓 dyspnea 呼吸困难; pneumothorax 气胸; inspiration 吸气 |
| 鼻 nose | rhin(o)-<br>naso- | rhinitis 鼻炎 rhinorrhoea 鼻漏; nasobronchial 鼻支气管 nasoscope 鼻镜 endonasopharyngeal 鼻咽内的 |
| 喉 larynx | laryng(o)- | laryngitis 喉炎 laryngectomy 喉切除术 |
| 咽 pharynx | pharyng(o)- | pharyngeal 咽部 pharyngitis 咽炎 pharyngoplasty 咽成形术 |
| 气管 windpipe | trache(o)- | tracheotomy 气管切开术 tracheobronchitis 气管支气管炎 |
| 支气管 bronchi | bronch(o)- | bronchiectasis 支气管扩张 bronchitis 支气管炎 bronchoscope 支气管镜 bronchogenic 支气管原的 |
| 肺 lung | pneumon(o)-;<br>pulmo(n)- | pneumonia 肺炎 bronchopneumonia 支气管肺炎; pulmonary 肺的 bronchopulmonary 支气管肺的 |
| 胸膜 pleura | pleur(o)- | pleuritis 胸膜炎 pleural 胸膜的 |

1. The word "windpipe" is related to ________.

A. trachy-　B. trachelo-　C. teacho-　D. tracheo-

2. In medical terms, the combining form strictly related to "larynx" is ________.

A. laryngo-　B. larygo-　C. pharyngo-　D. pharygo-

3. Which word in the following has nothing to do with "breath"?

A. Inspiration.　B. Spirochaeta.　C. Expiration.　D. Respiration.

4. The correct spelling form for "支气管炎" is ________.

A. bronchoitis　B. brancheitis　C. bronchitis　D. bronchoeitis

5. Which word in the following represents the abnormal respiration?

A. Pneumoperitonue.　B. Orthopnea.

C. Expiration.　D. Pneumaturia.

6. The combining form "spiro-" is related to ________.

A. breath　B. air　C. lung　D. chest

7. The combining form only denoting relationship to "lung" is ________.

A. pleur(o)-　B. pneumati-　C. pneumono-　D. alve(o)-

8. The English term for "气管切开术" is ________.

A. tracheotomy  B. tracheoectomy  C. bronchiectomy  D. bronchoectomy

9. The word "breath" is not related to ________.

A. pneum(o)-  B. pneumat(o)-  C. pneumon(o)-  D. -pnea

10. The expression for lung function which is used most often is ________.

A. pneumonofunction  B. pneumofunction

C. pulmonary function  D. pulmofunction

# Unit Three

## Learning Objectives

1. To seek and gather information about medical equipment, human skeleton and first aid about wound from the pictures and charts.
2. To understand how to admit a patient in English.
3. To remember the commonly used medical terms and understand the texts.
4. To know how to write a case report in English.

# Part One　Pictures & Charts

## Ⅰ. Medical Instruments

**Direction: Label the pictures below using the words in the box.**

| | | |
|---|---|---|
| dressing（敷料） | drain tube（引流管） | ice pack（冰袋） |
| oxygen mask（氧气面罩） | heat pack（热敷袋） | syringe driver（注射器泵） |

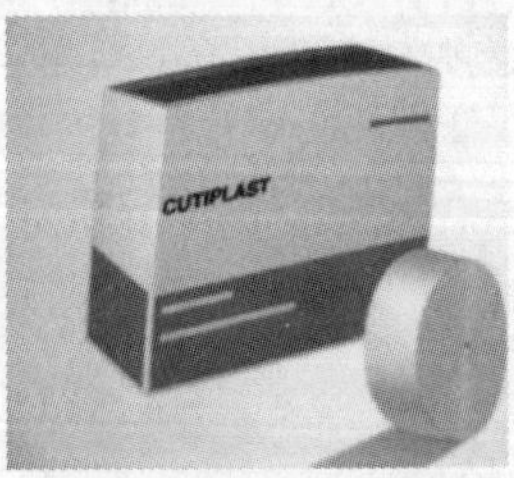


1

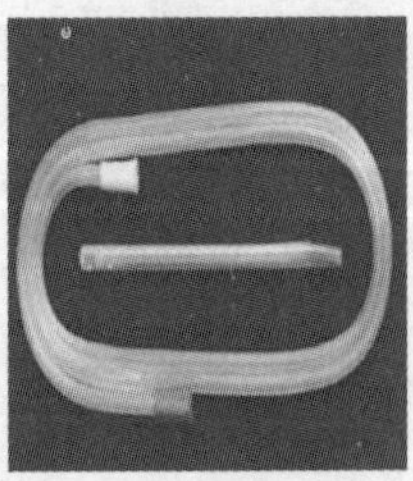

2

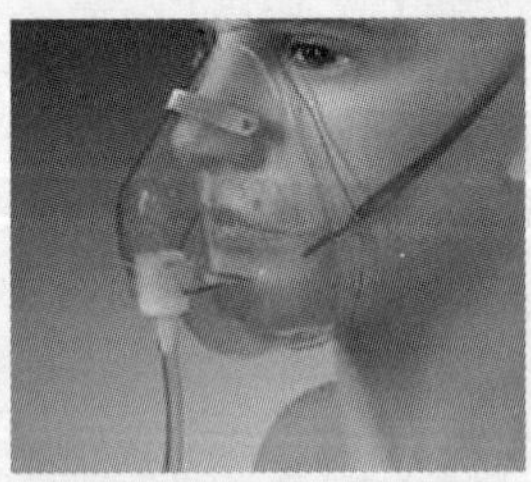

3

4

5

6

1. ______________________________
2. ______________________________
3. ______________________________
4. ______________________________
5. ______________________________
6. ______________________________

## New Words & Phrases

tube/tjuːb/*n.* 管,管状物
oxygen/ˈɒksɪdʒən/*n.* 氧气
syringe/sɪˈrɪndʒ/*n.* 注射器,注射筒

## Ⅱ. Human Skeleton

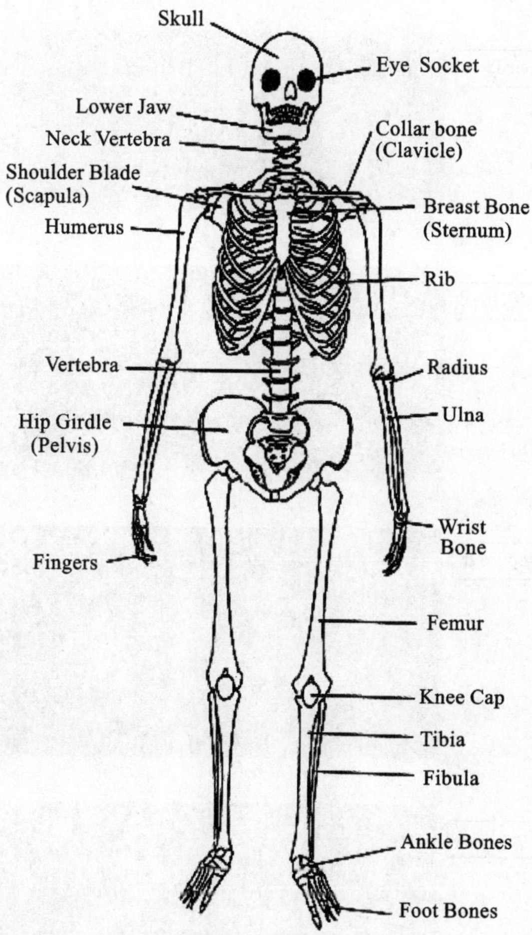


**Direction: Translate the following words into Chinese.**

1. vertebra/ˈvɜːtɪbrə/ ______________

2. collarbone/ˈkɔləbəun/ ________________

3. humerus/ˈhjuːmərəs/ ________________

4. radius/ˈreɪdiəs/ ________________

5. ulna/ˈʌlnə/ ________________

6. femur/ˈfiːmə(r)/ ________________

7. tibia/ˈtɪbiə/ ________________

8. fibula/ˈfɪbjələ/ ________________

## Ⅲ. First Aid: Embedded Objects in Wounds

Step One

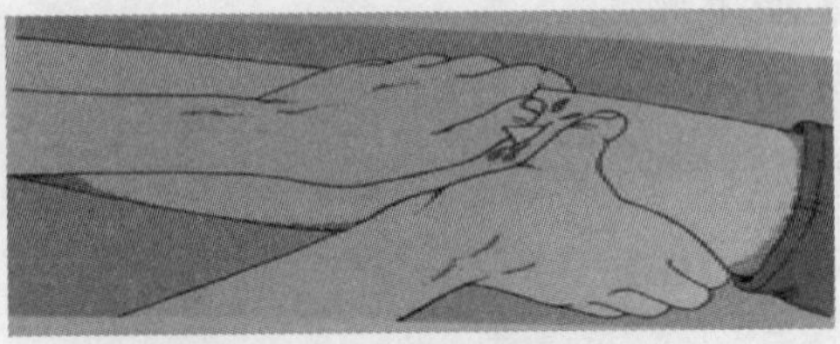

Step Two

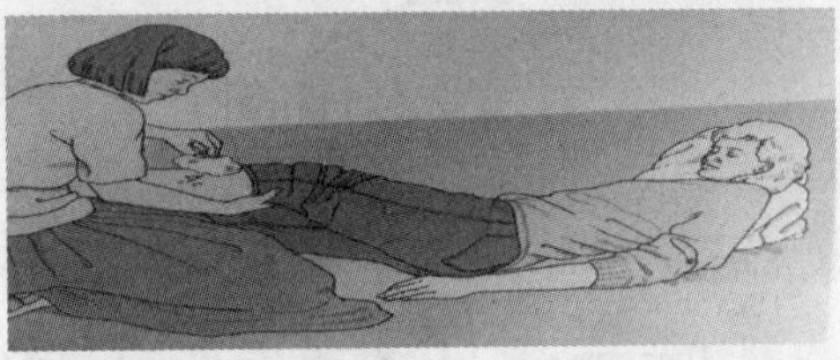

Step Three

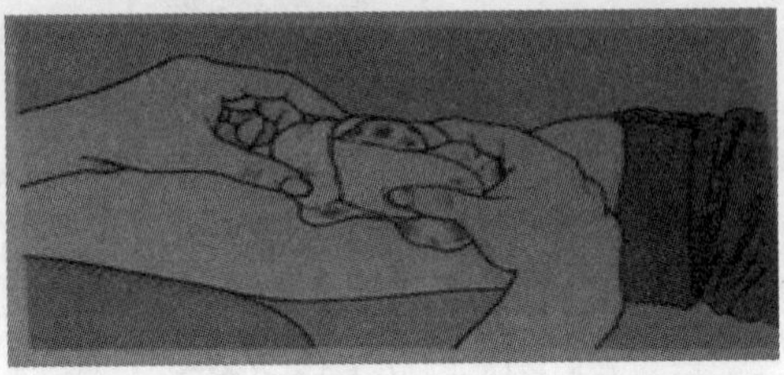

Step Four

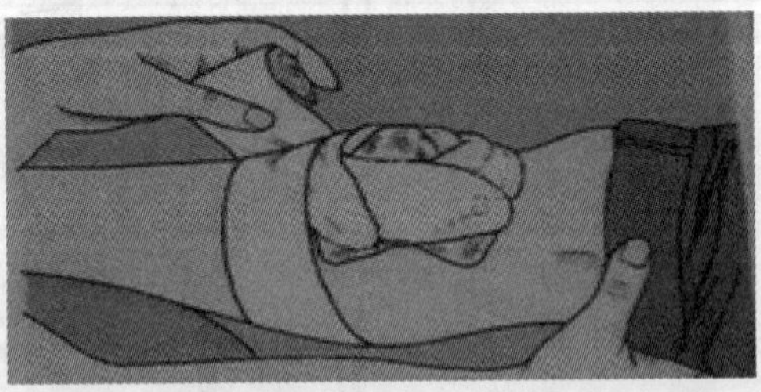

Step Five

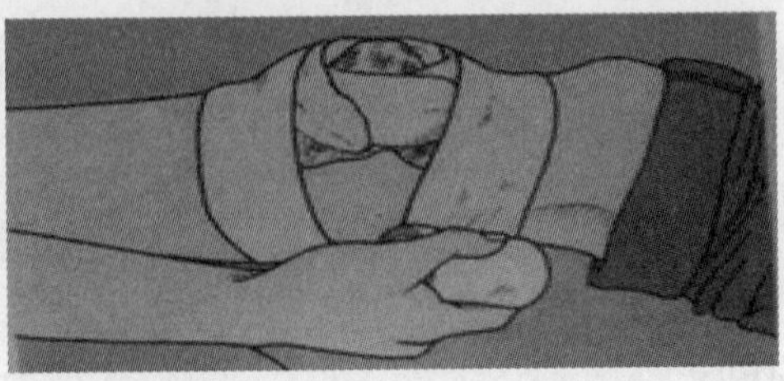

Step Six

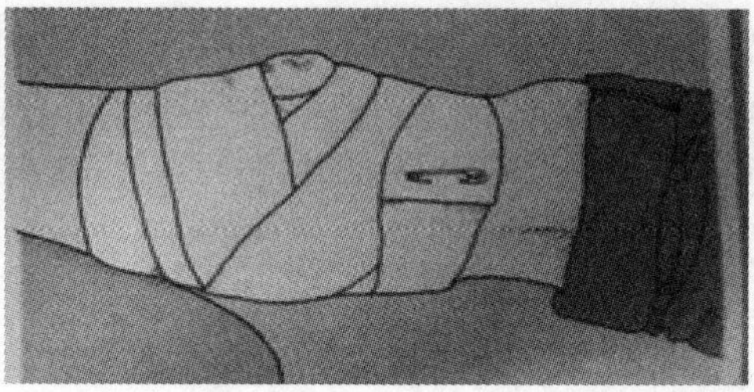

**Direction: Arrange the following steps in a proper sequence based on the medical procedure.**

________ Help the casualty lie down and raise and support the injured part. Drape a piece of gauze over the wound and object.

________ Control severe bleeding by pressing the area immediately above and below the object.

________ Place the end of a roller bandage over the part of the built-up dressing nearest you and make two straight turns around the limb.

________ Very carefully build up pads of cotton wool around the object until they are at least the same height as the object. Do not pull the gauze down as you do this. If it is not possible to build up the dressing high enough, leave the embedded object protruding.

________ Pass the bandage under the limb and bring it up over the upper edge of the dressing.

________ Continue making these diagonal turns until the dressing is firm, then secure the bandage.

________ Transfer the casualty to hospital.

________ Keeping the injured part raised, immobilize the limb as for a broken bone.

## New Words & Phrases

embed/ɪmˈbed/*v.* 把……嵌入
drape/dreɪp/*v.* (用布等)遮盖或装饰某人或某物
gauze/gɔːz/*n.* 纱布
protrude/prəˈtruːd/*v.* (使)突出,(使)伸出
immobilize/ɪˈməʊbəlaɪz/*v.* 使不动,使不能移动

# Part Two Listening Comprehension

## Situation Dialogue: Admitting a Patient

**Task One Watch Episode One and fill in the missing words referring to the original text. Then check your writing against the original.**

Nurse: Good morning, Mrs. Wilson. I am the nurse of the ________. My name is Emily.

I'll be ________ you to the ward today.

Patient: Good morning, Emily. What should I do now?

Nurse: Would you please come with me to the nurses' office so I can finish the paperwork first?

Patient: Sure. May I sit down?

Nurse: Yes, of course. Please sit down and make yourself comfortable, OK? Can you tell me your full name and your date of birth?

Patient: My full name is Rose Wilson. And I was born on ________, 1968.

Nurse: Can you tell me why you are here today?

Patient: Well, um. I've had a duodenal ulcer for about five years. My ________ have been black for the past two days. I feel weak, too. My occult blood test is ________, so my doctor suggested for me to come here.

**Task Two Watch Episode Two and complete the answers according to the questions.**

1. What causes Mrs. Wilson's duodenal ulcer?
   It came from too much ________ in her job.
2. What's the result of Mrs. Wilson's BP?
   It's ________.
3. Why does Mrs. Wilson think her pulse is too fast?
   Because she always feels ________ these days.

# Part Three Reading Comprehension

## Ⅰ. Medical Horizon

### Doctors' Dirty Hands and Patients' Deaths

A study in the United States found that doctors and nurses fail to wash their hands with alarming frequency, contributing to the 247 deaths caused each day by preventable hospital infections.

An agency has joined with eight major hospitals to address low hand washing rates nationwide. The program began in the spring, when the hospitals conducted rigorous assessments of hand washing compliance among their staff. They found that doctors and nurses washed their hands only 30 to 70 percent of the time when they entered or exited a patient's room, averaging 50 percent.

Hand washing upon entering and exiting a room is a key part of the requirements and has been recommended by both the Centers for Disease Control and Prevention and the World Health Organization.

The hospitals then assessed what obstacles were preventing health care providers from adequately washing their hands. In some cases, the problems were logistical and easy to fix by means such as moving hand washing stations to more convenient locations or adding stands where workers could put down objects they might be carrying. In other cases, problems seem to stem from an attitude and are harder to fix.

Hospitals have tried to address these problems through techniques such as constant monitoring. Since the implementation of corrective strategies, hand washing compliance at the participating hospitals has risen to 74 percent, still short of the long-term goal of 90 percent.

## New Words & Phrases

infection/ɪnˈfekʃən/*n*. 传染，传染病
rigorous/ˈrɪgərəs/*adj*. 严厉的，(指天气等)严酷的
compliance/kəmˈplaɪəns/*n*. 服从，听从
obstacle/ˈɔbstəkl/*n*. 障碍，妨碍
logistical/ləˈdʒɪstɪkəl/*adj*. 后勤方面的
address/əˈdrɛs/*v*. 对付，满足
monitor/ˈmɔnɪtə/*v*. 监控，监视
implementation/ˌɪmpləmenˈteɪʃən/*n*. 履行，完成，成就

## Exercises

**Task One Choose the best answer to each of the following questions according to the text.**

1. What causes the 247 deaths every day?

A. Operation failure.

B. Doctors and nurses fail to wash their hands.

C. The patients are seriously ill.

D. Medical mistakes.

2. What did the hospitals find in the program?

A. They found that doctors and nurses washed their hands every time when they entered or exited a patient's room.

B. They found that doctors and nurses washed their hands 50 percent of the time when they entered or exited a patient's room.

C. They found that doctors and nurses washed their hands 74 percent of the time when they entered or exited a patient's room.

D. They found that doctors and nurses washed their hands only 30 to 70 percent of the time when they entered or exited a patient's room.

3. What's one of the key parts of the requirements recommended by the two authorities?

A. Hand washing upon entering and exiting a room.

B. Be patient to the patients.

C. Be professional as a doctor or a nurse.

D. Putting on uniform when reporting duties.

4. What obstacles were preventing health care providers from adequately washing their hand?

A. The problems were logistical.

B. Problems seem to stem from an attitude.

C. They are too busy to wash hands.

D. Both A and B.

5. How can we fix the problem of hand washing logistically?

A. Setting rules to monitor.

B. Moving hand washing stations to more convenient locations.

C. Adding stands where workers could put down objects they might be carrying.

D. Both B and C.

**Task Two  Fill in the blanks with the words given below. Make changes if necessary.**

**rigorous  stem from  compliance  obstacle  preventable**

1. She felt that her family was an ________ to her work.

2. The planes have to undergo ________ safety checks.

3. These injuries are entirely ________.

4. The present wave of strikes ________ discontent among the lower-paid.

5. ________ with the rules is expected of all members.

## Ⅱ. Hospital Story

### Notes and Lives

Everyone has a favorite song whether it's from Street Boys, Beethoven or the Beatles. Music can motivate you, soothe you or call forth a range of emotions. Now it's being applied to healthcare as therapy to treat anxiety, reduce pain and improve communication skills.

Patricia Turse has seen what music can do. As a certified music therapist, Patricia spends her days working with children making them less afraid and more comfortable while they're in the hospital.

Music was always part of her life and she wanted to do something special with her talent.

"I wanted to help people and music was always beneficial for me. I was convinced it could be helpful in many ways," says Patricia.

Patricia currently works with children, but she has also treated mentally ill and chemically addicted adults. She sees 10 to 15 children a day on a one-to-one basis since each child has a different set of needs to be addressed.

"I help them manage pain, separation or anxiety. Sometimes I only get one day to get to know and assess a child before he or she goes home," states Patricia.

"I feel like I have something to give by using music to calm and heal others." Patricia may play the harp for them or teach breathing techniques to help them deal with whatever they're going through. "Sometimes we sing or they write a song with me," says Patricia.

She recalls treating a 5-year-old girl who had autism.

"She loved drumming so we sang and drummed all day. She didn't want to give up the drum at the end of the session. I really enjoyed her. Music therapy can help to improve a child's communication and socialization skills," notes Patricia.

Patty certainly helps to add beautiful notes to these children's lives.

## New Words & Phrases

motivate/ˈməʊtɪveɪt/*vt.* 给……动机，刺激，激发

therapy/ˈθerəpɪ/*n.* 治疗，疗法

beneficial/ˌbenɪˈfɪʃ(ə)l/*adj.* 有益的，有利的，有帮助的

convince/kənˈvɪns/*vt.* 使确信，使信服，说服

harp/hɑːp/*n.* 竖琴

autism/ˈɔːtɪz(ə)m/*n.* 自闭症

## Exercises

**Task One　Translate the following sentences into Chinese.**

1. Now it's being applied to healthcare as therapy to treat anxiety, reduce pain and improve communication skills.

2. Patricia currently works with children, but she has also treated mentally ill and chemically addicted adults.

3. Patricia may play the harp for them or teach breathing techniques to help them deal with whatever they're going through.

# Ⅲ. Human Disease

### Bird Flu

Bird flu is also called avian flu, avian influenza, H5N1. "Bird flu" is a phrase similar to "swine flu","dog flu","horse flu",or "human flu" in that it refers to an illness caused by any of many different strains of influenza viruses that have adapted to a specific host.

Birds, just like people, get the flu. Bird flu viruses infect birds, including chickens, ducks, other poultry and wild birds. However, bird flu can pose health risks to people. The first case of a bird flu virus infecting a person directly, H5N1, was in Hong Kong, China in 1997. Since then, the bird flu virus has spread to birds in countries in Asia, Africa and Europe.

Human infection is still very rare, but the virus that causes the infection in birds might change, or mutate, to more easily infect humans. This could lead to a pandemic, or a worldwide outbreak of the illness.

During an outbreak of bird flu, people who have contact with infected birds can become sick. It may also be possible to catch bird flu by eating poultry that is not well cooked or through contact with a person who has it. Bird flu can make people very sick or even cause death. There is currently no vaccine.

Avian influenza viruses occur naturally among birds. Wild birds worldwide carry the viruses in their intestines, but usually do not get sick from them. However, avian influenza is very contagious among birds and can make some domesticated birds, including chickens, ducks, and turkeys, very sick and kill them.

Infected birds shed influenza virus in their saliva, nasal secretions, and feces. Susceptible birds become infected when they have contact with contaminated secretions or excretions or with surfaces that are contaminated with secretions or excretions from infected birds. Domesticated birds may become infected with avian influenza virus through direct contact with infected waterfowl or other infected poultry, or through contact with surfaces (such as dirt or cages) or materials (such as water or feed) that have been contaminated with the virus.

Symptoms of avian influenza in humans have ranged from typical human influenza-like symptoms (e. g., fever, cough, sore throat, and muscle aches) to eye infections, pneumonia, severe respiratory diseases (such as acute respiratory distress), and other severe and life-threatening complications. The symptoms of avian influenza may depend on which virus caused the infection.

Studies done in laboratories suggest that some of the prescription medicines should work in treating avian influenza infection in humans. However, influenza viruses can become resistant to these drugs, so these medications may not always work. Additional studies are needed to demonstrate the effectiveness of these medicines.

## New Words & Phrases

avian/ˈeɪviə/*adj*. 鸟类的　*n*. 鸟

mutate/mjuːˈteɪt/*v*. 变异

poultry/ˈpəʊltri/*n.* 家禽
intestine/ɪnˈtestɪn/*n.* 肠
domesticate/dəˈmestɪkeɪt/*vt.* 驯养,教化
saliva/səˈlaɪvə/*n.* 口水,唾液
secretion/sɪˈkriːʃn/*n.* 分泌,分泌物(液)
feces/ˈfiːsiːz/*n.* 粪,屎,渣滓
susceptible/səˈseptəbl/*adj.* 易受影响的　*n.*(因缺乏免疫力)易得病的人
contaminate/kənˈtæmɪneɪt/*v.* 污染
resistant/rɪˈzɪstənt/*adj.* 有耐药性的

## Exercises

**Task One　Vocabulary Exercise**

**Direction: Match the words or phrases with similar meaning in the two columns.**

| A | B |
|---|---|
| 1. isolate | a. death rate |
| 2. hepatitis | b. muscle pain |
| 3. mutate | c. pollute |
| 4. sore | d. doctor's order for the use of a medicine |
| 5. myalgia | e. liver trouble |
| 6. mortality | f. change |
| 7. host | g. separate |
| 8. prescription | h. aching |
| 9. poultry | i. animals or plants on which a parasite lives |
| 10. contaminate | j. domesticated bird |

# Part Four　Practical Writing

### Case Report

**Direction: Read the following writing sample carefully. Design and finish an imitated writing task with the similar style.**

与其他应用文相比,写病情报告、病例等短文一般都会提供较为详细的信息,学生只要连词成句即可。写作时常用一般现在时、现在完成时和一般过去时;同时也常使用被动语态。

**【Sample】**

Patient's name: Peter Morgan
Sex: Male

Occupation: Driver

DOB: Oct. 5, 1980

Chief Complaint: Fever for three days, got worse today; seizure at home this morning

History: Oral ulcer noted for 3 days

Hand, foot and buttock rash noted for 2 days

Activity and appetite normal in the first few days

Vomiting since this morning

Mild headache

**Case Report**

The patient's name is Peter Morgan, male, 30 years old, and is currently a driver for a living. He got a fever three days ago and became worse today. Moreover, he has attacked by a seizure at home this morning. He has suffered oral ulcer for 3 days, and rash can be seen on his hands, legs, and buttock. His activity and appetite are both normal in the first few days, but he vomited a number of times since this morning. He also complained about a mild headache.

**【Assignment】**

Read the patient discharge summary. Use the information in the summary to write a case report in about 100 words.

---

DISCHARGE SUMMARY

---

| | |
|---|---|
| **Patient**: Mrs Martha | **D. O. B.** 17/9/21 |
| **Date of Discharge**: 10 May, 2009 | **Date of Admission**: 23 April, 2009 |

---

**Problems**:

1. Has been suffering from hypertension & degenerative bone disease.
2. Needs to urinate frequently.
3. Diagnosed—left pneumonia & urinary tract infection.

---

**Close Relative**:

4. No immediate family.

---

**Needs**:

5. Bath seat and safety rails in bathroom.
6. Nurse to visit 2 x week to monitor medications.
7. Physiotherapy 3 x week.

---

**Strengths and Resources**:

8. Independent-minded woman, fully alert and articulate, can cook.

---

# Part Five　Prefixes, Suffixes & Roots

**Direction: Learn the prefixes, suffixes or roots in the table by heart and then choose the best answers to finish the exercises.**

**Digestive System（消化系统）**

| 汉语/英语 | 常用词根 | 例　词 |
|---|---|---|
| 食管 esophagus | esophag(o)- | esophagoscope 食管镜　gastroesophageal 胃食管的 |
| 胃 stomach | gastr(o)-; stomach(o)- | gastritis 胃炎　gastroscopy 胃镜检查　gastropathy 胃病; stomachache 胃痛 |
| 肠 intestine | enter(o)- | enteritis 肠炎　enterovirus 肠道病毒　enterobacteria 肠道菌 |
| 十二指肠 duodenum | duoden(o)- | duodenal 十二指肠的 |
| 结肠 colon | col(o)-; colon(o)- | colocentesis 结肠穿刺术　colitis 结肠炎; colonoscopy 结肠镜检查 |
| 消化 digestion | peps(o)-; -gest(o)- | dyspepsia 消化不良　pepsin 胃蛋白酶; digestive 消化的　digestible 可消化的 |
| 直肠 rectum | rect(o)-; procto- | rectocele 直肠膨出　rectouterine 直肠子宫; proctoptosis 直肠脱垂　proctoscopy 直肠镜检查 |
| 胆囊 gallbladder; cholecyst | cholecyst(o)- | cholecystitis 胆囊炎　cholecystolithiasis 胆囊结石病 |
| 肝 liver | hepat(o)- | hepatitis 肝炎　hepatorrhexis 肝破裂 |
| 胆管 bile duct | cholangi(o)- | cholangitis 胆管炎　cholangiography 胆管造影术 |
| 阑尾 appendix | appendic(o)- | appendicitis 阑尾炎　appendicectomy 阑尾切除术 |

1. The Chinese meaning for "pepsin" is ________.

A. 胃蛋白酶　　B. 胃泌素　　C. 胃蛋白酶原　　D. 胃酶抑素

2. Fill in the blank with the combining part for the medical term "结肠镜检查": ________ scopy.

A. entero B. recto C. colono D. colo

3. The Chinese meaning for "cholecystitis" is ________.

A. 胆囊炎 B. 膀胱炎 C. 肝炎 D. 胆管炎

4. The English term for "直肠脱落" is ________.

A. rectouterine B. proctoptosis C. colitis D. rectocele

5. The term "duodenum" is so called because it is about twelve ________.

A. fingerlengths B. fingerbreadths

C. fingercircle D. fingercircumferrence

6. The word which has nothing to do with liver is ________.

A. hepatitis B. hepatolithiasis

C. hepatorrhexis D. pancreatitis

7. To make a word for "胆管造影术",its correct spelling is ________.

A. cholangiopancreatography B. cholangiocarcinoma

C. cholangiography D. cholecystectomy

8. The following words have the meaning of inflammation except ________.

A. pancreatitis B. hepatitis C. cholangiitis D. gastropathy

9. Which word has the meaning of "胆囊切除术"?

A. Hepatolithiasis. B. Cholecystectomy.

C. Cholecystolithiasis. D. Cholecystoctomy.

10. Which word has nothing to do with stomach?

A. Gastritis. B. Gastropathy.

C. Stomatitis. D. Stomachache.

# Unit Four

## Learning Objectives

1. To seek and gather information about medical equipment, brain cross-sections and first aid about eye injury from pictures and charts.

2. To understand two conversations in the nurses' office.

3. To remember the commonly used medical terms and understand the texts in Part Three.

4. To know how to write a history of illness.

# Part One  Pictures & Charts

## Ⅰ. Medical Instruments

**Direction: Label the pictures below using the words in the box.**

| nebulizer (雾化器)  air tank (氧气筒)  air sterilization machine (空气消毒机)<br>hypodermic syringe (皮下注射器)  ultraviolet sterilizer (紫外线消毒车)<br>scales (磅秤) |
|---|

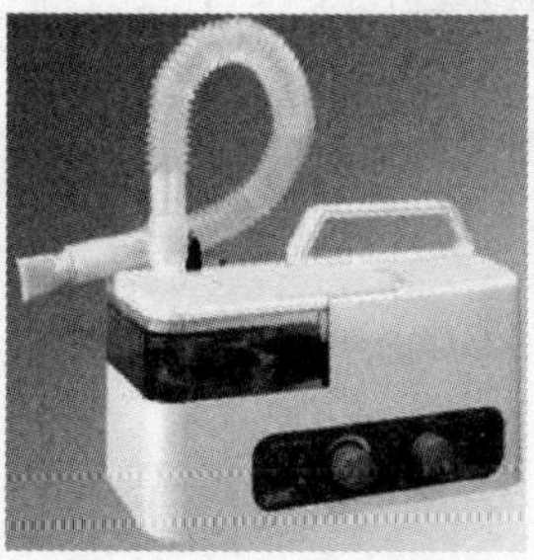

1

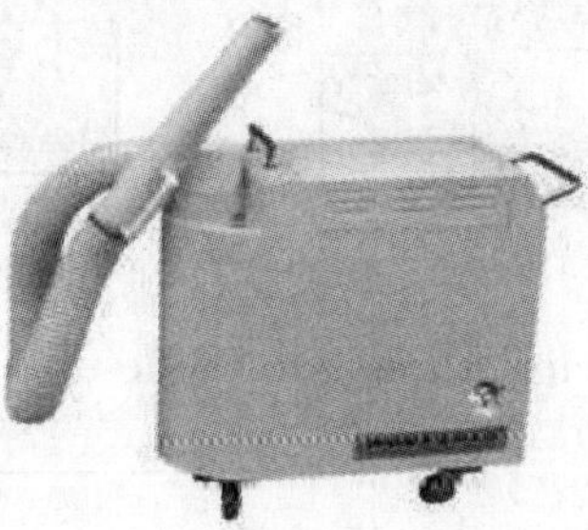

2

3

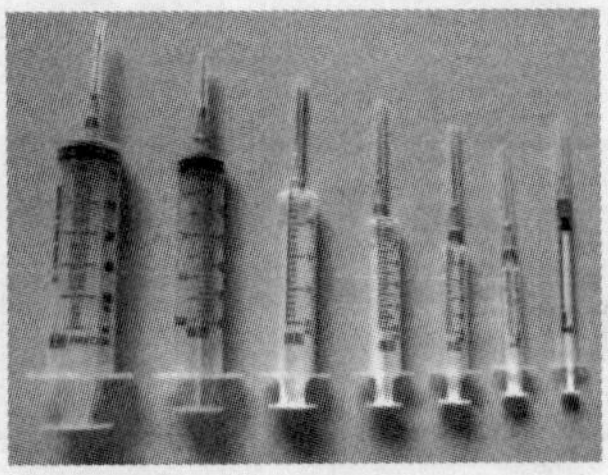
4

5

6

1. ______
2. ______
3. ______
4. ______
5. ______
6. ______

## New Words & Phrases

nebulizer/ˈnebjʊlaɪzə/*n*. 喷雾器
sterilization/ˌsterəlaɪˈzeɪʃn/*n*. 杀菌，绝育
hypodermic/ˌhaɪpəˈdɜːmɪk/*adj*. 皮下注射用的
ultraviolet/ˌʌltrəˈvaɪələt/*adj*. 紫外的，紫外线的　*n*. 紫外线

## Ⅱ. Brain Cross-Sections

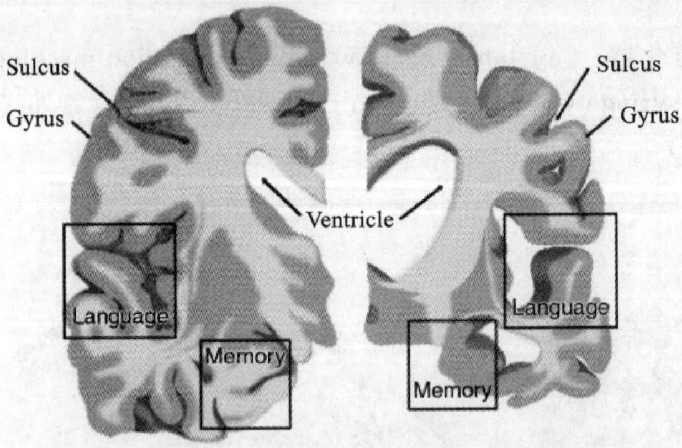


**Direction: Translate the following words into Chinese.**

1. cross-section ______
2. sulcus/ˈsʌlkəs/ ______
3. gyrus/ˈdʒaɪrəs/ ______
4. ventricle/ˈventrɪkl/ ______

## Ⅲ. First Aid: Eye Injury

Step One

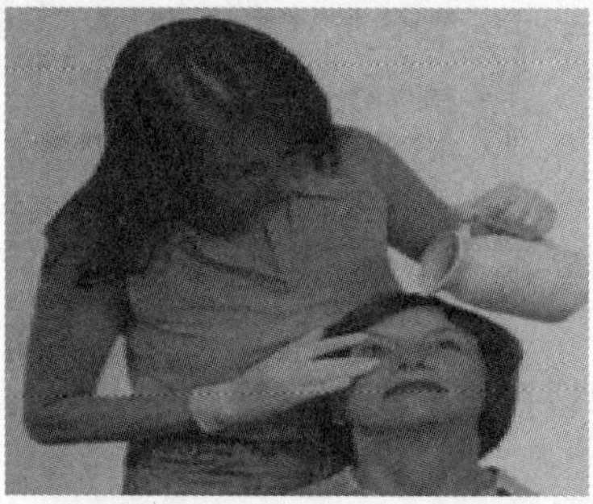

Step Two

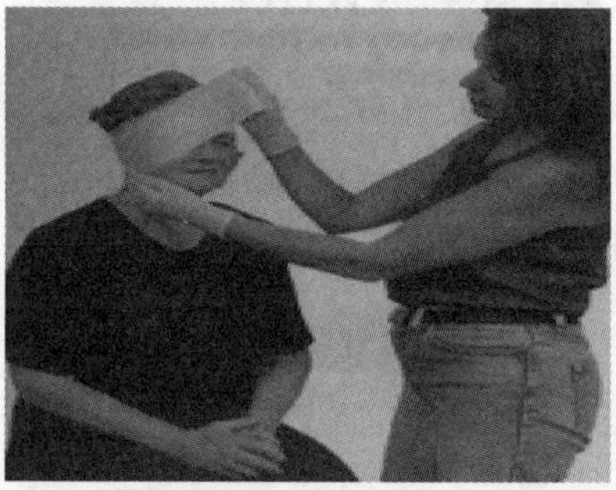

Step Three

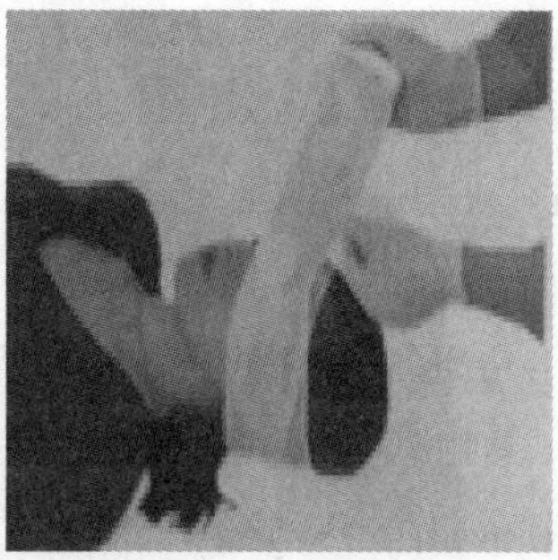

**Direction: Arrange the following steps in a proper sequence based on the medical procedure.**

________ Support the casualty's head: Support the casualty's head to keep it as still as possible, ask the casualty to try not to move eyes.

________ Call 120 for an ambulance.

________ Place a dressing over the eye: Place a sterile pad or dressing over the injured eye, ask the casualty to hold this in place, and bandage the dressing in place, covering the injured eye. If there is an embedded object in the eye, lie the casualty on his/her back, place a pad around the object and bandage it in place.

________ Flush the eye with cool, flowing water: if it is chemical or heat burn, or smoke in the eyes, flush them with water.

## New Words & Phrases

sterile/'steraɪl/*adj*. 无菌的

pad/pæd/*n*. 垫,衬垫

flush/flʌʃ/*v*. (以水)冲刷,冲洗

# Part Two Listening Comprehension

## Situation Dialogue: In the Nurses' Office

**Task One Watch Episode One and fill in the missing words referring to the original text. Then check your writing against the original.**

Doctor: Hello. Mary, are you looking after Mr. John today?

Nurse: Yes. Any questions?

Doctor: Oh, can we take a few minutes to talk about his situation?

Nurse: Sure. Have a seat, please.

Doctor: Thank you. He was back from the OR an hour ago and there are a lot of orders for him. Let's make sure they are clear.

Nurse: OK. Let me see. ________, ________, ________ every 30 minutes, temperature every 4 hours. And monitor the GCS every 4 hours.

Doctor: And also monitor his I & O, OK?

Nurse: Sure. How about his ________?

Doctor: Now his potassium levels are very low according to his blood result. Would you please give him a liter of normal saline with 20 millimoles of KCL?

Nurse: Sure. Please fill out the patient's ________ first.

**Task Two Watch Episode Two and complete the answers according to the questions.**

1. How will the nurse run the antibiotics for Mr. John?

   She will run them through a ________.

2. Besides antibiotics, what does the doctor want to give to Mr. John?

   He wants to give him some ________ with the fluids.

3. Why can these nutrients not be run through the cannula?

   Because these nutrients are ________, and it's easy to cause ________.

# Part Three Reading Comprehension

## Ⅰ. Medical Horizon

### Student Awareness and Mental Health

More than 16 million young people attend colleges and universities in the United States. According to the Suicide Prevention Resource Center, one-fifth of college students experience a mental illness, and more and more students arrive on campus these days having received mental health services before starting their college careers. Also, increasing numbers of students are seeking help for emotional problems that occur after they arrive at college. Clinical depression often emerges for the first time in adolescence.

Suicide, the eighth leading cause of death for all Americans, is the second leading cause of death for college-age individuals. College-age adults are especially vulnerable to mental health problems, in part because many mental health issues first emerge in the late teens or early 20s. Overall, an estimated 27 percent of young adults between the ages of 18 and 24 have diagnosable mental health problems.

By teaming up with a school's campus counseling services, psychology club, office of disability, office of student affairs, office of diversity, or other groups, students can raise awareness of mental health problems and the importance of good mental health—especially during May (Mental Health Month) and the first week in October (Mental Illness Awareness Week).

In addition, these ideas have been used on college campuses across the country:

- Add signage to high-traffic areas on campus.
- Make a presentation to your psychology class.
- Incorporate mental health into Freshman Orientation.
- Write a letter to the editor of your school newspaper.
- Ask your campus radio station to highlight mental health issues.
- Train campus leaders.
- Show a movie that spurs conversation around mental health issues.
- Offer free mental health screenings.
- Organize a run/walk.
- Organize a benefit concert.
- Organize a "De-Stress Fest".
- Establish your own group.

Making participation enjoyable, publicizing events, and recruiting others are central to the effectiveness of your events.

## New Words & Phrases

awareness/əˈweənis/*n.* 察觉，觉悟，意识

mental/ˈment(ə)l/*adj.* 精神的，心理的，智力的

suicide/ˈs(j)uːɪsaɪd/*n.* 自杀，自杀行为

emotional/ɪˈməʊʃ(ə)n(ə)l/*adj.* 感情的

emerge/ɪˈmɜːdʒ/*vi.* 浮现，出现，发生

adolescence/ˌædəˈles(ə)ns/*n.* 青春期，青少年期

vulnerable/ˈvʌln(ə)rəb(ə)l/*adj.* 易受伤的，易受攻击的

psychology/saɪˈkɒlədʒɪ/*n.* 心理学，心理

spur/spɜː/*v.* 刺激，激励，鼓舞

## Exercises

**Task One Choose the best answer to each of the following questions according to the text.**

1. What often emerges for the first time in adolescence according to the text?

A. Suicide. B. Clinical depression.

C. Rebellion. D. Sensitiveness.

2. What's the second leading cause of death for college-age individuals?

A. Diseases. B. Traffic accident.

C. Disasters. D. Suicide.

3. What's the percentage of young adults between 18 and 24 having diagnosable mental health problems?

A. 27%. B. 20%. C. 16%. D. 30%.

4. How many college students experience a mental illness?

A. 1/4. B. 1/3. C. 1/5. D. 1/2.

5. Why are college-age adults vulnerable to mental health problem according to the text?

A. Because mental health problem is very serious.

B. Because many mental health issues first emerge in the late teens or early 20s.

C. Because there is no doctor to help them.

D. Because the family can't give them enough support.

**Task Two Fill in the blanks with the words given below. Make changes if necessary.**

**emerge vulnerable team up with awareness adolescence**

1. Your arguments are ________ to criticism.
2. Women are often more ________ of their feelings than men.
3. I've ________ Jane to write the book.
4. It ________ that the driver of the car had been drunk.

5. Her remarks seemed a bit ________.

## Ⅱ. Hospital Story

### Facing H1N1

Ten-year-old Benjamin Oback has the typical face of swine flu in its more serious stages. He lies in the intensive care unit at Davis Children's Hospital. His parents pray. For nearly two weeks, their son has been fighting for his life.

"I feel awful. I feel like part of my soul has been crushed," said Benjamin's father Eric Oback.

It started out like a normal flu. On Sunday, Oct. 4, after riding his bike, Benjamin felt out of breath.

"On Sunday, he complained his chest hurt. He was seen to have a minor case of the flu," his mother Julie Oback said. "His pediatrician listens to his lungs. He said his lungs were clear. I asked him about giving him Tamiflu, and he said, 'No, he's not that sick. He should be better by the end of the week.' Nine hours later, he took a turn for the worse."

Benjamin had passed out and was rushed to the hospital.

"So that night, Tuesday night and early Wednesday morning was the worst," said Julie Oback. "This wasn't the normal course. Most people who get H1N1 are fine, but you don't know who's going to take a turn for the worse. That's what's so scary about it."

"In Benjamin's case, the main symptom was that fluid built up on the outside of his lung rather than the inside of his lung, and I think that's probably why his pediatrician didn't catch it with a stethoscope." Benjamin's father said.

Already, H1N1 is proving far more deadly for children than the seasonal flu.

"When Benjamin first presented to the hospital, he was gravely ill," said Dr. Joanne Natale, who treated Benjamin. "He wasn't conscious. Now, he's recovered significantly."

After his near death experience, Benjamin's prognosis is good. His mother said she's learned a valuable lesson. For now, Benjamin is fortunately winning the battle that is overcoming so many, who are so young.

## New Words & Phrases

swine flu 猪流感

pediatrician/ˌpidiəˈtrɪʃən/*n.* 小儿科医师

Tamiflu 特敏福(药品名称)

stethoscope/ˈsteθəskəʊp/*n.* 听诊器

prognosis/prɒgˈnəʊsɪs/*n.* (对病情的)预断,预后

# Exercises

**Task One  Translate the following sentences into Chinese.**

1. Benjamin had passed out and was rushed to the hospital.

2. In Benjamin's case, the main symptom was that fluid built up on the outside of his lung rather than the inside of his lung.

3. Already, H1N1 is proving far more deadly for children than the seasonal flu.

# Ⅲ. Human Disease

## Diabetes Mellitus

Diabetes mellitus is a group of metabolic diseases characterized by high blood sugar (glucose) levels, which result from defects in insulin secretion, or action, or both.

Diabetes can lead to blindness, kidney failure, and nerve damage. These types of damage are the result of damage to small vessels, referred to as microvascular disease. Diabetes is also an important factor in accelerating the hardening and narrowing of the arteries (atherosclerosis), leading to strokes, coronary heart disease, and other large blood vessel diseases.

The early symptoms of untreated diabetes are related to elevated blood sugar levels, and loss of glucose in the urine. High amounts of glucose in the urine can cause increased urine output and lead to dehydration. Dehydration causes increased thirst and water consumption. The inability of insulin to perform normally has effects on protein, fat and carbohydrate metabolism. Insulin is an anabolic hormone, that is, one that encourages storage of fat and protein. A relative or absolute insulin deficiency eventually leads to weight loss despite an increase in appetite. Some untreated diabetes patients also complain of fatigue, nausea and vomiting. Patients with diabetes are prone to developing infections of the bladder, skin, and vaginal areas. Fluctuations in blood glucose levels can lead to blurred vision. Extremely elevated glucose levels can lead to lethargy and coma.

There are two major types of diabetes, called type 1 and type 2. Type 1 diabetes was also called insulin dependent diabetes mellitus (IDDM), or juvenile onset diabetes mellitus. In type 1 diabetes, the pancreas undergoes an autoimmune attack by the body itself, and is rendered incapable of making insulin. Type 2 diabetes was also referred to as non-insulin dependent diabetes mellitus (NIDDM), or adult onset diabetes mellitus (AODM). In type 2 diabetes, patients can still produce insulin, but do so relatively inadequately for their body's needs, particularly in the face of insulin resistance.

Aggressive and intensive control of elevated levels of blood sugar in patients with type 1 and type 2 diabetes decreases the complications of nephropathy, neuropathy, retinopathy, and may reduce the occurrence and severity of large blood vessel diseases. Aggressive control with intensive therapy means achieving fasting glucose levels between 70-120 mg/dL; glucose levels of less than 160 mg/dL after meals.

The goal of diabetes management is to keep blood glucose levels as close to normal as safely possible. In addition, since diabetes may greatly increase a person's risk for heart disease, preventative measures for tightly controlling blood pressure and cholesterol levels are now an essential part of diabetes treatment as well.

## New Words & Phrases

atherosclerosis/ˌæθərəusklɪˈrəusɪs/*n.* [医]动脉硬化症

dehydration/ˌdiːhaɪˈdreɪʃn/*n.* 脱水

carbohydrate/ˌkɑːbəʊˈhaɪdreɪt/*n.* [化]碳水化合物

insulin/ˈɪnsjəlɪn/*n.* 胰岛素

hormone/ˈhɔːməun/*n.* 荷尔蒙，激素

onset/ˈɒnset/*n.* 攻击　*n.* [医]发作

nephropathy/nəˈfrɒpəθɪ/*n.* [医] 肾病

neuropathy/ˌnjʊəˈrɒpəθɪ/*n.* 神经病

retinopathy/ˌretɪˈnɒpəθɪ/*n.* [医]视网膜病

fasting/ˈfɑːstɪŋ/*adj.* 禁食的　*n.* 禁食

glucose/ˈgluːkəʊs/*n.* 葡萄糖

cholesterol/kəˈlestərɒl/*n.* 胆固醇

## Exercises

**Task One　Vocabulary Exercise**

**Direction: match the word with its Chinese meaning in the two columns.**

| A | B |
|---|---|
| 1. hardening | a. 冠状的 |
| 2. rupture | b. 畸形 |
| 3. coronary | c. 组织 |
| 4. abnormality | d. 胰岛素 |
| 5. cerebellum | e. 硬化 |

6. glucose　　　　f. 波动
7. tissue　　　　g. 破裂
8. insulin　　　　h. 小脑
9. traumatic　　　　i. 葡萄糖
10. fluctuation　　　　j. 外伤的

# Part Four　Practical Writing

## History of Illness

**Direction: Read the following writing sample carefully. Design and finish an imitated writing task with the similar style.**

病史是病人病程记录的第一部分。它由六部分组成:主诉、现病史、过去、家族史、社会史和系统回顾。写病史应基本掌握本专业内可能有的常用词汇和表达法;在转述患者的话语时,一定要注意时态的正确运用。

**【Sample】**

××× Hosptial

**Patient's Name:**
**Chart Number:**
**Date of Birth:**
**Sex:**
**Race:**
**Date of Examination: mm/dd/yy**
**Date of Admission: mm/dd/yy**
**Chief Complaint:**
**Present Illness:**
**Past History:**
**Family History:**
**Review of Systems:**
**Impressions:**

**【Assignment】**

Write a history of illness according to the following information.

中国第一医院住院部

患者姓名:约翰
病历号:15672
出生日期:1993 年 6 月 4 日
出生地点:美国纽约

性别:男

入院日期:2006 年 6 月 7 日

主诉:咳嗽、哮喘伴呼吸困难

现病史:这是该患者(13 岁)首次住院,从三岁起开始有哮喘,但未住过院。入境后一直很好,入院前游长城发生气短,使用咳嗽药无效。哮喘逐渐加重,孩子被带到中国第一医院急症室,接受肾上腺素和氧气治疗。然后送回希尔顿饭店。三小时后,孩子又被带回急症室并住院。

过去史:孩子八个半月出生。免疫接种:完全。过敏史:灰尘、洋葱。

家族史:母亲 37 岁,父亲 40 岁,都健在。哥哥、妹妹均身体健康。家族中无哮喘及糖尿病史。

系统回顾:除随时有结膜炎及哮喘外,其他为阴性。

诊断:哮喘。

# Part Five Prefixes, Suffixes & Roots

**Direction: Learn the prefixes, suffixes or roots in the table by heart and then choose the best answers to finish the exercises.**

**Circulatory System (循环系统)**

| 汉语/英语 | 常用词根 | 例词 |
|---|---|---|
| 心 heart | cardi(o)-<br>-cardium | electrocardiogram 心电图 carditis 心肌炎 phonocardiogram 心音图 cardiology 心脏病学;<br>myocardium 心肌层 pericardium 心包膜 |
| 心房 atrium | atri(o)- | atriotomy 心房切开术 periatrial 心房周的<br>transatrial 经心房的 atrial 心房的 |
| 心室 ventricle | ventricul- | supraventricular 室上的 ventriculocentesis 心室穿刺术<br>ventriculofiberscopy 心室纤维镜检查 |
| 瓣膜 valve | valvul(o)- | valvulitis 瓣膜炎 multivalvular 多瓣膜的<br>valvulopathy 心瓣病 |
| 血管 vessel | vas(o)-; angi(o)- | vasculitis 血管炎 vasopressin 血管升压素;<br>angiotensin 血管紧张素 angiography 血管造影 |
| 动脉 artery | arteri(o)- | arteriography 动脉造影术 arteritis 动脉炎<br>endoarteritis 动脉内膜炎 arteriosclerosis 动脉硬化 |
| 静脉 vein | ven(o)-; phleb(o)- | venous 静脉的 intravenous 内静脉的;<br>phlebitis 静脉炎 phlebography 静脉造影 |
| 脉搏 pulse | puls(o)- | pulseless 无脉的 pulsed 脉冲的 |

1. The Chinese meaning for the word "angiotensin" is ________.

A. 血管紧张素原 B. 血管成型 C. 血管舒缩活动 D. 血管紧张素

2. The correct spelling form for “静脉造影” is ________ graphy.

A. veino　B. arteri　C. vaso　D. phlebo

3. Fill in the blank the combining form for the medical term “心音图”: phono ________ gram.

A. heart　B. cardi　C. cardio　D. cor

4. The Chinese explanation for “endoarteritis” is ________.

A. 动脉炎　B. 脉管炎　C. 动脉内膜炎　D. 主动脉炎

5. The English term for “静脉炎” is ________.

A. phlebitis　B. veinitis　C. venitis　D. venulitis

6. The word combining “arterio” with “graphy” means ________.

A. 动脉成形术　B. 动脉造影术　C. 动脉石　D. 动脉内膜炎

7. To make a word pertaining to the heart and blood vessels is ________.

A. cardioventricular　B. cardioversion

C. cardiovalvular　D. cardiovascular

8. Which word in the following means inflammation of artery?

A. Arteritis.　B. Atritis.　C. Arthritis.　D. Angitis.

9. The English equivalent for the word “血管炎” is ________.

A. phlebitis　B. vessel inflammation

C. vasculitis　D. angitis

10. Which form in the following has nothing to do with “脉搏”?

A. “pulse”.　B. “impulse”.　C. “pulso-”.　D. “sphygmo-”.

# Unit Five

## Learning Objectives

1. To seek and gather information about medical equipment, oral cavity and first aid about broken hands or fingers from the pictures and charts.
2. To know how to administer medication in English.
3. To remember the commonly used medical terms and understand the texts.
4. To understand how to write a prescription.

## Part One　Pictures & Charts

### Ⅰ. Medical Instruments

**Direction: Label the pictures below using the words in the box.**

| | |
|---|---|
| roller clamp（轮钳） | IV stand（静脉输液架） |
| IV solution bag（静脉输液药袋） | catheter（输液管，导管） |

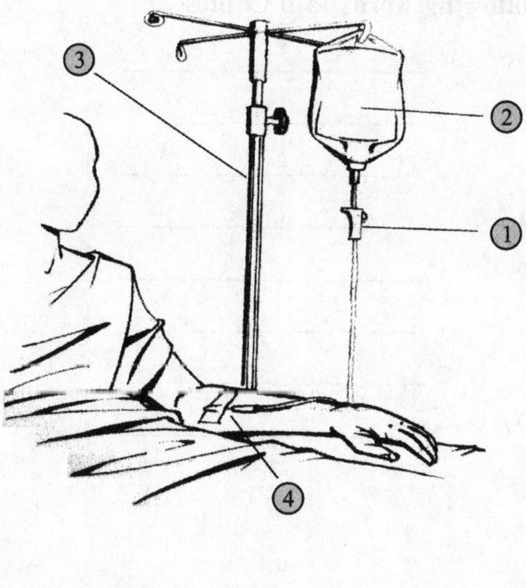

1. ______________________________
2. ______________________________
3. ______________________________
4. ______________________________

## New Words & Phrases

clamp/klæmp/*n.* 钳,夹子

IV abbr. intravenous/ˌɪntrəˈviːnəs/*adj.* 静脉注射的

solution/səˈluːʃn/*n.* 溶液

catheter/ˈkæθɪtə(r)/*n.* 导管

## Ⅱ. Oral Cavity

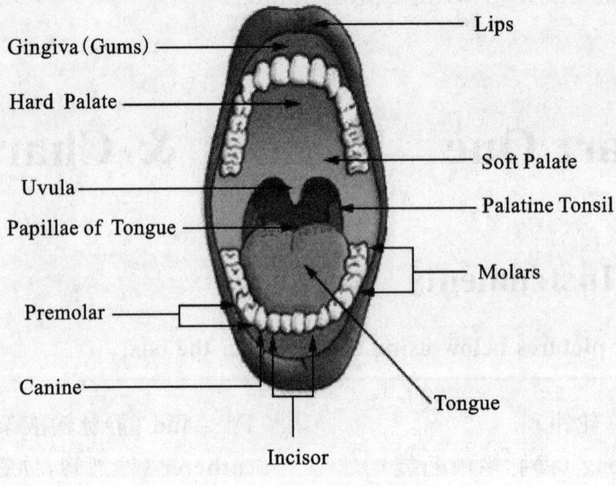


**Direction: Translate the following words into Chinese.**

1. gingiva/dʒɪnˈdʒaɪvə/ ______________
2. uvula/ˈjuːvjələ/ ______________
3. papillae/ˌpəpɪˈliː/ ______________
4. palatine/ˈpælətaɪn/ ______________
5. premolar/priːˈməʊlə/ ______________
6. molar/ˈməʊlə(r)/ ______________
7. canine/ˈkeɪnaɪn/ ______________
8. incisor/ɪnˈsaɪzə(r)/ ______________

## Ⅲ. First Aid: Broken Hands or Fingers

Step One

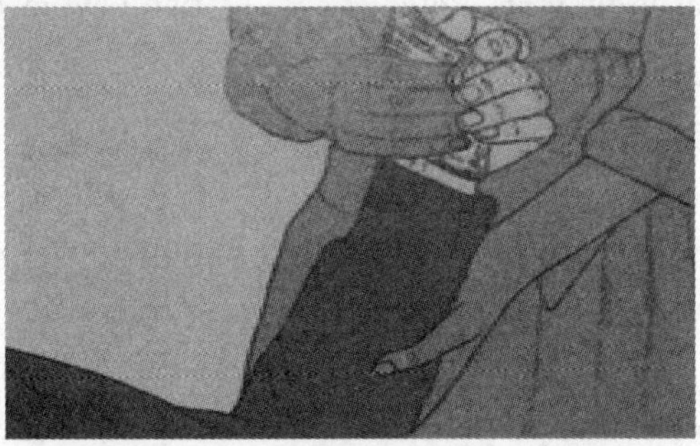

Step Two

**Direction: Arrange the following steps in a proper sequence based on the medical procedure.**

________ Take the casualty to hospital.

________ Raise the injured hand to control bleeding and apply a dressing.

________ Place the casualty's hand in soft padding and in an elevation sling and a broad-fold bandage.

### New Words & Phrases

padding/ˈpædɪŋ/*n*. 衬垫

elevation/ˌelɪˈveɪʃn/*n*. 高处,高地,高度

sling/slɪŋ/*n*. 悬带

# Part Two Listening Comprehension

## Situation Dialogue: Administering Medications

**Task One Watch Episode One and fill in the missing words referring to the original text. Then check your writing against the original.**

Nurse: How are you doing today?

Patient: Not good, I have a ________ and feel ________ today. My blood pressure was one eighty over one ten (180/110) this morning. That's really high, isn't it?

Nurse: Oh, I see. That's the reason why Dr. Peter ________ two new medications for you. One is Metoprolol, to ________ your BP, and the other is Lasix, a diuretic.

Patient: Oh, I can't remember the names. Would you please repeat them?

Nurse: Sure, and I'll tell more about them. Metoprolol is in the green box, and I already wrote down the ________ for you. You take these 2 pills once, twice a day; that's 8am before your breakfast and 8pm before your bedtime. Got it?

Patient: Mm, but I have a very poor memory. Instructions on the box are good for me.

**Task Two　Watch Episode Two and complete the answers according to the questions.**

1. Why should the patient put this medicine in a cool place?
   Because it would be ________ at 45 ℃.
2. What's the function of Lasix?
   It prevents the body from ________ too much ________.
3. What's the nurse's suggestion for diet?
   The patient would better eat diet with more ________.

# Part Three　Reading Comprehension

## Ⅰ. Medical Horizon

### Antibiotic Resistance and Human Health

Experts fear antibiotic resistance puts humans in danger of becoming nearly defenseless against some bacterial infections. The World Health Organization calls antibiotic resistance one of the three greatest threats to human health.

The improper use of antibiotics has led to strains of bacteria that are resistant to antibiotics. Experts say if efforts to combat the problem are not launched now, infections that were curable could make a dangerous comeback. Dr. Thomas Frieden, director of the U. S. Centers for Disease Control and Prevention, calls on American lawmakers to address the problem.

"If we don't improve our response to the public health problem of antibiotic resistance, we may enter a post-antibiotic world in which we will have few or no clinical interventions for some infections," he says.

Specialists are concerned that the more an antibiotic is used, the less effective it becomes. The genetic mutation of bacteria, which makes them resistant to antibiotics, is a natural process. But drug overuse has accelerated the process.

"You end up with very resistant bacteria in the urinary tract. That's only one example. Skin infections, lung infections, different bacteria causing these types of infections as they become more and more resistant, and then you get to more severe problem like tuberculosis in many parts of the world," says Dr. Donald Poretz, an infectious disease specialist. "People are given little of this and little of that to treat tuberculosis and tuberculosis germs develop resistance."

"You can have worldwide resistance, different resistance to different drugs in different parts of the world," he says. "And with rapid travel you can communicate those resistant bacteria to anyone here or there."

Experts say the solution lies in educating patients and doctors to stop using antibiotics when they are not necessary.

## New Words & Phrases

resistance/rɪˈzɪstəns/*n.* 抗性，耐性
mutation/mjuːˈteɪʃən/*n.*（生物细胞内的）突变
urinary/ˈjʊərɪnəri/*adj.* 尿的，泌尿系统的
tuberculosis/tjʊˌbɜːkjʊˈləʊsɪs/*n.* 结核病
germ/dʒɜːm/*n.* 细菌，病菌

## Exercises

**Task One Choose the best answer to each of the following questions according to the text.**

1. What is called one of the three greatest threats to human health by WHO?

A. Natural disasters. B. Environmental pollution.

C. Antibiotic resistance. D. Diseases.

2. The specialists are concerned that ________.

A. the more an antibiotic is used, the less effective it becomes

B. the more an antibiotic is used, the more effective it becomes

C. the less an antibiotic is used, the less effective it becomes

D. the less an antibiotic is used, the more effective it becomes

3. If the response to the public health problem of antibiotic resistance doesn't be improved, what will happen?

A. There is no change at all.

B. There is few or no clinical interventions for some infections.

C. It will produce new medicine.

D. There is no mentioned.

4. What will accelerate the process of antibiotic resistance?

A. Environment pollutions. B. Bad habits.

C. Drug overuse. D. Psychological factors.

5. Why does the tuberculosis get more severe in many parts of the world?

A. Because there is no advanced medical facilities.

B. Because there is lack of advanced medical techniques.

C. Because the people there are lack of money to receive the treatment.

D. Because people overuse the drug to treat and the germs develop resistance.

**Task Two Fill in the blanks with the words given below. Make changes if necessary.**

**launch intervention end up with resistant severe**

1. The government refused to ________ in the dispute between British Coal and the miners.

2. Many teachers are ________ to new ideas.

3. The drought is becoming increasingly ________.

4. How many pages did you ________?

5. The company is ________ a new model next month.

## Ⅱ. Hospital Story

### The Truth about Nursing

Raleigh, a nurse at Johns Hopkins Hospital, recalls taking her niece to a movie in which one of the characters was a nurse.

"In the movie, the little girl is dying. It's a very sad situation and the nurse comes in and says to the family quite abruptly, 'You all need to go home, visiting hours are over.' And she walks out of the room," says Raleigh.

"I was thinking to myself, 'Gosh, does my niece think this is what really happens? All nurses are like this or this is how we act towards patients?' It just made me sad. It just embarrassed me in front of my niece."

Raleigh's co-worker at the hospital, Neysa Ernst, says nurse portrayals on television are not much better.

"There are 2.9 million nurses in the United States. There are 790,000 physicians. And yet when you watch the TV programs, you see the physicians doing all of the work that nurses normally do," says Ernst.

"Nurses are the ones that are doing the EKGs. Nurses are the people who are taking the patient back and forth to the tests, making sure that procedures are administered appropriately. I don't see that on television."

A group of nursing students founded The Truth about Nursing nine years ago to encourage the media to present a more realistic portrayal of their profession. This year, the group released its "Decade Awards"—a list of the best and worst media portrayals of nursing since 2000.

NBC's new hospital drama, *Mercy*, comes in at the top of the list. Some of the most popular hospital dramas—for example, ABC's *Grey's Anatomy*—made the Worst of the

Decade list. And when that care is shown in these dramas, it often does not reflect the education and specialization of today's nurses. She says unless that changes, nursing will not be able to attract talented students who want to make it their career.

## New Words & Phrases

niece/niːs/*n.* 侄女,外甥女
abruptly/əˈbrʌptli/*adv.* 突然地,鲁莽地
embarrass/ɪmˈbærəs/*vt.* 使窘迫,使尴尬
portrayal/pɔːˈtreɪəl/*n.* 描绘,描写
physician/fɪˈzɪʃ(ə)n/*n.* 医师
EKG(Abbr. electrocardiogram)*n.* 心电图

## Exercises

**Task One Translate the following sentences into Chinese.**

1. Nurses are the people who are taking the patient back and forth to the tests, making sure that procedures are administered appropriately.

2. A group of nursing students founded The Truth about Nursing nine years ago to encourage the media to present a more realistic portrayal of their profession.

3. She says unless that changes, nursing will not be able to attract talented students who want to make it their career.

# Ⅲ. Human Disease

### Acute Kidney Failure

Acute kidney failure is the sudden loss of your kidneys' ability to perform their main function—eliminate excess fluid and waste material from your blood. When your kidneys lose their filtering ability, dangerous levels of fluid and waste accumulate in your body.

Acute kidney failure is most common in people who are already hospitalized, particularly people who need intensive care. Acute kidney failure tends to occur after complicated surgery, after a severe injury or when blood flow to your kidneys is disrupted.

Loss of kidney function may also develop gradually over time, with few signs or symptoms in the early stages. In this case, it's referred to as chronic kidney failure. High blood pressure and diabetes are the most common causes of chronic kidney failure.

Acute kidney failure can be serious and generally requires intensive treatment. Unlike the chronic form, however, acute kidney failure is reversible and if you're otherwise in good health you should recover normal kidney function within a few weeks. If acute kidney failure occurs in the context of severe chronic illness—a heart attack, stroke, overwhelming infection—the outcome is often worse.

Signs and symptoms of acute kidney failure may include:

• Decreased urine output, although occasionally urine output remains normal;

• Fluid retention, causing swelling in your legs, ankles or feet;

• Drowsiness;

• Shortness of breath;

• Fatigue;

• Confusion;

• Seizures or coma in severe cases;

• Chest pain related to pericarditis, an inflammation of the sac-like membrane that envelops your heart...

Some people don't notice any early signs or symptoms, or are more bothered by the underlying problem causing the sudden kidney failure.

Your kidneys are two bean-shaped organs, each about the size of your fist. They're located at the back of your upper abdomen, one on either side of your spine. Your kidneys are part of a system that removes excess fluid and waste material from your blood. Initially, blood enters your kidneys through the renal arteries, which are branches of the aorta—the main artery carrying oxygenated blood from your heart to the rest of your body. From there, blood moves through structures in your kidneys known as nephrons.

Each kidney contains approximately 1 million nephrons, each consisting of a tuft of capillary blood vessels (glomerulus) and tiny tubules that lead into larger collecting tubes. Each tuft of capillaries filters fluid from your bloodstream.

The filtered material, which contains both waste products and substances vital for your health, passes into the tubules. From there, waste byproducts—urea, uric acid and creatinine—are excreted in your urine, while substances your body needs—sugar, amino acids, calcium and salts—are reabsorbed back into your bloodstream.

## New Words & Phrases

eliminate/ɪ'lɪmɪneɪt/*vt*. 排除，消除

retention/rɪ'tenʃn/*n*. 潴留

pericarditis/ˌperɪkɑː'daɪtɪs/*n*. [医]心包炎

inflammation/ˌɪnfləˈmeɪʃn/*n.* 炎症,发炎
envelop/ɪnˈveləp/*vt.* 包封,遮盖,包围
spine/spaɪn/*n.* 脊骨
aorta/eɪˈɔːtə/*n.* 大动脉
oxygenate/ˈɒksɪdʒəneɪt/*v.* [化]以氧处理,氧化
nephron/ˈnefrɒn/*n.* [解]肾单位,肾元
capillary/kəˈpɪləri/*n.* 毛细血管
glomerulus/glɒˈmerjʊləs/*n.* [解](肾)小球
tuft/tʌft/*n.* 一丛,一簇
tubule/ˈtjuːbjuːl/*n.* 小管,细管
urea/jʊˈriːə/*n.* [化]尿素
uric/ˈjʊərɪk/*adj.* 尿的,取自尿中的
amino/əˈmiːnəʊ/*adj.* [化]氨基的

## Exercises

**Task One Vocabulary Exercise**

**Direction: Match the words with similar meanings in the two columns.**

| A | B |
|---|---|
| 1. peptic ulcers | a. capillary blood vessels as nephrons in kidney |
| 2. Helicobacter pylori | b. ward the road of something through |
| 3. perforation | c. flow in blood vessel |
| 4. hemorrhage | d. exceed range of natural blood pressure |
| 5. obstruction | e. a urease-enzyme-producing bacterium |
| 6. glomerulus | f. holes in the lining of the stomach and duodenum |
| 7. high blood pressure | g. break a blood vessel |
| 8. bloodstream | h. penetrate the stomach or duodenal wall |

# Part Four Practical Writing

## Prescription

**Direction: Read the following writing sample carefully. Design and finish an imitated writing task with the similar style.**

In the United States, a doctor sometimes may dictate prescriptions to nurses through phone calls, and signs his/her name on them later. Such a prescription should include the doctor's name, the patient's name, address and age, the date of the prescription made, etc. The following sample is a prescription. Read it and learn the meaning of the abbreviations of Rx. ,Sig. and Disp.

**Sample**

Name: *Sue White* Age: *23* Date: *06/11/2009*

Address: *2020 5th Street, Seattle*

Rx.: *Throat lozenge X100mg/tab*

Sig.: *Six tabs. daily*

Disp.: *50 tabs.*

Name of Doctor: *Williams Lang*

Signature: *Williams Lang*

**【Assignment】**

Jenny Duncun,35 years old,lives on 5th Ave. ,New York. She's got a cold and went to see the doctor on July 28,2009. As she's also got a sore throat and a fever,Kate Longley,the doctor,prescribed 8 tablets of aspirin,0. 5 gram per tablet and 30 tablets of throat lozenge,100 mg per tablet for her. She told Jenny that she should take the aspirin 1 tablet each time,three times a day after meals and the lozenge 1 tablet six times a day.

Name: ________ Age: ________ Date: ________

Address: ____________________

Rx. : ____________________

Sig. : ____________________

Disp. : ____________________

Name of Doctor:

Signature: ____________________

# Part Five Prefixes,Suffixes & Roots

**Direction: Learn the prefixes,suffixes or roots in the table by heart and then choose the best answers to finish the exercises.**

**Urinary System(泌尿系统)**

| 汉语/英语 | 常用词根 | 例词 |
| --- | --- | --- |
| 尿 urine | urin(o)-;ur(o)- | urinary 尿的 urinogenital 泌尿生殖的;<br>hematuria 血尿 polyuria 多尿症 |
| 肾 kidney | ren(o)-;nephr(o)- | suprarenal 肾上的 renovascular 肾血管的;<br>hydronephrosis 肾积水 nephritis 肾炎 |
| 膀胱 bladder | vesic(o)-;cyst(o)- | vesical 膀胱的 rectovesical 直肠膀胱的;<br>cystitis 膀胱炎 cystostomy 膀胱造瘘术 |

续表

| 汉语/英语 | 常用词根 | 例 词 |
|---|---|---|
| 尿道 urethra | urethr(o)-; meat(o)- | urethritis 尿道炎 urethroscopy 尿道镜检查; meatotomy 尿道口切开术 meatorrhaphy 尿道口缝合术 |
| 睾丸 testis | test(o)-; testicul(o)-; orchi(o)-; didym(o)- | testosterone 睾酮; testicular 睾丸的; orchitis 睾丸炎; epididymis 附睾 |
| 前列腺 prostate | prostat(o)- | prostatic 前列腺的 prostatitis 前列腺炎 prostatectomy 前列腺切除术 prostatalgia 前列腺痛 |
| 肾盂 renal pelvis | pelvi(o)-; pyel(o)- | pelvioplasty 肾盂造影术; pyelonephritis 肾盂肾炎 pyelography 肾盂造影术 |

1. Fill in the blank with the combining part for the medical term "尿道造影术": ________ graphy.

A. urino B. ureter C. urethro D. urethra

2. The correct spelling form for the word "尿道炎" is ________.

A. uteritis B. urinitis C. ureteritis D. urethritis

3. The correct spelling form for the word "肾积水" is ________.

A. hydrorenosis B. hydronephrosis C. hydrorenitis D. hydronephritis

4. The word with Chinese meaning as "血尿" is ________.

A. hematuria B. hemaurine C. hemaurinati D. hemaurinary

5. Inflammation of the prostate is given the term as ________.

A. orchitis B. orchotitis C. prostatitis D. prostatotitis

6. Which word in the following has the meaning of "no urine"?

A. Anuria. B. Polyuria. C. Anurine. D. Polyurine.

7. Inflammation of the testis is given the term as ________.

A. epididymoorchitis B. orchitis

C. epididymitis D. epididymis

8. Fill in the blank with the combining part for the medical term "膀胱造影术": ________ graphy.

A. gall bladder B. bladder C. vesico D. cysto

9. Which form in the following has nothing to do with "睾丸"?

A. "testiculo-". B. "testo-". C. "cysto-". D. "orchi-".

10. The correct spelling form for the word "膀胱输尿管的" is ________.

A. cystocoureteral B. vesicoureteral

C. vesicourethral D. bladderureteral

# Unit Six

## Learning Objectives

1. To seek and gather information about medical equipment, respiratory system and recovery position from the pictures and charts.
2. To understand two conversations about preoperative nursing.
3. To remember the commonly used medical terms and understand the texts.
4. To know how to write a discharge summary in English.

# Part One  Pictures & Charts

## Ⅰ. Medical Instruments

**Direction: Label the pictures below using the words in the box.**

| | |
|---|---|
| shower chair（沐浴椅） | walking frame（助行架） |
| crutches（拐杖） | walking stick（手杖） |
| wheelchair（轮椅） | commode chair（流动坐便椅） |

1

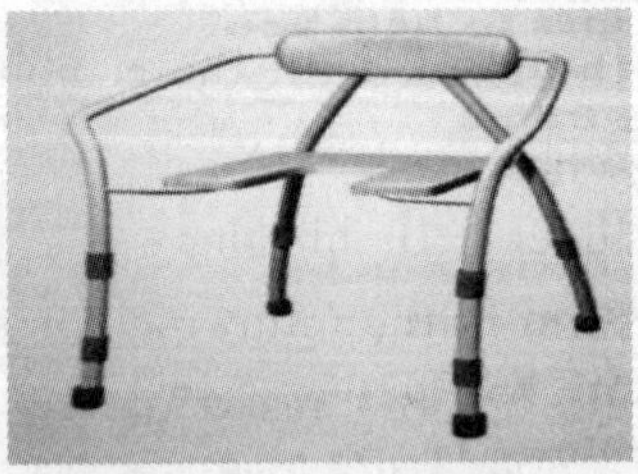

2

3

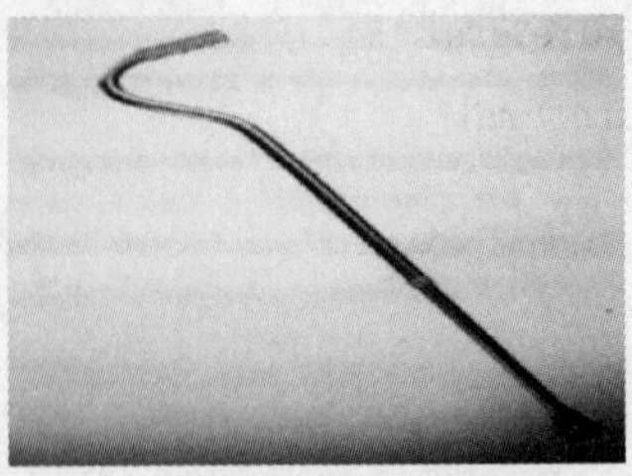

4

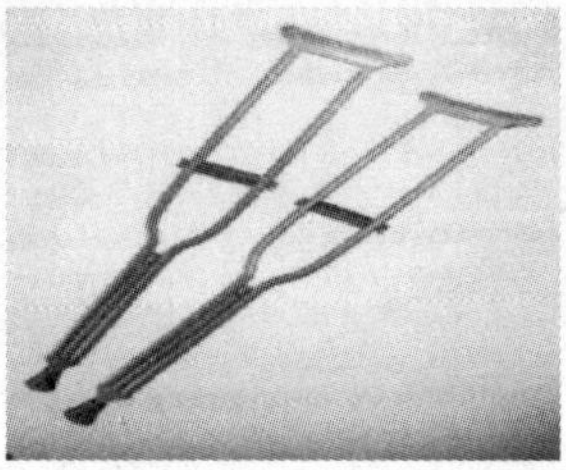

5

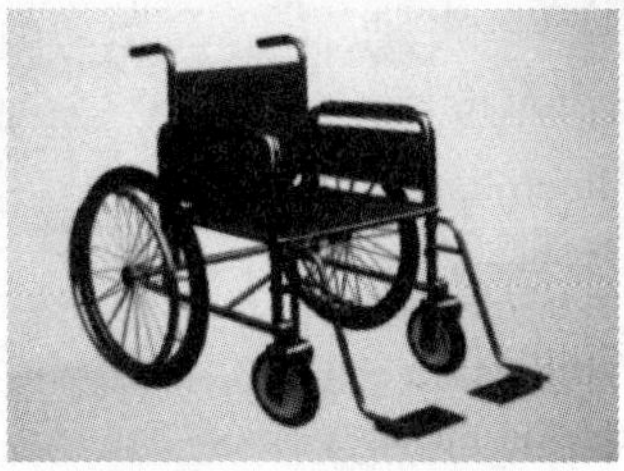

6

1. ______________________
2. ______________________
3. ______________________
4. ______________________
5. ______________________
6. ______________________

## New Words & Phrases

commode/kə'məʊd/*n.* 洗脸台，便桶
crutches/krʌtʃ/*n.* 拐杖；支持

# Ⅱ. Respiratory System

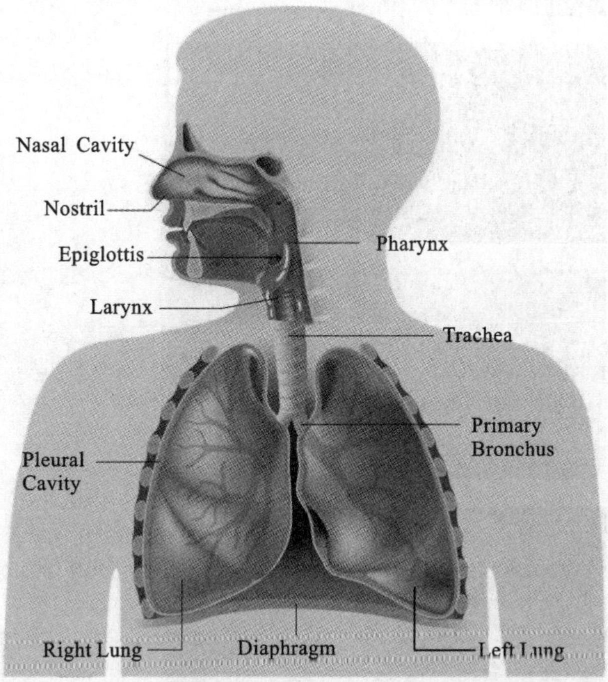


**Direction: Translate the following words into Chinese.**

1. nostril/'nɒstrəl/ ______________

2. epiglottis/epɪ'glɒtɪs/ ______________________
3. pharynx/'færɪŋks/ ______________________
4. larynx/'lærɪŋks/ ______________________
5. trachea/trə'kiːə/ ______________________
6. pleural/'plʊrəl/ ______________________
7. bronchus/'brɒŋkəs/ ______________________
8. diaphragm/'daɪəfræm/ ______________________

## Ⅲ. First Aid: Recovery Position

Step One

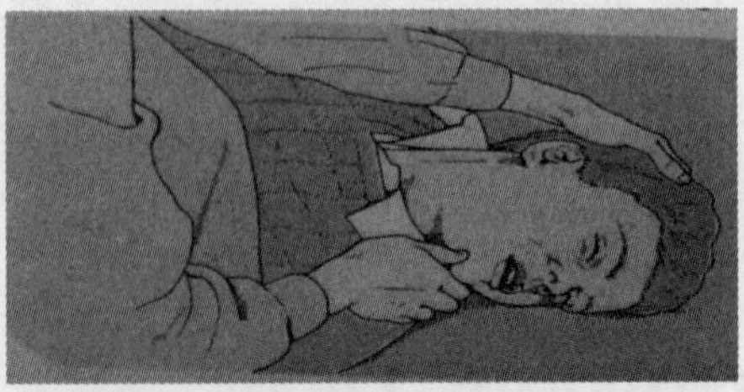

Step Two

Step Three

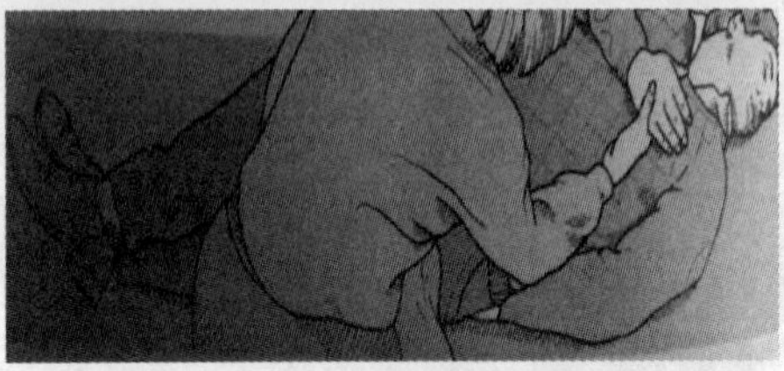

Step Four

Step Five

Step Six

**Direction: Arrange the following steps in a proper sequence based on the medical procedure.**

________ Turn the casualty's head towards you and tilt it back slightly to open the airway.

________ Re-adjust the casualty's head so that it is now well back to make sure the airway stays open.

________ Place the arm nearest you by the casualty's side. Keeping his hand flat, slide it well under his buttock.

________ Kneel beside the casualty. About 22.5cm from his chest and support his head with one hand. Grasp the casualty's clothes at the hip farthest from you and pull him towards you until he is resting against your knees.

________ Slightly raise the farthest leg at the heel, bring it towards you and cross it over his other leg. Then bring the casualty's other arm up and lay it across his chest with the hand, pointing towards his opposite shoulder.

________ Working on the uppermost limbs, bond first the arm, then the leg into a convenient position to prevent the casualty rolling on to his face.

________ The arm behind the casualty should now be free. If it is not, carefully case it out from under his back and leave it lying parallel to his body to prevent him rolling on to his back.

## New Words & Phrases

tilt/tɪlt/*v.* 使倾斜
buttock/ˈbʌtək/*n.* 臀部，屁股
bond/bɒnd/*v.* 使结合
parallel/ˈpærəlel/*adj.* 平行的

# Part Two Listening Comprehension

## Situation Dialogue: Preoperative Nursing

**Task One Watch Episode One and fill in the missing words referring to the original text. Then check your writing against the original.**

Nurse: Morning, Mrs. Peter. I am Cathy. Did you sleep well last night?

Patient: Morning, Cathy. I was a little nervous about the ________, so I didn't sleep that well.

Nurse: Yes, it's hard for everyone at this point. Do you have any questions about the surgery?

Patient: Mm, I signed the consent form two days ago, and I saw the ________ of the operation in the form, such as the complications from the ________, the ________, and even death. I am a little afraid of these things.

Nurse: (smiles and touches the patient's hand) I understand it's not easy for you. Actually the consent form tells us all kinds of the possibilities during the surgery, but these risks are very small and not likely to happen to you. It's just ________ hospital procedure.

Patient: I see. I hope my surgery is successful. Especially my child is only five years old.

Nurse: (smiles) It will be fine. You should trust the doctors. And you have been on a ________ diet for 3 days, right?

Patient: Yes. May I eat today?

Nurse: Yes, but only clear ________ for today. Then you'll start NPO after midnight.

**Task Two Watch Episode Two and complete the answers according to the questions.**

1. When will the patient be given an enema?

   The patient should be given an enema tonight ________.

2. Why will the patient be given an enema?

   The enema causes the patient to have a ________ and then lower the risk of contamination from the bowel content.

3. What are two more things before the surgery?

   Tomorrow morning the patient will be given a nasogastric tube to keep the ________ empty. And the patient will keep the tube for a few days for gastric decompression.

# Part Three Reading Comprehension

## Ⅰ. Medical Horizon

### Childhood Cancer Rates on the Rise

Health experts have warned the public that pollution and environmental worsening are causing rising cancer rates among Chinese children aged under 14.

The Chinese mainland now has more than 32,000 children aged under 14 suffering cancer of various kinds, which translates into a prevalence of 104 in 1 million, according to a secretary of the Chinese Anti-Cancer Association.

"Notably, the fatal disease, long considered a problem in senior years, is striking more and more children. Major risk factors include pollution and unhealthy lifestyles. The most common kinds of cancer among children are leukemia, lymphoma and brain cancer. The incidence of bone cancer is higher among teenagers than younger children. Personally, I've seen more cases of children developing leukemia after home decoration. Long-term exposure to harmful chemicals from decoration materials would substantially raise the cancer risks, particularly for children," he said.

Similarly, parents' occupations are also related, studies have found people such as drivers and painters are more likely to be exposed to lead and this means their children face higher risks of cancer, experts said.

Child cancer patients show common symptoms, including persistent low fever, weight loss for unknown reason and nose bleeds.

Also, unhealthy lifestyles greatly increase the risk of cancer, which is "a lifestyle chronic disease". It has been scientifically proven that factors such as obesity, physically inactive lifestyle and high-calorie diet are also factors in the development of childhood cancer.

"Early intervention in children's unhealthy lifestyles will greatly lower their risk of developing cancer both in childhood and adulthood. For instance, without intervention, overweight children, who are usually meat lovers, often become obese adults, who face much higher risks of breast and colon cancers. Cancers of the breast, skin and colon are more related to unhealthy lifestyles than lung and liver cancers," the secretary said.

"The rates of these cancers are rising rapidly among Chinese people, who have become richer in recent decades and have then adopted a Western lifestyle," he added.

## New Words & Phrases

prevalence/ˈprevələns/*n.* 流行,盛行,普遍
lymphoma/lɪmˈfəumə/*n.* 淋巴瘤
chronic/ˈkrɒnɪk/*adj.* (病)慢性的,长期的
obesity/əuˈbisɪti/*n.* 肥胖,过胖
obese/əuˈbiːs/*adj.* 肥胖的,过胖的
breast/brest/*n.* 乳房,胸部

## Exercises

**Task One Choose the best answer to each of the following questions according to the text.**

1. According to the passage, which statement is not true?

A. Pollution is causing rising cancer rates among Chinese children aged under14.

B. The most common kinds of cancer among children are leukemia, lymphoma, and brain cancer.

C. Parents' occupations are not related to childhood cancer rates.

D. Persistent low fever is one of common symptoms of childhood cancer.

2. Which of the following cancer are most related to pollution and unhealthy lifestyle according to the third paragraph?

A. Lung cancer. B. Breast cancer. C. Liver cancer. D. Brain cancer.

3. Major risk factors of the fatal disease don't include ______.

A. healthy lifestyles B. physically inactive lifestyle

C. pollution D. high-calorie diet

4. Having adopted a Western lifestyle, Chinese people may ______.

A. become richer B. become healthier

C. become happier D. become unhealthier

5. Child cancer patients show common symptoms, not including ______.

A. persistent low fever B. weight gain

C. nose bleeding D. weight loss for unknown reason

**Task Two Fill in the blanks with the words given below, changing the form if necessary, fill in each blank with one word only.**

**chronic prevalence obesity lymphoma symptom**

1. The ______ of lower back pain among adults in our society may well have its origins in childhood punishment.

2. Hodgkin's disease(or lymphoreticuloma) is the most common malignant ______.

3. Anorexia nervous probably represents a weight phobia—the fear of ______.

4. A fever is a ______ of illness.

5. ______ diseases usually develop slowly, last a long time.

## Ⅱ. Hospital Story

### From a Patient to a Nurse

When it comes to hospital care, Jody Baker has a unique perspective—as both a caregiver and a patient.

Twenty-three years ago, Jody Baker, then 24, was on her way home from work when her life was changed forever. A catastrophic car accident left her with multiple injuries, including broken bones and a traumatic brain injury.

Taken to JFK Medical Center in Edison, Jody wasn't expected to live. She spent a month in the intensive care unit in a coma. And while she doesn't recall the accident or much about her stay at JFK, she has no doubt that the great care she received there helped save her life.

Once stable enough to travel, Jody was transferred to Underwood-Memorial Hospital in Woodbury so she could continue her recovery closer to home. While at Underwood, she endured months of painful rehabilitation and physical therapy.

"The nurses at Underwood were wonderfully caring and vigilant in attending to the needs of this bedridden, brain injured patient," said Jody.

But from tragedy came triumph. When Jody was finally able to return to work she realized she wanted to do something meaningful with her second chance at life. Jody wanted to become a nurse.

She earned her Associate's degree in Nursing from Gloucester County College. She has been working as the critical care clinical nurse specialist at a medical center and recently accepted a position as a registered nurse in CT angiography.

Jody feels the accident was meant to be. She believes she has been blessed with the gift to help others who were also given a second chance at life. She's held hands with families as their loved ones were permitted to die with dignity, has calmed confused patients and supported those who thought there was no hope.

"What goes around comes around," said Jody. "Someday, I will be the patient again. I have no doubt that some wonderful nurse will be my guardian angel."

## New Words & Phrases

catastrophic/ˌkætəˈstrɒfɪk/*adj*. 灾难的，激变的
traumatic/traʊˈmætɪk/*adj*. 外伤的，创伤（性）的
coma/ˈkəʊmə/*n*. 昏睡（状态），昏迷
bedridden/ˈbedrɪd(ə)n/*adj*. 卧床不起的
registerd nurse 注册护士
angiography/ˌændʒɪˈɒgrəfi/*n*. 血管造影法

## Exercises

**Task One Translate the following sentences into Chinese.**

1. When it comes to hospital care, Jody Baker has a unique perspective—as both a caregiver and a patient.

2. The nurses at Underwood were wonderfully caring and vigilant in attending to the needs of this bedridden, brain injured patient.

3. She's held hands with families as their loved ones were permitted to die with dignity, has calmed confused patients and supported those who thought there was no hope.

## Ⅲ. Human Disease

### Constipation

Constipation is a common digestive system problem in which you have infrequent bowel movements, pass hard stools, or strain during bowel movements. There may not be defecation for more than a few days.

Not having a bowel movement every day doesn't necessarily mean you're constipated. You're likely constipated, however, if you:

- Pass a hard stool fewer than three times a week;
- Strain frequently during bowel movements;
- Have abdominal bloating or discomfort.

To understand constipation, it helps to know how the colon, or large intestine, works. As food moves through the colon, the colon absorbs water from the food while it forms waste products, or stool. Muscle contractions in the colon then push the stool toward the rectum. By the time stool reaches the rectum it is solid, because most of the water has been absorbed.

Constipation occurs when the colon absorbs too much water or if the colon muscle contractions are slow or sluggish, causing the stool to move through the colon too slowly. As a result, stools can become hard and dry. Common causes of constipation are:

- Inadequate fluid intake,
- A low-fiber diet,
- Inattention to bowel habits,
- Age,
- Lack of physical activity,
- Pregnancy,
- Illness.

When you are constipated you feel that passing stools has become more difficult than it used to be. Passing stools may feel more difficult for one, or more, reasons. For example, passing stools may have become significantly less frequent, or significantly less effective (you feel that you are unable to completely empty your bowel).

Most people do not need to worry extraordinarily. Only a small number of patients with constipation have a more serious medical problem. If you have constipation for more than two weeks, you should see a doctor so he or she can determine the source of your problem and treat it. If constipation is caused by colon cancer, early detection and treatment is very important.

A diagnosis of constipation generally depends on your medical history and physical exam. Your doctor will first want to make sure you don't have a blockage in your small intestine or colon (intestinal obstruction), an endocrine condition, such as hypothyroidism, or an electrolyte disturbance. He or she will also want to check your medications in case they may be causing your constipation.

In people without medical problems, the main intervention is to increase the intake of fluids (preferably water) and dietary fiber. The latter may be achieved by consuming more vegetables and fruit and whole meal bread, and by adding linseeds to one's diet. The routine non-medical use of laxatives is to be discouraged as this may result in bowel action becoming dependent upon their use. Enemas can be used to provide a form of mechanical stimulation. However, enemas are generally useful only for stool in the rectum, not in the intestinal tract.

## New Words & Phrases

constipation/ˌkɒnstɪˈpeɪʃn/*n.* 便秘
bowel/ˈbaʊəl/*n.* 肠
stool/stuːl/*n.* 大便，厕所
colon/ˈkəʊlən/*n.* 大肠，结肠，冒号
rectum/ˈrektəm/*n.* 直肠
contraction/kənˈtrækʃn/*n.* 收缩，缩写式，紧缩
intestinal/ˌɪnteˈstaɪnl/*adj.* 肠的，肠内的，(疾病)侵袭肠的
hypothyroidism/ˌhaɪpəʊˈθaɪrɔɪdɪzəm/*n.* [医]甲状腺机能减退
electrolyte/ɪˈlektrəlaɪt/*n.* 电解质，电解液
linseed/ˈlɪnsiːd/*n.* 亚麻子，亚麻仁
laxative/ˈlæksətɪv/*adj.* 放松的，通便的
enema/ˈenəmə/*n.* 灌肠剂
stimulation/ˌstɪmjʊˈleɪʃn/*n.* 激励，鼓舞，刺激

## Exercises

**Task One Vocabulary Exercise**

**Direction: There are ten incomplete sentences in this part. For each sentence there are four choices marked A, B, C, D, and choose the correct one to complete the sentence.**

1. ________ is a condition characterized by inflammation of the appendix.
A. Appendicitis B. Appendectomy
C. Appendix D. Peritonitis

2. The causes of constipation do not include ________.
A. inadequate fluid intake B. a low-fiber diet
C. inattention to bowel habits D. quantity of diet

3. By the time stool reaches the ________ it is solid.
A. intestinal B. rectum C. colon D. bowel

4. Constipation occurs when the ________ absorbs too much water.

A. bowel B. rectum C. colon D. intestinal

5. The cause of appendicitis relates to ________ of the inside of the appendix.

A. blockage B. gangrene C. rupture D. inflammation

6. Surgery to remove the appendix is called a(an) ________.

A. enema B. peritonitis C. appendectomy D. anesthesia

7. The symptoms of constipation do not include ________.

A. passing a hard stool fewer than three times a week

B. straining frequently during bowel movements

C. having abdominal bloating or discomfort

D. pregnancy

8. ________ is(are) given before an appendectomy to fight possible peritonitis.

A. Irrigate B. Antibiotics C. Anesthesia D. Enema

9. In people without medical problems on constipation, the main intervention is to increase the ________ of fluids (preferably water) and dietary fiber.

A. intake B. intestinal C. inflammation D. incision

10. If the appendix is lateral to or behind the ________, the tenderness may be in the right flank.

A. navel B. pelvis C. lumen D. cecum

# Part four Practical Writing

## Discharge Summary

**Direction: Read the following writing sample carefully. Design and finish an imitated writing task with the similar style.**

**Study the following sample discharge summary and learn to write one.**

**【Sample】**

| Patient: Zhang Jun | Sex: Male Age: 18 |
|---|---|
| HOD (hospital day): | 6 days |
| DOA (date of admission): | October 7th, 2008 |
| Attending Physician: | Yu Bai |
| Conditions on Admission: | Vomiting for unknown reason |
| AD (admitting diagnosis): | Acute gastroenteritis |
| Hospital Course: | The patient was admitted and placed on fluid rehydration and mineral supplement. |

续表

| | |
|---|---|
| DOD (date of discharge): | October 12th,2008 |
| Conditions on Discharge: | The patient improved,showing gradual resolution of nausea and vomiting. The patient was discharged in stable condition. |
| DD (discharge diagnosis): | Acute gastroenteritis |
| Prognosis: | Good. No medications needed after discharge. But if this patient cannot get used to Chinese food,she had better return to UK as soon as possible to prevent the relapse(复发) of acute gastroenteritis. |

The patient is to follow up with Dr. Yu Bai in one week. ________

Yu Bai D:12/10/2008

**【Assignment】**

**Direction:read the information below and fill in the discharge summary**

A patient's information: The patient was called Tom Smith, 15 years old. He was admitted because of high fever, dry cough and no appetite on April 5, 2008. First, he was diagnosed as pneumonia and placed on erythromycin by attending physician Dr. John. After 15 days, the patient improved, showing general state of health. And the patient had good appetite. The patient was discharged in stable condition. At last, he was diagnosed as pneumonia and Dr. John told the patient that no medications needed after discharge. The patient is to follow up with him in one week.

| Patient: | Sex: Age: |
|---|---|
| HOD (hospital day): | |
| DOA (date of admission): | |
| Attending Physician: | |
| Conditions on Admission: | |
| AD (admitting diagnosis): | |
| Hospital Course: | |
| DOD (date of discharge): | |
| Conditions on Discharge: | |
| DD (discharge diagnosis): | |
| Prognosis: | |

The patient is to follow up with Dr. John in one week.

________________________

John D:20/04/2008

# Part Five  Prefixes, Suffixes & Roots

**Direction: Learn the prefixes, suffixes or roots in the table by heart and then choose the best answers to finish the exercises.**

## Reproductive System (生殖系统)

| 汉语/英语 | 常用词根 | 例词 |
|---|---|---|
| 生殖 reproduction | genit(o)- | genital 生殖的  urogenital 泌尿生殖的 |
| 子宫 womb | uter(o)-; hyster(o)-; metr(o)- | uterine 子宫的  extrauterine 子宫外的; hysterotomy 子宫切开术; perimetrium 子宫外膜 |
| 膀胱 bladder | vesic(o)-; cyst(o)- | vesical 膀胱的  rectovesical 直肠膀胱的; cystitis 膀胱炎  cystostomy 膀胱造瘘术 |
| 阴道 vagina | vahin(o)-; colp(o)- | vaginitis 阴道炎; colposcopy 阴道镜检查 colpoperineoplasty 阴道会阴成形术 |
| 月经 menstruation | men(o)- | menopause 绝经  amenorrhea 闭经 |
| 胚胎 embryo | embry(o)- | embryology 胚胎学 |
| 羊膜,羊水 amnion | amni(o)- | amniotic 羊膜的  amniocentesis 羊膜穿刺术 amnioscopy 羊膜镜检查 |
| 胎盘 placenta | placent(o)- | placental 胎盘的  uteroplacental 子宫胎盘的 |
| 胎儿 fetus | fet(o)- | fetal 胎儿的  fetocardiogram 胎儿心动图 |
| 产次 parity | -para | primipara 初产妇  multipara 多产妇 |
| 卵泡 follicle | follicul(o)- | follicular 卵泡的  folliculosis 卵泡增殖 |
| 卵巢 ovary | ovari(o)- | ovariotomy 卵巢切除术  ovariotubal 卵巢输卵管的 |
| 精子 semen | semin(o)- | seminal 精液的  insemination 受精 |
| 阴囊 scrotum | scrot(o)- | scrotitis 阴囊炎  scrotectomy 阴囊切除术 |
| 阴茎 penis | phall(o)- | phallalgia 阴茎痛 |

1. The Chinese meaning for the word "genital" is ________.

A. 生殖  B. 泌尿生殖的  C. 生殖的  D. 生殖器

2. The correct medical term for "阴道炎" is ________.

A. vulvitis  B. vulvovaginitis  C. vulvaginiti  D. vaginitis

3. "子宫切开术" is called as ________.

A. hysterotomy  B. uterotomy  C. metrotomy  D. wombotomy

4. The correct interpretation of the word "amenorrhea" is ________.

A. 月经　B. 绝经　C. 闭经　D. 月经不调

5. The correct spelling of the word for Chinese "羊膜" is ________.

A. amino　B. amnion　C. ammino　D. annion

6. Fill in the blank with the combining part for the medical term "羊膜穿刺术": ________ centesis.

A. amnio　B. amnion　C. ammio　D. annio

7. The correct interpretation of the word "scrotitis" is ________.

A. 阴茎痛　B. 阴茎炎　C. 阴囊炎　D. 阴囊肿大

8. The correct Chinese equivalent for the word "tubalembryo" is ________.

A. 胚胎学　B. 胚胎　C. 输卵管　D. 胚胎输卵管

9. The woman delivering the baby for the first time is called as ________.

A. deutiapara　B. nullipara　C. primipara　D. multipara

10. The correct spelling form for the word "胎儿心动图" is ________.

A. fetocardiogram　B. fetal cardiogram

C. fetus cardiogram　D. embryo cardiogram

# Unit Seven

## Learning Objectives

1. To seek and gather information about medical equipment, digestive system and first aid about severe bleeding from the pictures and charts.
2. To understand two conversations about postoperative nursing discussion.
3. To remember the commonly used medical terms and understand the texts.
4. To know how to write a recommendation letter.

# Part One　Pictures & Charts

## Ⅰ. Medical Instruments

**Direction: Label the pictures below using the words in the box.**

| | |
|---|---|
| cotton swab (棉签) | alcohol wipe (酒精棉) |
| lancet (刺血针) | acupuncture (针灸) |
| medical rubber gloves (医用橡胶手套) | glucometer (血糖仪) |

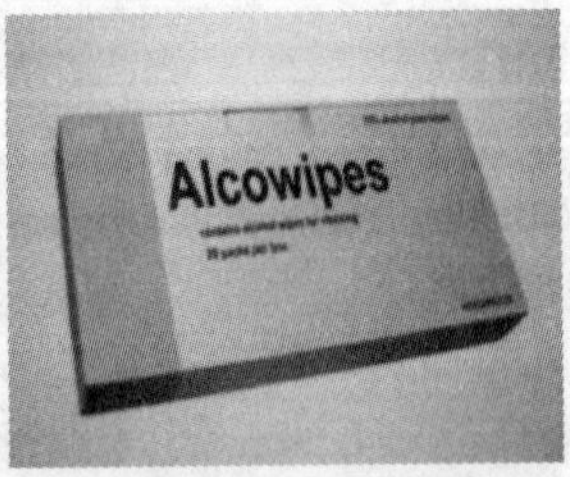


1

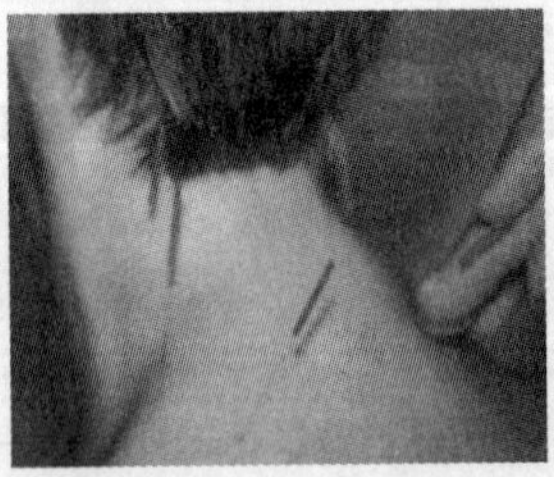

2

3

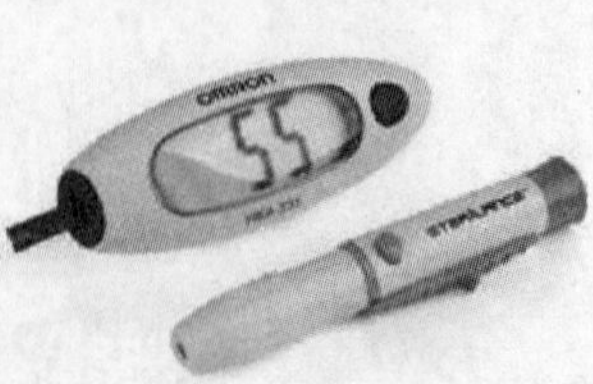

4

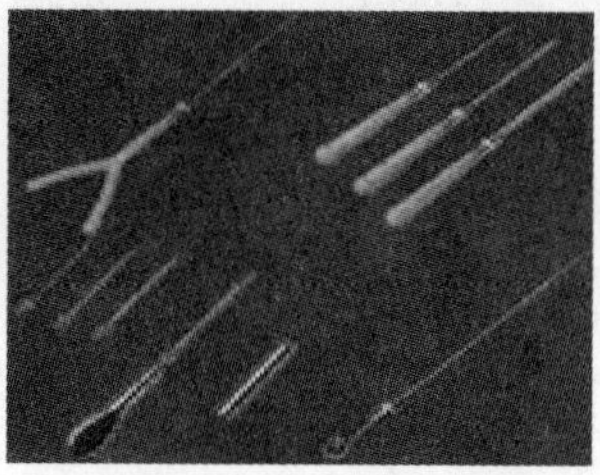

5

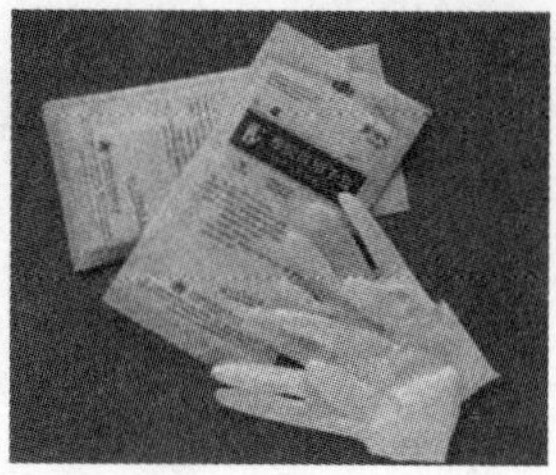

6

1. ______________________
2. ______________________
3. ______________________
4. ______________________
5. ______________________
6. ______________________

## New Words & Phrases

swab/swɒb/*n.* 拭子，药签
lancet/ˈlɑːnsɪt/*n.* 刺血针
acupuncture/ˈækjʊpʌŋktʃə(r)/*n.* 针灸（疗法）
glucometer/gluːˈkɒmɪtə/*n.* 血糖仪

# Ⅱ. Digestive System

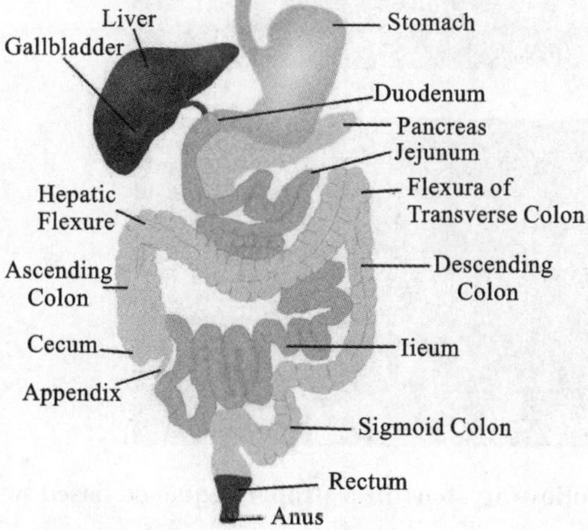


**Direction: Translate the following words into Chinese.**

1. esophagus/ɪˈsɒfəgəs/ ______________
2. gallbladder/ˈgɔːlblædə/ ______________

3. duodenum/ˌdjuːəˈdiːnəm/ ________________
4. jejunum/dʒɪˈdʒuːnəm/ ________________
5. colon/ˈkəʊlən/ ________________
6. cecum/ˈsiːkəm/ ________________
7. ileum/ˈɪlɪəm/ ________________
8. rectum/ˈrektəm/ ________________

## Ⅲ. First Aid: Severe Bleeding

Step One

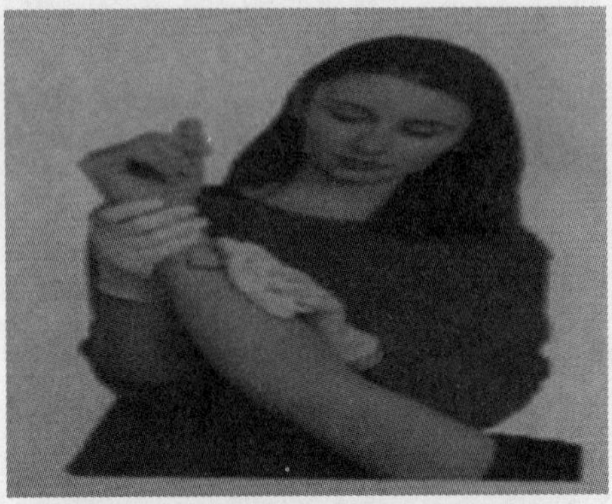

Step Two

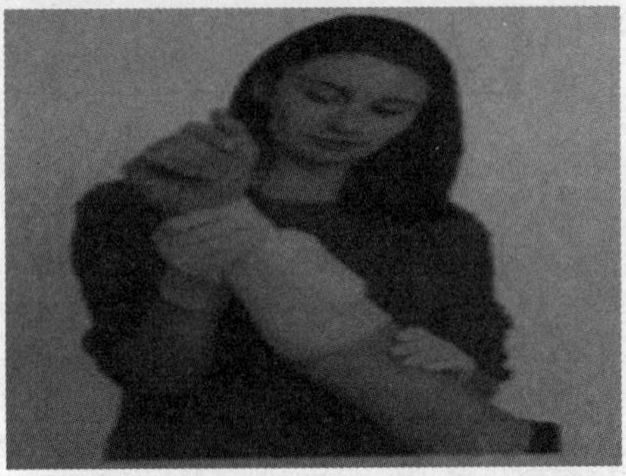

Step Three

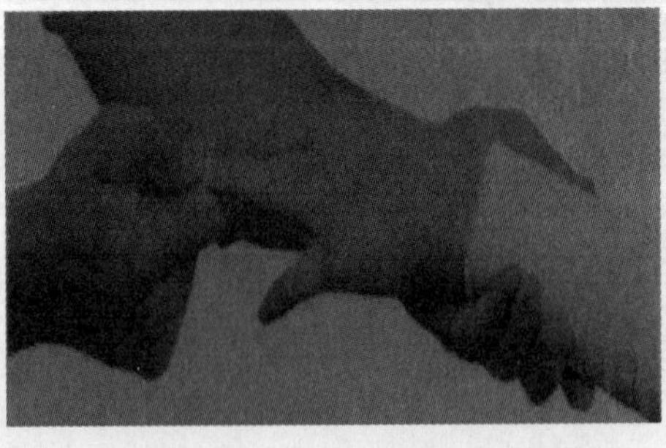

**Direction: Arrange the following steps in a proper sequence based on the medical procedure.**

________ Apply pressure to the wound: Remove or cut the casualty's clothing to expose the wound. Apply direct pressure over the wound. Cover the wound with a sterile dressing. Apply a pad.

________ Bandage the wound: Bandage firmly in place. Apply another dressing or pad if bleeding continues.

________ Raise and support the injured part: Lie the casualty down. Raise the injured part above the level of the heart. Handle gently if you suspect a fracture.

________ Check circulation below the wound.

________ Call 120 for an ambulance if severe bleeding persists.

## New Words & Phrases

expose/ɪkˈspəʊz/*v.* 使暴露
sterile/ˈsteraɪl/*adj.* 无菌的
fracture/ˈfræktʃə(r)/*n.* 骨折
circulation/ˌsɜːkjəˈleɪʃn/*n.* 血液循环
persist/pəˈsɪst/*v.* 坚持，继续存在

# Part Two Listening Comprehension

## Situation Dialogue: Postoperative Nursing Discussion

**Task One Watch Episode One and fill in the missing words referring to the original text. Then check your writing against the original.**

Head Nurse: Hello, everyone. Let's start with Mrs. John. Mrs. John is a 40-year-old American lady and was ________ last Friday. From her biopsy she was diagnosed with rectum cancer 6 months ago in our hospital. A colostomy was performed on her at 10am yesterday. She is fully awake and ________ from the procedure. We are going to talk about her nursing implementation, especially the stoma care after the surgery.

Nurse 1: Mm, I examined her yesterday after she came back from the OR. I feel that she's doing well. Her ________ signs are good, except for a slight fever. But that's ________ after the surgery. The stoma is swollen, but the ________ ________ around the stoma is good.

Nurse 2: Yes, we need to pay close attention to the stoma.

Head Nurse: What kind of stoma is normal, post-op?

Nurse 1: Stoma is initially edematous and shrinks over next 4 to 6 weeks. A normal stoma is moist and reddish pink. I think Mrs. John's is a standard.

Head Nurse: Any other signs? How about the skin?

**Task Two Watch Episode Two and complete the answers according to the questions.**

1. What's the first step of the pouching system?

The first step is ________ hands and apply ________ ________.

2. What should be done after the removal of the protective backing?

Apply pouch ________ ________.

3. What should be done, if the pouch is open?

Don't forget to ________ the end of pouch if it is open.

# Part Three Reading Comprehension

## Ⅰ. Medical Horizon

### Tongrentang's Presence in the West

Beijing Tongrentang Group Co. Ltd., a traditional Chinese medicine (TCM) producer, plans to open three more stores in Europe and is looking for partners to set up shop in the United States, a company executive said.

From its origins as a pharmacy which served the Chinese royal family for nearly two centuries, the company will open three stores in Europe this year—one each in Germany, Poland and Hungary.

Beginning its overseas expansion in 1993, the company now has 45 joint venture or wholly-owned stores in 16 countries and regions.

Most of the company's overseas shops are in Asia where Chinese culture and TCMs are popular, partly thanks to the presence of large Chinese communities.

Tongrentang's presence in the West is smaller. It has one store in Europe—in London—and two in Canada. It also has two stores in Australia.

Tongrentang is looking for partners in the US to set up its first shop. "We have sales agencies in the US now and pay lots of attention to the market. To set up a store there is our next stage of development," the executive said.

Non-Chinese customers have also increased. In Canada, about 10 percent of the customers are local and the proportion is 20 percent in Australia.

But experts said the Western venture faces a lot of challenges.

"The TCM's global journey has never been smooth and its future could be worse as global supervision on medicines will become stricter," some expert said.

"TCMs are recognized by some people in the West. But the principles of Western and Chinese medicines are totally different, and it is hard for TCMs to fit the conditions of Western medicine," said a professor at Beijing University of Chinese Medicine.

### New Words & Phrases

TCM (Traditional Chinese Medicine) 中医,中药

executive/ɪgˈzekjʊtɪv/*n.* 经理，主管
pharmacy/ˈfɑːməsi/*n.* 配药学，制药业，药房
wholly-owned 全资的

# Exercises

**Task One Choose the best answer to each of the following questions.**

1. What's the Tongrentang's origin?

A. A pharmacy which served the Chinese royal family.
B. A pharmacy which served the Chinese general family.
C. A pharmacy which served the Chinese royal hospital.
D. A pharmacy which served the Chinese general family.

2. Tongrentang hasn't yet opened stores in ________.

A. China B. Australia C. Canada D. Poland

3. Why is it hard for TCMs to fit the conditions of Western medicine?

A. TCMs are recognized by some people in the West.
B. The TCM's global journey has never been smooth.
C. The principles of Western and Chinese medicines are totally different.
D. TCMs are not popular in West.

4. Most of Tongrentang's overseas shops are in Asia, partly thanks to ________.

A. Chinese culture and TCMs are popular in Asia
B. the presence of large Chinese communities
C. the presence of large Chinese people
D. Tongrentang expanded its overseas shop in Asia firstly

5. Where does Tongrentang plan to open three more stores?

A. In China. B. In England. C. In Asia D. In Europe.

**Task Two Fill in the blanks with the words given below. Make changes if necessary.**

**executive pharmacy wholly-owned presence overseas**

1. The Chinese residents ________ are much in the thoughts of the people at home.
2. Solutia (Shanghai) is a ________ foreign company.
3. Her ________ greatly brightened up the evening party.
4. A ________ compound drug is made from prescribed ingredients.
5. A hotel manager is a business ________.

## Ⅱ. Hospital Story

### My Visit to a TCM Doctor in Beijing

High on my list of things to do when I visited Beijing, China, was to have a check-up done by a TCM (Traditional Chinese Medicine) doctor. Is it possible to be diagnosed without taking off my clothes, without a blood test, and without x-rays?

I signed up for a visit to a traditional Chinese medicine hospital in Beijing. Nine other people joined me and the tour guide.

It's said TCM includes herbal medicine, acupuncture, massage and moxibustion. Our most charming tour guide told us what a real TCM doctor should look like. First, a TCM doctor should be much older as it takes years to study the practice. Next, she told us that gray hair is desirable as proof of age. The most interesting feature was the stomach—it should have a small pouch. A TCM doctor with a small stomach pouch proves that he knows how to breathe properly.

My turn came. It took less than five minutes for the doctor to diagnose me.

First, he checked my pulse. The accompanying nurse told me that, historically, rich women had no intentions of taking off their clothes to be diagnosed—so doctors developed diagnostic skills based on external signs.

Next, the doctor looked at my tongue which had a bit of cookie on it but that did not matter. The nurse explained that tongue diagnosis ranks second to the pulse diagnosis. Different parts of the tongue relates to different parts of the body. For example, the root of the tongue relates to the kidney and bladder

My diagnosis? My doctor told me I had pain across my back and shoulders as well as a serious case of brain fog. This was true. In fact I have had a pain, particularly in my right shoulder, for so long that I no longer think about it. Nevertheless, I bought a two months supply of herbal medicine. The results? For the first time in many years, after taking the herbs, the shoulder pain, along with the brain fog, went away and hasn't come back.

## New Words & Phrases

moxibustion/ˌmɒksɪˈbʌstʃən/*n*. 艾灸

pulse/pʌls/*n*. 脉搏　*vi*. 搏动，跳动

diagnostic/ˌdaɪəgˈnɔstɪk/*adj*. 诊断的

kidney/ˈkɪdni/*n*. 肾脏，(动物的可食用的)腰子

bladder/ˈblædə(r)/*n*. 膀胱，囊状物

herbal/ˈhəːbəl/*a*. 草本的

## Exercises

**Task One　Translate the following sentences into Chinese.**

1. My doctor told me I had pain across my back and shoulders as well as a serious case of brain fog.

2. Is it possible to be diagnosed without taking off my clothes, without a blood test, and without x-rays?

3. It took less than five minutes for the doctor to diagnose me.

4. The doctor looked at my tongue which had a bit of cookie on it but that did not matter.

5. The accompanying nurse told me that, historically, rich women had no intentions of taking off their clothes to be diagnosed—so doctors developed diagnostic skills based on external signs.

## Ⅲ. Human Disease

### Bone Fracture

When external forces are applied to bone it has the potential to fail. Fractures occur when bone cannot withstand those external forces. When fracture happens, the integrity of the bone has been lost and the bone structure fails.

There are many classifications of fractures according to characteristics such as where they occur and their appearance. A closed fracture means the skin around the fractured bone is not broken. An open one does include a break in the skin, revealing the bone and making the wound more susceptible to infection. A fracture is called complete if the break is the whole way through the bone, and incomplete (or greenstick) if the break is partial. Greenstick fractures are more commonly seen in children. Stress fractures are small cracks in a bone that occur over time as a result of repeated activities that put stress on the bone. According to the way the fracture line goes across the bone, we have transverse fracture, oblique fracture or spiral fracture. If the fracture is in multiple pieces, it is comminuted fracture. Actually, a person can have just one fracture or multiple fractures at the same time.

Generally speaking, a bone fracture results in pain, swelling, and sometimes, bruising from internal bleeding. The patient cannot bear weight or pressure on the injured area, and may be unable to move it without severe pain. The soft tissues around the broken bone may also be injured. The area around or below the fracture may feel numb or paralyzed due to a loss of pulse in that area.

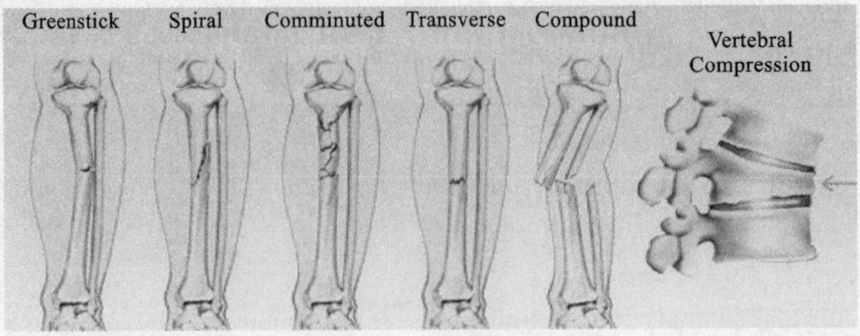


A bone fracture is diagnosed by a physical examination and X-rays of the injured area. However, some types of fractures are difficult to see on an X-ray. In this case, your doctor may order other diagnostic imaging tests, such as computed tomography, magnetic resonance imaging, or bone scans. Open fractures require additional laboratory tests to determine whether blood has been lost and if there is infection.

Initial treatment for fractures of the arms, legs, hands and feet in the field include splinting the extremity in the position it is found, elevation and ice. Immobilization will be very helpful with initial pain control. For injuries of the neck and back, first responders or paramedics may choose to place the injured person on a long board and in a neck collar to protect the spinal cord from potential injury.

Surgery on fractures is very much dependent on what bone is broken and where it is broken. The bones are manipulated by surgeons so that alignment is restored and a cast is placed to hold the bones in that alignment. Sometimes, the bones are broken in such a way that they need to have metal hardware inserted to hold them in place. Depending on the fracture, some of these pieces of metal are permanent, and some are temporary until the healing of the bone is complete and surgically removed at a later time.

## New Words & Phrases

transverse/ˈtrænzvɜːs/*adj*. 横向的，横断的

oblique/əˈbliːk/*adj*. 倾斜的

spiral/ˈspaɪrəl/*adj*. 螺旋形的　*n*. 螺旋

multiple/ˈmʌltɪpl/*adj*. 多样的，多重的

comminute/ˈkɒmɪnjuːt/*v*. 使成粉末，粉碎

paralyze/ˈpærəlaɪz/*vt*. 使瘫痪，使麻痹

tomography/təˈmɒɡrəfi/*n*. X线断层摄影术

splint/splɪnt/*n*. 薄金属片，(外科用的)夹板　*v*. 用夹板夹

immobilization/ɪˌməʊbəlaɪˈzeɪʃn/*n*. 固定

surgery/ˈsɜːdʒəri/*n*. 外科手术

manipulate/məˈnɪpjʊleɪt/*vt*. (熟练地)操作，使用(机器等)

alignment/əˈlaɪnmənt/*n*. 排成直线，队列

## Exercises

**Task One  Vocabulary Exercise**

**Direction: Match the words or phrases with similar meaning in the two columns.**

| A | B |
|---|---|
| 1. initial | a. everlasting |
| 2. poisonous | b. nursing staff |
| 3. pulmonary | c. operation |
| 4. fracture | d. man-made |
| 5. immobilization | e. first, beginning |
| 6. permanent | f. toxic |
| 7. paramedic | g. of lung(s) |
| 8. surgery | h. continuous |
| 9. artificial | i. break |
| 10. sequential | j. fixation |

# Part four  Practical Writing

### A Recommendation Letter

**Direction: Read the following writing sample carefully. Design and finish an imitated writing task with the similar style.**

Study the following format and sample of a recommendation letter and learn how to write one.

| Format |
|---|
| Date of the letter |
| Salutation of the letter |
| Body of the letter |
| Complementary close of the letter |
| Signature |
| |

**【Sample】**

June 1st, 2008

Dear Mr. Lee,

This is to introduce Ms. May Jones, head nurse from the Department of Gynecology and Obstetrics of our hospital who will be on business in London from April 5 to mid

April. We shall appreciate any help you can give Ms. May Jones and will always be happy to reciprocate.

Yours faithfully,

Teng Fei Hospital

**【Assignment】**

**Write a recommendation letter according to the following information.**

兹介绍我院儿科护士长许华女士前往纽约市的希尔顿医院出差三周,请接洽。

秋阳医科大学

2008 年 5 月 5 日

# Part Five Prefixes, Suffixes & Roots

**Direction: Learn the prefixes, suffixes or roots in the table by heart and then choose the best answers to finish the exercises.**

**Endocrine System (内分泌系统)**

| 汉语/英语 | 常用词根 | 例词 |
|---|---|---|
| 分泌 secretion | crin(o)-; secret(o)- | endocrine 内分泌; secretive 分泌的 |
| 腺 gland | aden(o)- | adenoma 腺瘤 adenomyosis 子宫腺肌病 |
| 垂体 pituitary | pitui-; hypophys- | pituicyte 垂体细胞 pituitary 垂体<br>hypopituitarism 垂体功能减退; hypophyseal 垂体的 |
| 甲状腺 thyroid | thyr(o)- | thyroiditis 甲状腺炎 thyroxine 甲状腺素<br>thyrotrophin 促甲状腺激素 |
| 肾上腺 adrenal | adren(o)- | adrenalitis 肾上腺炎 adrenaline 肾上腺素 |
| 胸腺 thymus | thym(o)- | thymosin 胸腺素 thymoma 胸腺瘤 |
| 葡萄糖 glucose | gluc(o)- | glucagon 胰高血糖素 glucokinase 葡萄糖激酶 |
| 钙 calcium | calc(i)- | calcification 钙化 cholecalciferol 胆钙化醇 |

1. The correct spelling form of the word “内分泌” is ________.

A. endocrine B. intracrine C. intercrine D. introcrine

2. Fill in the blank with the combining part for the medical term “子宫腺肌病”: ________ myosis.

A. crino B. gland C. adeno D. utero

3. The Chinese explanation for the word “hypopituitarism” is ________.

A. 下丘脑促垂体 B. 垂体功能亢进

C. 下丘脑垂体 D. 垂体功能减退

4. The Chinese meaning for the word “adenoma” is ________.

A. 腺瘤 B. 腺癌 C. 腺素 D. 肾上腺素

5. The correct Chinese equivalent for the word “thymosin” is ________.

A. 胸腺瘤 B. 胸腺素 C. 胸腺生成素 D. 胸腺生成

6. Which version of Chinese is right for the term “adrenaline”?

A. 去甲肾上腺素 B. 肾上腺皮质激素

C. 肾上腺素 D. 类肾上腺素

7. The English word defined as the inflammation of the thyroid is ________.

A. thyroiditis B. adrenalitis C. gonaditis D. thymitis

8. The word formation of “calc(i)-” means ________.

A. kalium B. natrium C. calcium D. iodium

9. The definition of “thymoma” is ________.

A. any disease of thymus B. tumour of thymus

C. enlargement of thymus D. hypertrophy of thymus

10. Which term is equal to the English term “cholecalciferol” in the following choice?

A. 钙化 B. 高钙 C. 降钙素 D. 胆钙化醇

# Unit Eight

## Learning Objectives

1. To seek and gather information about medical equipment, blood circulatory system and first aid about spinal injury from the pictures and charts.
2. To understand two conversations about enema.
3. To remember the commonly used medical terms and understand the texts.
4. To know how to write an application letter.

# Part One Pictures & Charts

## Ⅰ. Medical Instruments

**Direction: Label the pictures below using the words in the box.**

| slide sheet（患者移动床单） vomit bowl（痰盂） light（灯） |
|---|
| grab bar（扶手，抓条） non-slip mat（防滑垫） non-tip cup（不倒杯） |

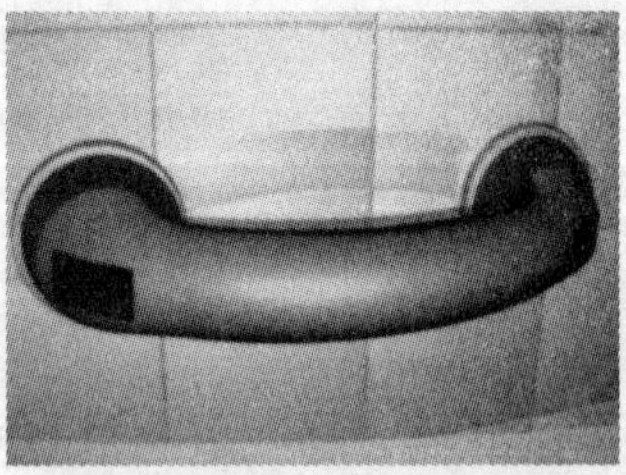

1

2

3

4

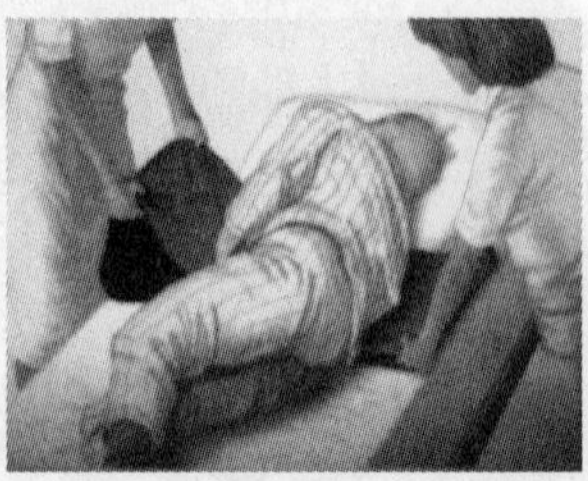

5

6

1. ______________________________
2. ______________________________
3. ______________________________
4. ______________________________
5. ______________________________
6. ______________________________

## New Words & Phrases

slide/slaɪd/*n*. 滑动
vomit/ˈvɒmɪt/*v*. 呕吐
mat/mæt/*n*. 席子，垫子
non-tip 固定的

## Ⅱ. Blood Circulatory System

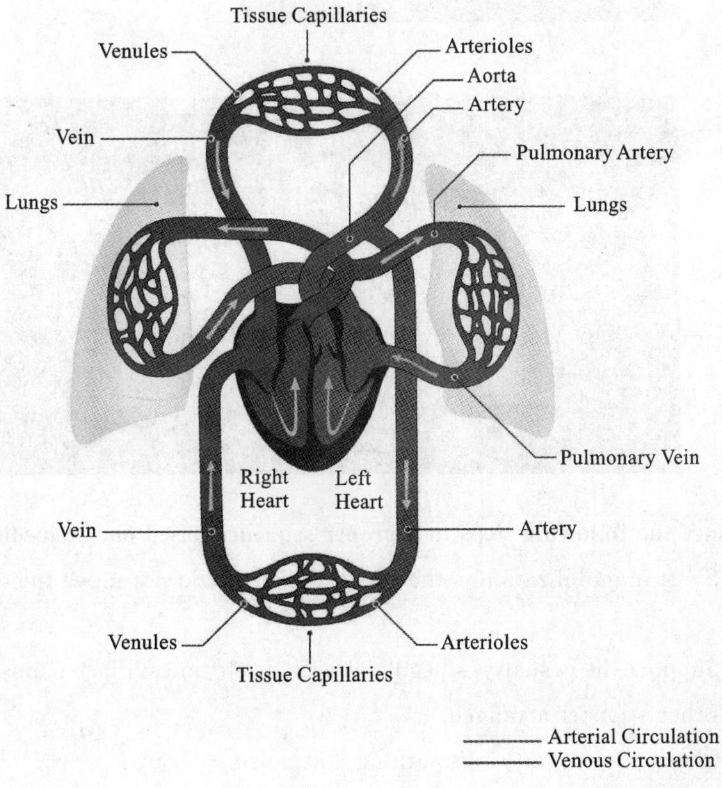


**Direction: Translate the following words into Chinese.**

1. venule/ˈvenjuːl/ ______________
2. vein/veɪn/ ______________
3. capillary/kəˈpɪləri/ ______________

4. arteriole/ɑːˈtɪərɪəʊl/ ________________
5. aorta/eɪˈɔːtə/ ________________
6. artery/ˈɑːtəri/ ________________
7. pulmonary/ˈpʌlmənəri/ ________________

## Ⅲ. First Aid: Spinal Injury

Step One

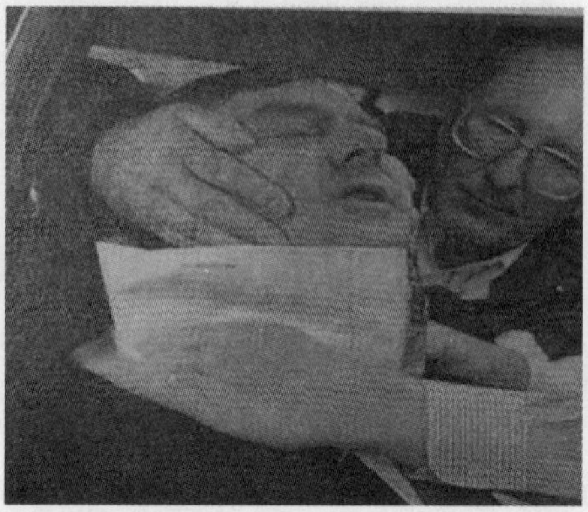

Step Two

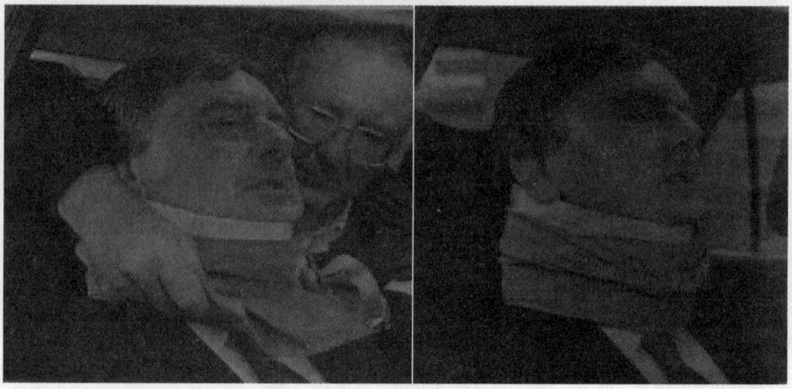

**Direction: Arrange the following steps in a proper sequence based on the medical procedure.**

________ Swift immobilization is the highest priority; do not move the casualty unless in danger.

________ Support the casualty's head and neck at all times. Place hands on the side of the head until other support arranged.

________ Check the casualty's breathing and pulse.

________ Apply a cervical or improvised collar to minimize the neck movement.

________ Call 120 for an ambulance.

________ Give reassurance: calm the casualty.

## New Words & Phrases

spinal/ˈspaɪnl/*adj*. 脊柱的，与脊柱有关的

immobilization/ɪˌməubɪlaɪˈzeɪʃən/*n*. 固定

priority/praɪˈɒrəti/*n*. 优先，优先权

cervical/ˈsɜːvɪkl/*adj*. 颈的

improvise/ˈɪmprəvaɪz/*v*. 临时提供，临时凑成

minimize/ˈmɪnɪmaɪz/*v*. 把……减至最低数量[程度]

# Part Two  Listening Comprehension

## Situation Dialogue: Enema

**Task One  Watch Episode One and fill in the missing words referring to the original text. Then check your writing against the original.**

Nurse: Hi, Mrs John. How are you today?

Patient: Not bad. How are you?

Nurse: Good. I hear you've been constipated for a few days.

Patient: Yes. I haven't had bowel movement at least 4 days, so my abdomen feels distended and painful. I ________ ________ ________ but it doesn't work.

Nurse: That must be uncomfortable. Dr. Peter ________ an enema for you.

Patient: Oh, what is ________ ________? Will it hurt?

Nurse: An enema is a tube of liquid inserted into the rectum through the anus to help your bowel movements. It won't hurt. I am sure you can ________ it.

Patient: OK, I hope so. What should I do now?

Nurse: You should go to the bathroom first. I'll go to prepare the stuff and come back later.

**Task Two  Watch Episode Two and complete the answers according to the questions.**

1. What does the nurse ask the patient to show to her?

   The nurse asks the patient to show her ________ bracelet.

2. How should the patient lie?

   The patient should take off her pants to the knees and lie ________ ________ ________.

3. How long is the patient asked to keep the position?

   The nurse asks the patient to keep the position for ________ ________ ________ minutes.

# Part Three Reading Comprehension

## Ⅰ. Medical Horizon

### Loneliness: an Infection or Not?

Loneliness has been linked to depression and other health problems. Now, a study says it can also spread. A friend of a lonely person was fifty-two percent more likely to develop feelings of loneliness. And a friend of that friend was twenty-five percent more likely to do the same.

Earlier findings showed that happiness, obesity and the ability to stop smoking can also spread like infections within social groups. The findings all come from a major health study in the American town of Framingham, Massachusetts.

The study began in nineteen forty-eight to investigate the causes of heart disease. Since then, more tests have been added, including of loneliness and depression.

The new findings involved more than five thousand people in the second generation of the Framingham Heart Study. The researchers examined friendship histories and reports of loneliness.

For example, loneliness can affect relationships between next-door neighbors. The loneliness spreads as neighbors who were close friends now spend less time together. The study also found that loneliness spreads more easily among women than men.

The findings appeared last month in the Journal of *Personality and Social Psychology*.

The average person is said to experience feelings of loneliness about forty-eight days a year. The study found that having a lonely friend can add about seventeen days. But every additional friend can decrease loneliness by about five percent, or two and a half days.

Lonely people become less and less trusting of others. This makes it more and more difficult for them to make friends—and more likely that society will reject them.

An expert at the University of Chicago led the study. He says it is important to recognize and deal with loneliness. He says people who have been pushed to the edges of society should receive help to repair their social networks.

The aim should be to aggressively create what he calls a "protective barrier" against loneliness. This barrier, he says, can keep the whole network from coming apart.

### New Words & Phrases

depression/dɪ'preʃən/*n.* 消沉，沮丧

barrier/ˈbærɪə/*n.* 障碍物，路障，障碍
personality/ˌpɜːsəˈnælɪti/*n.* 人格，个性

# Exercises

**Task One Choose the best answer to each of the following questions.**

1. This passage is most probably ________.

A. an advertisement B. a news item

C. part of a lecture D. a story

2. It can be concluded from the passage that ________.

A. we should create a "protective barrier" against loneliness

B. lonely people become more and more trusting of others

C. we should help people who have been pushed to the edges of society to repair their social networks

D. A & C

3. According to the passage, which of the following is not true?

A. The average person is said to experience feelings of loneliness about forty-eight days a year.

B. Earlier findings showed that happiness, obesity and the ability to stop smoking can also spread like infections within social groups.

C. Loneliness cannot spread.

D. Lonely people become less and less trusting of others.

4. The word "this" (in the last paragraph) refers to ________.

A. a protective barrier B. an aggressive barrier

C. a damaged barrier D. a wonderful barrier

5. What's the effect of a "protective barrier"?

A. It is important to recognize and deal with loneliness.

B. It can keep the whole network from coming apart.

C. It can keep the loneliness from spreading.

D. It can help people make more friends.

**Task Two Fill in the blanks with the words given below. Make changes if necessary.**

**obesity infection spread barrier loneliness**

1. Mumps is an acute contagious viral ________.
2. The ________ of urban areas endangers wildlife.
3. Social activities usually preserve old people from the ________ of old age.
4. ________ patients are advised to change their diet.
5. Children would bring them close together and break down this invisible ________.

## Ⅱ. Hospital Story

### A Special Gift

Anthony Murphy got a gift he'll never forget-a kidney from his wife, Dina.

Anthony was born with only one kidney which didn't function very well. Two years ago, Anthony went to his doctor who was alarmed to see that his blood pressure was abnormally high. Then later in 2008, blood tests indicated that a transplant was necessary. Soon, a search began for a match.

At first, due to health reasons or lack of a tissue match, many potential donors were passed over. Then a miracle happened. Dina was tested and turned out to be a match for her husband.

"I was very surprised that I was a match, but very relieved to know it was going to be me," says Dina.

When there are children involved and both parents are undergoing surgery at the same time, it raises some complex issues. Even though their children, Colin and Kyle, are young, they seemed to understand that this was something that was important for their dad.

"We told them that mommy was giving daddy a very important part of her body that he needs to feel better. They just thought it was cool that we were able to do such a thing," says Anthony.

"Everyone was very caring and understanding," adds Dina. "The nurses and the doctors for both Anthony and I were just great. They were very encouraging and told us that everything was going to fall into place and be OK."

The transplant took place in January 2009. It took Anthony about six months before he felt like himself again, but the kidney is functioning well and everyone is healthy again.

"I was given the best gift in the world from the love of my life, and now I will be here for Dina and my children. Being able to see it all come true is a wonderful feeling," says Anthony.

"It was truly an amazing experience," adds Dina. "All of the love and support we received from family, friends and strangers was the most beautiful way to heal. For Anthony and me to be able to see our young family grow is to me the most special feeling of all-love."

## New Words & Phrases

blood pressure 血压

abnormally/æb'nɔːməli/*adv*. 不正常地

match/mætʃ/*n*. 相配者

tissue/ˈtɪsjuː/*n.* (解剖)组织
donor/ˈdəunə/*n.* 捐赠者

## Exercises

**Task One  Translate the following sentences into Chinese.**

1. At first, due to health reasons or lack of a tissue match, many potential donors were passed over.

2. Dina was tested and turned out to be a match for her husband.

3. When there are children involved and both parents are undergoing surgery at the same time, it raises some complex issues.

4. I was given the best gift in the world from the love of my life, and now I will be here for Dina and my children.

5. For Anthony and me to be able to see our young family grow is to me the most special feeling of all-love.

# Ⅲ. Human Disease

### AIDS

People have been warned about HIV and AIDS for over twenty years now. AIDS has already killed millions of people. AIDS is one of biggest problems facing the world today and nobody is beyond its reach. Everyone should know the basic facts about AIDS.

AIDS stands for Acquired Immunodeficiency (or Immune Deficiency) Syndrome. It results from infection with a virus called HIV, which stands for Human Immunodeficiency Virus. This disease primarily spread through sexual intercourse and blood. This virus infects key cells in the human body called CD4 positive (CD4+) T cells. These cells are part of the body's immune system, which fights infections and various cancers.

**The latest statistics on the world epidemic of AIDS & HIV at the end of 2007**

| | | |
|---|---|---|
| People living with HIV/AIDS | total | 33,200,000 (30,600,000—36,100,000) |
| | adults | 30,800,000 (28,200,000—33,600,000) |
| | women | 15,400,000 (13,900,000—16,600,000) |
| | children ≤age 15 | 2,500,000 (2,200,000—2,600,000) |
| People newly infected with HIV/AIDS | total | 2,500,000 (1,800,000—4,100,000) |
| | adults | 2,100,000 (1,400,000—3,600,000) |
| | children≤age 15 | 420,000(350 —540,000) |
| Death toll of HIV infection | total | 2,100,000 (1,900,000—2,400,000) |
| | adults | 1,700,000 (1,600,000—2,100,000) |
| | children ≤age 15 | 330,000 (310,000—380,000) |

AIDS symptoms of infection vary because of the conditions of the internal organs and in different parts of the tumor. Common symptoms in the following areas: general symptoms include persistent fever, weakness, night sweats, general superficial lymphadenopathy, weight loss; respiratory symptoms: long-term cough, chest pain, dyspnea, sputum serious blood; gastrointestinal symptoms: such as anorexia, nausea, vomiting, diarrhea, severe blood in the stool; the nervous system symptoms: dizziness, headache, unresponsive, decreased intelligence, mental disorders, twitch, hemiplegia and dementia; damage to the skin and mucous membranes: diffuse papule, herpes zoster, inflammation and ulceration on oral and pharyngeal mucosa; and there will be a variety of malignant tumors, such as Kaposi's sarcoma that represents red or purple mucula, papules and invasive tumor. Therefore, the symptom of AIDS is very complex.

The diagnosis of HIV infection can be made by detecting the presence of disease-fighting proteins called antibodies in the blood. Two different types of antibody tests, enzyme-linked immunoassay (ELISA) and Western blot, are available.

You can decrease your chances of being infected with HIV by avoiding high-risk behaviors:

• Don't have sex, or have sex with only one partner who is also committed to having sex with only you.

• Use condoms with each act of sexual intercourse.

• If you use intravenous drugs, never share needles.

• If you are a health care worker, strictly follow universal precautions (the established infection-control procedures to avoid contact with bodily fluids).

• If you are a woman thinking about becoming pregnant, have a test for HIV beforehand, especially if you have a history of behaviors that put you at risk of HIV infection. Pregnant women who are HIV-positive need special prenatal care and medications to decrease the risk that HIV will pass to their newborn babies.

The prevention and treatment for people with HIV has improved enormously since the mid-1990s, but there is still no way to cure AIDS. The general principle of the treatment included anti-infection, anti-tumor, eliminating or restraint the HIV virus and enhancement organism immunity function.

## New Words & Phrases

lymphadenopathy/ˌlɪmfædəˈnɒpəθɪ/*n.* [医]淋巴结病

anorexia/ˌænəˈreksɪə/*n.* 食欲减退,厌食

diarrhea/ˌdaɪəˈrɪə/*n.* 痢疾,腹泻

hemiplegia/ˌhemɪˈpliːdʒɪə/*n.* [医]偏瘫,半身麻痹,半身不遂

dementia/dɪˈmenʃə/*n.* [医] 痴呆

herpes/ˈhɜːpiːz/*n.* 疱疹

zoster/ˈzɒstə/*n.* 带,带状疹子

ulceration/ˌʌlsəˈreɪʃn/*n.* 溃疡

malignant/məˈlɪgnənt/*adj.* 恶性的

macula/ˈmækjʊlə/*n.* 斑点,污点,黑点,斑疹

immunoassay/ˌɪmjʊnəʊˈæseɪ/*n.* 免疫测定

condom/ˈkɒndəm/*n.* 安全套

prenatal/ˌpriːˈneɪtl/*adj.* 出生以前的

## Exercise

**Task One Vocabulary Exercise**

**Direction: Match the words or phrases with similar meaning in the two columns.**

| A | B |
|---|---|
| 1. immature | a. being on or near the surface |
| 2. anorexia | b. existing or occurring before birth |
| 3. anemia | c. feeling of sickness or disgust |
| 4. superficial | d. physical or mental weariness resulting from exertion |
| 5. nausea | e. paralysis affecting only one side of the body |
| 6. hemiplegia | f. condition of the blood caused by a lack of red corpuscles |
| 7. prenatal | g. loss of appetite, esp. as a result of disease |
| 8. macula | h. of or relating to circulatory system |
| 9. fatigue | i. not fully grown or developed |
| 10. circulatory | j. a spot, stain |

# Part four　Practical Writing

## An Application Letter

**Direction: Read the following writing sample carefully. Design and finish an imitated writing task with the similar style.**

求职信是十分实用的一种应用文。第一段要直奔主题说明写信目的——求职,以及所求职位;第二段为中心段,说明求职条件——所学专业以及最后学历、工作经历,包括兼职,或做过的工作;结尾段要求面试,盼望回信,写清楚联系方式,并表示感谢。

**【Sample】**

1. 假如你是李明,某报社招聘新闻信件的编辑,你写信求职;
2. 毕业于四川大学新闻专业,硕士学位;
3. 曾担任校报体育编辑;现为华西出版社每月简报写稿,并担任编辑。

Dear Personnel Manager,

I notice your ad for a newsletter editor in the October 29 *China Daily*. Because writing and publication work have long been interests of mine, I wish to apply for this position.

I believe both my education and work experience qualify me for the job. In 2011, I graduated from Sichuan University; at the same time, I earned my master degree with a major in journalism and a minor in English. While in school, I was the sports editor on the campus newspaper. Since graduation, I have written and edited the monthly bulletin of the Huaxi Press.

I am currently available for an interview any weekday after 3:00 p. m. You can reach me at my home phone, 855-7382, and any day after 3:00 p. m. I'm looking forward to hearing from you and appreciate your consideration of my application.

Sincerely,

Li Ming

**【Assignment】**

假如你是王璐,某医学院护理专业大四学生,即将毕业,某医院正招聘护士,请写一封求职信。

______________________________________________

______________________________________________

______________________________________________

______________________________________________

______________________________________________

# Part Five Prefixes, Suffixes & Roots

**Direction: Learn the prefixes, suffixes or roots in the table by heart and then choose the best answers to finish the exercises.**

**Nervous System (神经系统)**

| 汉语/英语 | 常用词根 | 例 |
|---|---|---|
| 脑 brain | encephal(o)- | encephalitis 脑炎 encephalopathy 脑病<br>encephalomyelitis 脑脊髓炎 |
| 大脑 cerebrum | crecbr(o)- | crecbral 大脑的 crecbrovascular 脑血管的 |
| 小脑<br>cerebellum | cerebell(o)- | archicerebellum 原小脑 cerebrocerebellum 皮层小脑 |
| 丘脑 thalamus | thalam(o)- | metathalamus 后丘脑 epithalamus 上丘脑 |
| 髓质 marrow | medull(o)- | medullary 髓质的 adrenomedullin 肾上腺髓质素 |
| 脑膜,脊膜<br>membrane | mening(o)- | meningitis 脑膜炎 leptomeningitis 软脑膜炎<br>pachymeningitis 硬脑膜炎 |
| 脊柱 spine | spin(o)- | spinocerebellum 脊柱小脑 cerebrospinal 脑脊的 |
| 精神,意志<br>mind | psych(o)- | psychopathology 精神病理学<br>psychostimulant 精神兴奋剂 |
| 神经 nerve | neur(o)- | neurology 神经病学 neurotmesis 神经断伤 |
| 蛛网膜<br>arachnoid | arachn (o)- | arachnoidal 蛛网膜的 arachnoiditis 蛛网膜炎<br>subarachnoid 蛛网膜下 |
| 狂,癖<br>madness | -mania(c) | erotomania 色情狂 tocomania 产后躁狂<br>dipsomania 酒狂 |

1. Which is the correct meaning of the term "脑血管的": ________ vascular ?

A. encephalo B. brain C. cerebro D. cerebello

2. The term "leptomeningitis" can be translated into Chinese term ________.

A. 脑膜炎 B. 软脑膜炎 C. 硬脑膜炎 D. 脑膜膨出

3. The correct Chinese meaning of the word "arachnoid" is ________.

A. 蛛网膜卜 B. 蛛网膜炎 C. 蛛网膜下腔 D. 蛛网膜

4. The word "subthalamus" means the portion situated ________ the thalamus.

A. above B. over C. under D. below

5. The branch of medical science that is concerned with nerves is termed as ________.

A. neurology　B. neuroscience　C. neurobranch　D. nervescience

6. Any degenerative disease of the brain is termed as ________.

A. encephalitis　B. encephaloma

C. leukoencephalitis　D. encephalopathy

7. What does the inflammation in both the brain and the spinal cord mean in medicine?

A. Encephalomyelitis.　B. Leukoencephalitis.

C. Encephalalitis.　D. Cerebrospinauid.

8. The combining part "encephalo-" denotes the relationship to the ________.

A. brain stem　B. brain　C. large brain　D. small brain

9. The combining part which denotes relationship to the membranes covering the brain is ________.

A. encephalo-　B. cerebro-　C. meningo-　D. cerebello-

10. Which combining part in the choice denotes the relationship to the madness?

A. "-kinesia".　B. "-gnosis".　C. "-phobia".　D. "-mania".

# Unit Nine

## Learning Objectives

1. To seek and gather information about medical equipment, hospital departments and first aid about upper limb injury from the pictures and charts.
2. To understand two conversations about health education.
3. To remember the commonly used medical terms and understand the texts.
4. To know how to write a composition in English.

# Part One  Pictures & Charts

## Ⅰ. Medical Instruments

**Direction: Label the pictures below using the words in the box.**

| stretcher（担架） | first-aid kit（急救箱） | scissors（剪刀） |
|---|---|---|
| bandage（绷带） | scalpel（外科手术刀） | forceps（医用镊子） |

1

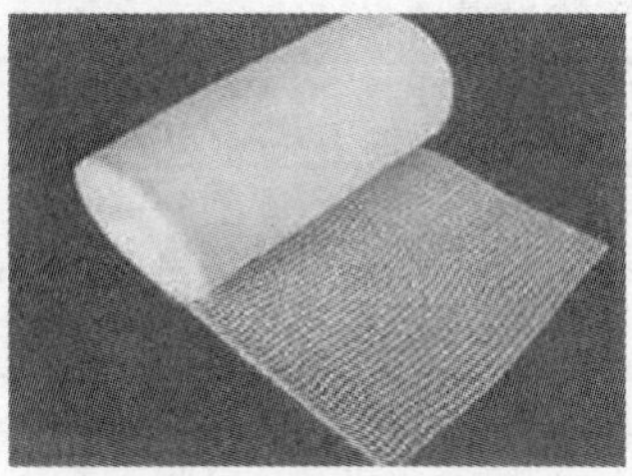

2

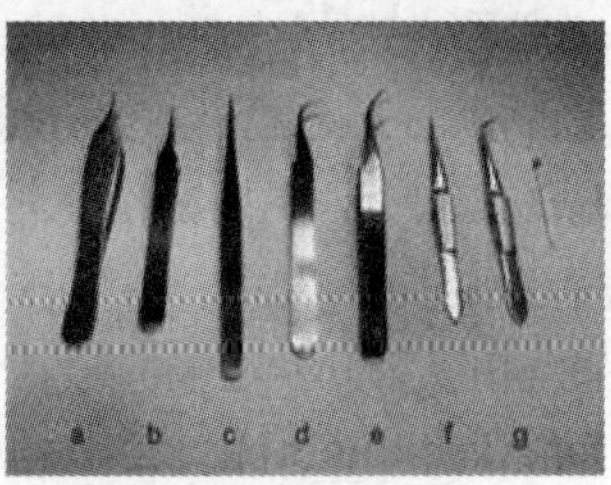


3

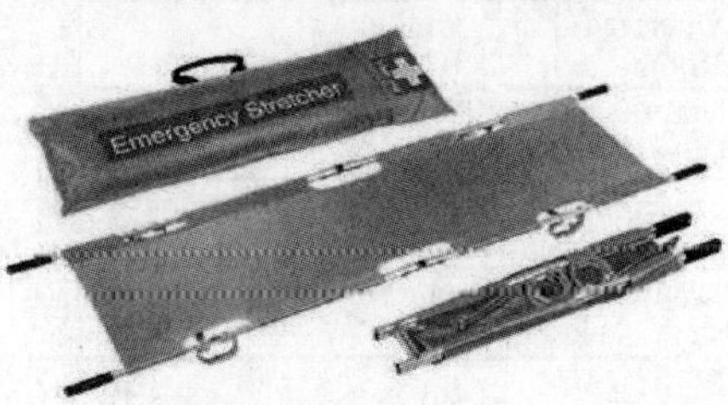


4

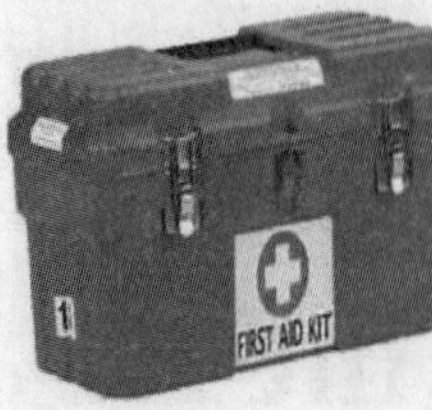


5

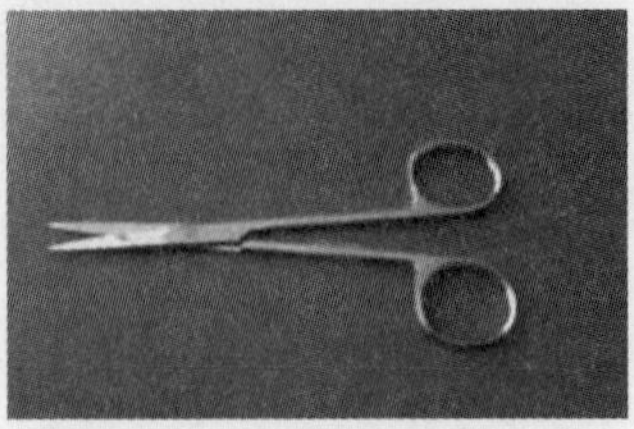

6

1. ______________________________
2. ______________________________
3. ______________________________
4. ______________________________
5. ______________________________
6. ______________________________

## New Words & Phrases

scissors/ˈsɪzəz/*n.* 剪刀
scalpel/ˈskælpəl/*n.* 外科手术刀
forceps/ˈfɔːseps/*n.* 医用镊子

## Ⅱ. Hospital Departments

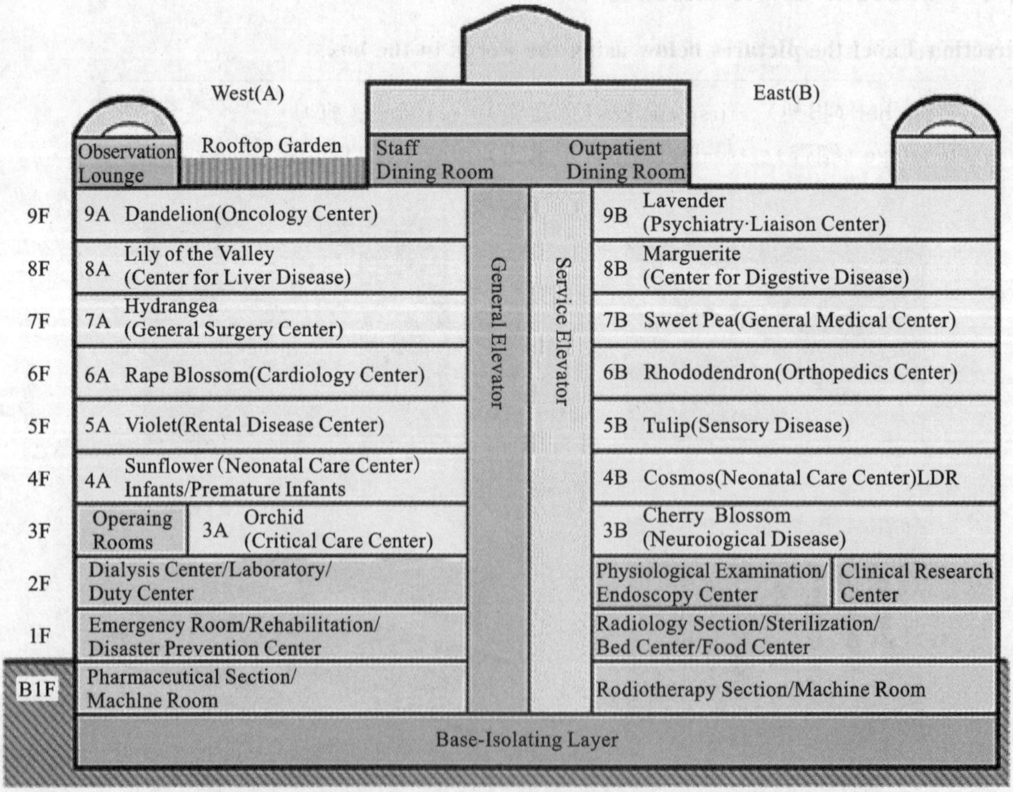

**Direction: Translate the following words into Chinese.**

1. premature/ˌpriməˈtjʊr/ ________
2. rehabilitation/ˌrihəbɪlɪˈteɪʃən/ ________
3. psychiatry/saɪˈkaɪətri/ ________
4. digestive/dɪˈdʒestɪv/ ________
5. orthopedics/ˌɔrθəˈpiːdɪks/ ________
6. neonatal/ˌniːəʊˈneɪtl/ ________
7. neurological/ˌnjʊrəˈlɒdʒɪkəl/ ________
8. endoscopy ________

# Ⅲ. First Aid: Upper Limb Injury

Step One

Step Two

Step Three

**Direction: Arrange the following steps in a proper sequence based on the medical procedure.**

________ If possible, gently bend the casualty's arm at the elbow so that her forearm is across her chest and place soft padding between the fracture site and her body.

________ Take the casualty to hospital.

________ For additional support, secure the casualty's arm to her trunk by applying a broad-fold bandage right around her arm and trunk. Avoid the fracture site.

________ Support her arm with an arm sling.

## New Words & Phrases

limb/lɪm/*n.* 肢
bend/bend/*v.* (使)弯曲,屈身
trunk/trʌŋk/*n.* 躯干

# Part Two Listening Comprehension

## Situation Dialogue: Health Education

**Task One Watch Episode One and fill in the missing words referring to the original text. Then check your writing against the original.**

Nurse: Hi, Mrs. Peter. How are you today?

Patient: Good. How are you?

Nurse: Very good. Thank you. I'd like to talk about your ________ management before your discharge.

Patient: Oh, thanks. I am really worrying about the complication of the diabetes after I go back home.

Nurse: I understand it's not easy for you to manage it now, so we need to ________ ________ you first.

Patient: I think so.

Nurse: OK, let's start. There are two types of diabetes, type 1 and type 2. Do you know what type you have?

Patient: Type 2. It's also called the non-insulin-dependent diabetes. And the doctor suggested me that I take the ________ injections.

Nurse: Good. Can you tell me how many units have been ________ for you?

Patient: 4 units of ________ insulin. But I am not sure.

**Task Two Watch Episode Two and complete the answers according to the questions.**

1. When should the patient inject the insulin?

   The patient should inject the insulin 30 minutes ________ ________ ________.

2. Why do most diabetics use insulin pen?

   Most diabetics use insulin pen because its prefilled devices are ________ ________ ________ for them.

3. According to doctors' orders, what must the patient do in case of hyperglycemia?
   The patient must have some ________ according to doctors' orders in case of hyperglycemia.

# Part Three Reading Comprehension

## Ⅰ. Medical Horizon

### Eating Less Salt

Eating less salt can reduce blood pressure, but can it cut heart disease, too?

Some scientists say a campaign to cut Americans' use of salt is an experiment with the health of millions of people.

Last month we reported about a study that showed eating even a little less salt could greatly help the heart. The study was published in the *New England Journal of Medicine*. The scientists used a computer model to predict how just three grams less salt a day would affect heart disease in the United States.

The scientists said the results would be thirteen percent fewer heart attacks, eight percent fewer strokes, four percent fewer deaths and eleven percent fewer new cases of heart disease. Researchers said it could prevent one hundred thousand heart attacks and ninety-two thousand deaths every year.

The researchers were from the University of California, San Francisco, Stanford University and Columbia University.

They and public health professionals in the United States are interested in a national campaign to persuade people to eat less salt. Such campaigns are already in place in Britain, Japan and Finland.

However, some scientists say such a campaign is an experiment with the health of millions of people.

Michael Alderman is among the critics. He is a high blood pressure expert and says that eating less salt results in lower blood pressure. But he says studies have not clearly shown that lowering salt means fewer heart attacks or strokes.

And he says salt has other biological effects. He says calling for reductions in the national diet could have good effects, but it could also have harmful results. He says there is not enough evidence either way.

Another critic is David McCarron, a nutrition and kidney disease expert. Doctor McCarron says the worldwide similarity suggests that a person's brain might decide how much salt to eat.

Both Doctor McCarron and Doctor Alderman have connections to the Salt Institute, a trade group for the salt industry. Doctor Alderman is a member of an advisory committee. But he says he receives no money from the group. Doctor McCarron is paid for offering scientific advice to the Salt Institute.

## New Words & Phrases

gram/græm/*n.* 克

biological/ˌbaɪəˈlɒdʒɪkəl/*adj.* 生物的，生物学的

nutrition/njuːˈtrɪʃən/*n.* 营养，营养物

stroke/strəuk/*n.* 中风

## Exercises

**Task One Choose the best answer to each of the following questions according to the text.**

1. Where was the report published about a study that showed eating even a little less salt could greatly help the heart?

A. *St. Francis Journal of Medicine*. B. *Southern Medical Journal*.

C. *New England Journal of Medicine*. D. *Journal of Laryngology & Otology*.

2. According to the scientists, which of the following is not the result of the prediction?

A. Thirteen percent fewer heart attacks.

B. Eight percent fewer strokes.

C. Four percent fewer deaths.

D. 13% fewer new cases of heart disease.

3. The word "it" in Para. 4 refers to ________.

A. a campaign to cut Americans' use of salt

B. an experiment with the health of millions of people

C. the scientists used a computer model to predict how just three grams less salt a day would affect heart disease in the United States

D. a national campaign to encourage people to eat more salt

4. What's the purpose of the national campaign mentioned in passage?

A. To prevent one hundred thousand heart attacks and ninety-two thousand deaths every year.

B. To predict how just three grams less salt a day would affect heart disease in the United States.

C. To persuade people to eat less salt.

D. To prevent a heart attack.

5. "Some scientists" mentioned in Para. 7 may include ________.

A. Doctor McCarron

B. Doctor Alderman

C. Doctor David

D. Both Doctor McCarron and Doctor Alderman

**Task Two Fill in the blanks with the words given below. Make changes if necessary.**

**biological nutrition heart attack harmful kidney**

1. He was carried away by a ________.
2. ________ activity in a soil is influenced by soil acidity and nutrient status.
3. Freezing winter is ________ to orange trees.
4. A primary function of the ________ is to remove unwanted substances from the blood.
5. It is easy to show that infection or disease may result in decreased ________.

# Ⅱ. Hospital Story

## Hospital Windows

Two men, both seriously ill, occupied the same hospital room.

One man was allowed to sit up in his bed for an hour each afternoon to help drain the fluid from his lungs.

His bed was next to the room's only window.

The other man had to spend all his time flat on his back.

The men talked for hours on end. They spoke of their wives and families, their homes, their jobs, where they had been on vacation.

Every afternoon when the man in the bed by the window could sit up, he would pass the time by describing to his roommate all the things he could see outside the window.

The man in the other bed began to live for those one hour periods where his world would be broadened and enlivened by all the activity and color of the world outside.

The window overlooked a park with a lovely lake. Ducks and swans played on the water while children sailed their model boats. Young lovers walked arm in arm amidst flowers of every color and a fine view of the city skyline could be seen in the distance.

As the man by the window described all this in detail, the man on the other side of the room would close his eyes and imagine the picturesque scene.

Days and weeks passed.

One morning, the day nurse arrived to bring water for their baths only to find the lifeless body of the man by the window, who had died peacefully in his sleep. She was saddened and called the hospital attendants to take the body away.

As soon as it seemed appropriate, the other man asked if he could be moved next to the window. The nurse was happy to make the switch, and after making sure he was comfortable, she left him alone.

Slowly, painfully, he propped himself up on one elbow to take his first look at the real world outside. He strained to slowly turn to look out the window beside the bed.

It faced a blank wall.

The man asked the nurse what could have compelled his deceased roommate who had described such wonderful things outside this window.

The nurse responded that the man was blind and could not even see the wall.

## New Words & Phrases

lung/lʌŋ/*n.* 肺,肺脏

enliven/ɪnˈlaɪvən/*vt.* 使有生气;使活跃;使快活

picturesque/ˌpɪktʃəˈresk/*adj.* 图画般的,美丽的

## Exercises

**Task One Translate the following sentences into Chinese.**

1. One man was allowed to sit up in his bed for an hour each afternoon to help drain the fluid from his lungs.

2. The man in the other bed began to live for those one hour periods where his world would be broadened and enlivened by all the activity and color of the world outside.

3. The window overlooked a park with a lovely lake.

4. The nurse was happy to make the switch, and after making sure he was comfortable, she left him alone.

5. The nurse responded that the man was blind and could not even see the wall.

# Ⅲ. Human Disease

### Stress

A decent coated white-collar may tell her friends gracefully: "Those days I feel depressed",which shocks her friends,"because the job imposes me great stress."

Lots of surveys have been carried out on stress. What is stress? Stress is a word coined by Hans Selye in 1936,who defined it as "the non-specific response of the body to any demand for change". Others defined it as a feeling that occurred when the body reacted to changes. Dictionaries defined it as "physical, mental, or emotional strain or tension" or "a condition or feeling experienced when a person perceives that demands exceed the personal and social resources the individual is able to mobilize". In medical science,stress is a disruption of homeostasis through physical and psychological ways.

Accordingly,when a person responses to stress,there are changes in emotion,mental and physical status. Medical science could give the primary causes of stressful events by stimulating the nervous system and some hormones. And some physical alterations would handle effectively the pressure. The hypothalamus sends off signs to the adrenal glands to produce more adrenaline and cortisol,subsequently entering into the bloodstream. These hormones would speed up heart rate, breathing rate, blood pressure, and metabolism. Blood vessels open larger. Pupils dilate. Livers release more stored glucose into bloodstream. Sweat produces. If a short time stress is not great,it can help the individual cope with some emergency events, enhancing the individual's ability to perform well. While excessive stress response can cause some problems when it overreacts and fails to reset properly.

Living in a rapid working-space society,individuals should not contradict stress but can learn to adapt to and live with it. There are some ways can help people deal with stress.

First of all,keep an eye on the symptoms of stress. Stress firstly has an impact on the inner emotions, causing the individual feel anxious, panic, oppressed, or excessively worried. Then the individual is irritable to anything,and distract to their hand working and be self-absorbed. If stress has not been taken under control,and the level increases over a long time,the individual would feel fatigued,upset in stomach,headache,pain in the chest,hard sleeping,even nausea and vomiting.

Secondly,know how to control it. Stress is coming with new changes or challenges. Take a review at the schedule,it's wise to omit those least important matters and make a best option. Set up a realistic expectation for professional achievements. Get enough and good night sleeping.

Finally,try to learn more about the causes. Both negative and positive events can lead to stress. When a sign of stress represents, try to detect the leading problems: work, study,family,society,life style,and environment. If you cannot give up the matter totally, you'd better make sure that you must slow down your pace while handling the event.

It is known that people with great stress have a tendency to take up unhealthy behaviors or habits. Therefore, stress can put health on risk. Stress comes in various forms, and it affects people of all ages. Time and space are the best recipes for stress.

## New Words & Phrases

strain/streɪn/n. 过度的疲劳 v.(使)紧张

perceive/pəˈsiːv/v. 感知,感到,认识到

mobilize/ˈməʊbəlaɪz/v. 动员

hypothalamus/ˌhaɪpəˈθæləməs/n. [解剖]视丘下部

adrenal/əˈdriːnəl/adj. 肾上腺的 n. 肾上腺

cortisol/ˈkɔːtɪsɒl/n. [生化]皮质(甾)醇

contradict/ˌkɒntrəˈdɪkt/vt. 同……矛盾,同……抵触

## Exercises

**Task One Vocabulary Exercise**

**Direction: Match the words or phrases with similar meaning in the two columns.**

| A | B |
|---|---|
| 1. fatigue | a. too heavy and fat |
| 2. hormone | b. having a baby growing inside her body |
| 3. overweight | c. a part of a cell in a living thing that controls what it looks like, how it grows, and how it develops |
| 4. pregnancy | d. very great tiredness |
| 5. obesity | e. having insufficient air |
| 6. apnea | f. a chemical substance produced by your body that influences its growth, development, and condition |
| 7. gene | g. general condition of body and how healthy you are |
| 8. appetite | h. a natural form of sugar that exists in |
| 9. health | i. a desire for food |
| 10. glucose | j. very fat in a way that is unhealthy |

# Part Four Practical Writing

### Essay Writing (1)

**Direction: Read the following writing sample carefully. Design and finish an imitated writing task with the similar style.**

一般意义上讲,英语议论文由于所阐释的重点不一样,各自具备不同的特点和板块结

构。在考试中英语议论文一直都是考试的重点，也是学生学习英语必须掌握的一种实用技能。英语议论文常见类型包括：总结类议论文、解决问题类议论文、个人观点类议论文和对比类议论文。总结类议论文常为三段式：第一段简明扼要地点明要论述的话题，并稍加阐述；第二段为中心段，主要分析原因或说明意义、实施的方法；第三段常称为结尾段，对所阐述的内容加以总结概括。

**【Sample】**

## Keep Health

**Outline**：

1. 健康十分重要；
2. 怎样保持健康；
3. 总结。

As a proverb says, "No one knows the value of health until he loses it." In other words, nothing is more valuable than health. If we are sick, it is impossible for us to pursue our career effectively.

Now that we know that health is the resource of our energy, what should we do to maintain our health? First, we should take exercise every day to strengthen our muscles, such as jogging every day, playing tennis at regular time, or climbing on holidays. Second, we should be in a good mood every day. If we get up early, we can breathe fresh air and see the sunrise. This habit can do wonders for our outlook on life. Last, there is a proverb that says, "Prevention is better than cure." If we pay close attention to our health, we can avoid getting sick.

From what has been discussed above, we may safely come to the conclusion that health is vital for us. If we want to make our dreams come true, health is the most important ingredient of our success.

**【Assignment】**

## Blood Donation

**Outline**：

1. 无偿献血的人越来越多；
2. 无偿献血的意义；
3. 总结。

______________________________________________

______________________________________________

______________________________________________

______________________________________________

______________________________________________

# Part Five Prefixes, Suffixes & Roots

**Direction: Learn the prefixes, suffixes or roots in the table by heart and then choose the best answers to finish the exercises.**

**Diseases (1)**

| 汉语/英语 | 常用词根 | 例　词 |
|---|---|---|
| 异常 abnormal | dys- | dysplasia 发育异常　dyspepsia 消化不良<br>dyspnea 呼吸困难　dysuria 排尿困难　dysfunction 机能失调 |
| 不良 bad | mal- | maladaptive 不适应的　malformation 畸形<br>malfunction 功能障碍　malnutrition 营养不良 |
| 慢 slow | brady- | bradypnea 呼吸过慢　bradycardia 心动过缓 |
| 快 rapid | tachy- | tachycardia 心动过速　tachypnea 呼吸急促<br>tachymeter 速度计（速测仪）　tachyuria 排尿急促 |
| 扩张 dilation | -cele | omphalocele 脐突出　hydrocele 积水（水囊肿）<br>bronchocele 支气管囊肿　hematocele 血肿 |
| 发炎 inflammation | -itis | cholecystitis 胆囊炎　nephritis 肾炎　neuritis 神经炎<br>myocarditis 心肌炎　phlebitis 静脉炎 |
| 出血 bleeding | -rrhagia<br>-staxis | colonorrhagia 结肠出血　cystorrhagia 膀胱出血<br>enterostaxis 肠渗血　bronchostaxis 支气管出血 |
| 溢出 discharge | -rrhea | diarrhea 腹泻（痢疾）　glycorrhea 糖溢<br>gastrorrhea 胃液溢出　hemorrhea 大出血 |
| 溶解 dissolving | -lysis | hydrolysis 水解　hemolysis 溶血（血细胞溶解）<br>bacteriolysis 溶菌作用 |
| 嗜好 like | -philia | hydrophilia 亲水性　pharmacophilia 嗜药性 |
| 恐惧 fear | -phobia | hydrophobia 恐水病　aerophobia 高空恐惧症<br>carcinomatophobia 癌病恐怖 |
| 下垂 dropping | -ptosis | gastroptosis 胃下垂　nephroptosis 肾下垂<br>gastroenteroptosis 胃肠下垂　cardioptosis 心下垂 |
| 病毒 virus | viro- | virocytology 病毒细胞学　virogene 病毒基因<br>viromembrane 病毒膜　virostatic 病毒抑制药 |

1. The Chinese meaning for "dysuria" is ________.

A. 排尿困难　　B. 发育异常　　C. 消化不良　　D. 呼吸困难

2. Fill in the blank with the combining part for the medical term "心动过缓": ________ cardia.

A. tachy B. brandy C. dys D. mal

3. The Chinese meaning for "tachypnea" is ________.

A. 心动过速 B. 心动过缓 C. 呼吸急促 D. 呼吸过慢

4. The English term for "结肠出血" is ________.

A. bronchostaxis B. enterostaxis

C. cystorrhagia D. colonorrhagia

5. The English term for "支气管囊肿" is ________.

A. omphalocele B. hydrocele C. hematocele D. bronchocele

6. The word which has nothing to do with "dropping" is ________.

A. hepatitis B. gastritis C. gastroptosis D. nephritis

7. To make a word for "心肌炎",its correct spelling is ________.

A. bronchitis B. myocarditis C. phlebitis D. cholecystitis

8. The following words have the meaning of virus except ________.

A. bacteriolysis B. virocytology C. viromembrane D. virogene

9. Which word has the meaning of "胃肠下垂"?

A. Gastroenteroptosis. B. Gastroptosis.

C. Nephroptosis. D. Cardioptosis.

10. The following words have the meaning of speeding except ________.

A. tachycardia B. bradypnea C. tachypnea D. tachyuria

# Unit Ten

## Learning Objectives

1. To seek and gather information about medical equipment, ICU and external chest compression from the pictures and charts.

2. To understand two conversations about intravenous therapy.

3. To remember the commonly used medical terms and understand the texts in Part Three.

4. To know how to write a composition in English.

# Part One Pictures & Charts

## Ⅰ. Medical Instruments

**Direction: Label the pictures below using the words in the box.**

| cupping jar（火罐） moxa stick（艾条） filiform needle（毫针） |
|---|

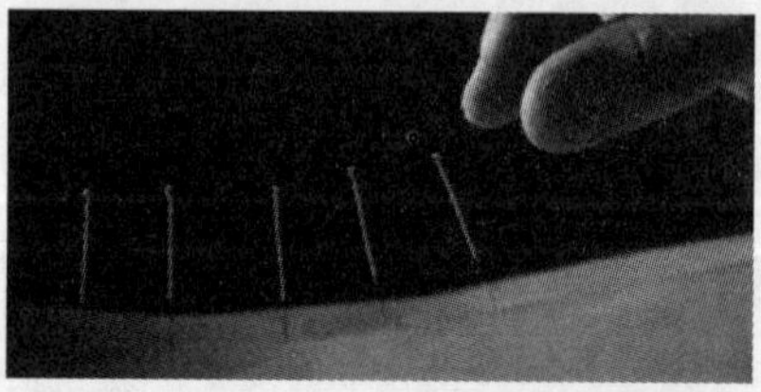

1

2

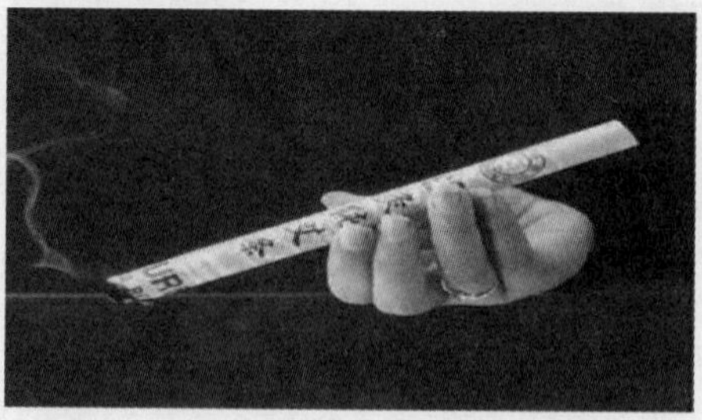

3

1. ______________________________
2. ______________________________
3. ______________________________

## New Words & Phrases

jar/dʒaː(r)/*n.* 罐子
moxa/ˈmɒksə/*n.* 艾，艾篙
filiform/ˈfɪlɪfɔːm/*adj.* 丝状的，纤维状的

# Ⅱ. ICU

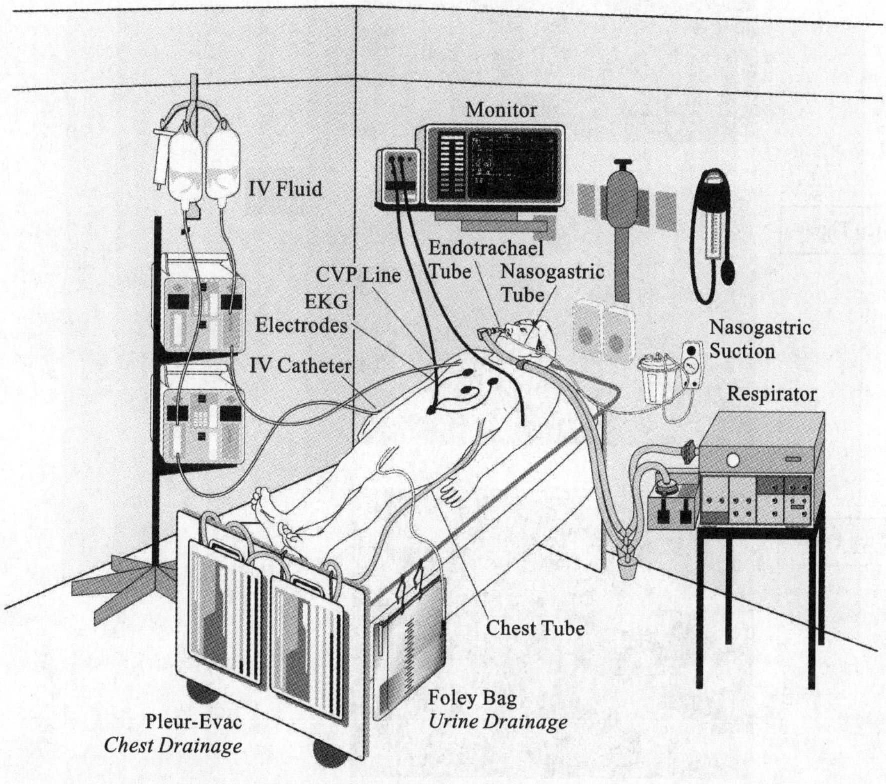


**Direction: Translate the following words into Chinese.**

1. endotracheal/ˌendəʊˈtreɪkɪəl/ ______________
2. respirator/ˈrespəreɪtə(r)/ ______________
3. catheter/ˈkæθɪtə(r)/ ______________
4. endotracheal tube ______________
5. nasogastric suction ______________
6. foley bag ______________
7. urine drainage ______________
8. Pleur-evac ______________

# Ⅲ. First Aid: External Chest Compression

Step One

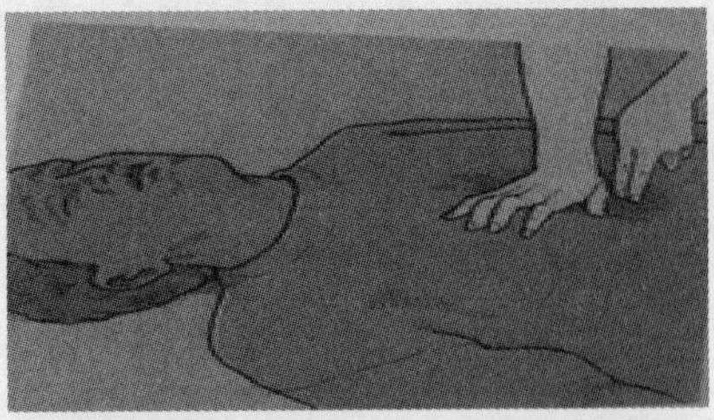

Step Two

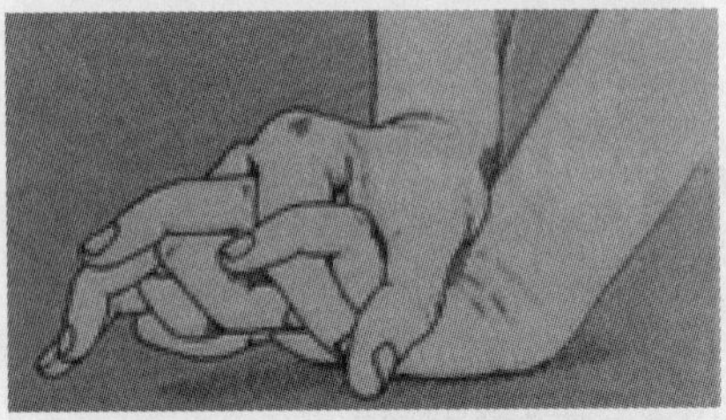

Step Three

Step Four

**Direction: Arrange the following steps in a proper sequence based on the medical procedure.**

________ Lay the casualty flat on the ground and kneel beside him facing his chest. To find his breastbone (the bone which runs down the centre of the chest), first locate the point where the end of his ribs meet in the middle. This is at the bottom of the breastbone. Measure two finger widths above this junction and place the heel of the other hand above them, keep your fingers off the ribs.

________ When you reach 15, move back to the casualty's head, tilt the chin back and give him two breaths of mouth-to-mouth.

________ Cover your hand with the heel of your other hand and lock your fingers together.

________ Kneel upright so that your shoulders are directly over the casualty's breastbone and your arms are straight. Press down about 4.50 m, then release the pressure but do not remove your hands. Complete 15 compressions at a rate of about 80 per minute by counting "one-and-two-and-" as you work.

________ When you can feel the pulse again, stop pumping immediately. Continue with mouth-to-mouth until natural breathing is restored, then stop assistance and place the casualty in the recovery position.

________ Continue giving 15 heart compressions followed by two breaths of mouth-to-mouth. Stop after one minute to check for the pulse; check it again every three minutes.

### New Words & Phrases

breastbone/ˈbrestbəʊn/*n.* 胸骨
pump/pʌmp/*v.* 用泵(或泵样器官等)输送
compression/kəmˈpreʃn/*n.* 压缩,压紧

# Part Two Listening Comprehension

## Situation Dialogue: Intravenous Therapy

**Task One Watch Episode One and fill in the missing words referring to the original text. Then check your writing against the original.**

Nurse: Morning, Miss Susan. I am Mary. I will be looking after you today.

Patient: Morning, Mary. Pleased to meet you. How does my ________ culture look? I can't handle the pain any more. Today I have to go to ________ more often.

Nurse: Your urine culture indicated you have a urinary tract ________. And Doctor Wilson prescribed intravenous ________ according to your sensitivity test.

Patient: You mean you will give me an IV right now?

Nurse: Yes, if you are ready.

Patient: OK. Do I need to take the ________ ________ first?

Nurse: No need. But you can go to the bathroom first and I will come back later.

Patient: Sure. See you later.

**Part Two Watch Episode Two and complete the answers according to the questions.**

1. What did the nurse do before giving the patient an IV?

   The nurse checked the patient's ________ ________ first.

2. What are the steps to have an IV?

   Lie down and make yourself comfortable. Hold your hand for a minute. Then ________ your hand.

3. If the patient needs help, what can he do?

   Ring the ________ ________ if he needs help.

# Part Three Reading Comprehension

## Ⅰ. Medical Horizon

### Your Doctor and Your Headache

Many headache sufferers do not consult a doctor. A recent US study showed that 50% of migraine sufferers had not sought medical advice and had not been diagnosed with migraine. As a result, they were not being treated for migraine.

Many people are disabled by headache. They may receive sympathy from relatives, friends and colleagues but this does not ease the pain. They may take various medications that do not really help. They may have consulted a doctor once and been prescribed medication that was not very effective.

It is important you consult your doctor to diagnose your headache. Any severe or constant headache that begins suddenly and is accompanied by weakness, dizziness, numbness or other strange physical sensations should be reported to a doctor immediately.

Your doctor should be consulted if you have frequent debilitating headaches or take an excessive number of pain relievers. The appointment should be made to specifically discuss the headache.

The role of your doctor is to accurately diagnose your headache and then to work with you to help minimize the effect it has on you and your lifestyle. Recommending medication is a part of this process. As with any medical problem, it is important to receive the best possible medical advice. You may find that your local doctor may not have enough specialized knowledge about headache or may not take headache seriously. Make sure your doctor is aware of the disability caused by headache to your quality of life and how it affects your partner, children, employer, work colleagues and friends.

Headache management is a great challenge. A number of treatment options, preparations and methods of administration may have to be tried to discover what works best for each headache sufferer. The role of the doctor is vital in this process. Once your headache is correctly diagnosed, your headache management plan can be developed. The plan should be evaluated and updated regularly.

Patient-doctor communication is vital for the best outcome. Effective communication on both sides can result in a trial-and-error process that leads to effective treatment that will minimize the pain and disability associated with headache.

## New Words & Phrases

migraine/ˈmiːgreɪn/*n.* 偏头痛
prescribe/prɪˈskraɪb/*v.* 开（药方）
debilitating/dɪˈbɪlɪteɪtɪŋ/*adj.* 使人衰弱的，削弱力量的
administration/ədmɪnɪsˈtreɪʃən/*n.* 给药
trial-and-error 试误法，反复尝试

## Exercises

**Task One Answer the following question according to the text.**

1. According to the passage, many people who suffered headache may ________.

A. be disabled B. be affected C. be concluded D. die

2. According to the passage, those who are disabled by headache may seek understanding from many people except ________.

A. relatives B. friends C. colleagues D. employees

3. What kind of headache should be reported to a doctor according to the text?

A. Mild headache.

B. Severe headache that begins suddenly.

C. Constant headache that begins suddenly.

D. Headache accompanied by weakness, dizziness, or numbness.

4. Whom does a person's headache affect?

A. Partner and children. B. Employer and work colleagues.

C. Friends. D. All of them.

5. Which statement is true according to the passage?

A. Headache management is a great challenge.

B. Few treatment options, preparations and methods of administration may have to be tried.

C. The role of the doctor is nothing in this process.

D. The plan doesn't have to be evaluated and updated regularly.

**Task Two Fill in the blanks with the words given below. Make changes if necessary.**

**prescribe minimize migraine headache affect**

1. I feel awful! I've had an excruciating ________ all day.
2. Remembering English words is a big ________ for English learners in China.
3. Patients should do as doctors ________.
4. Both diet and exercise ________ blood pressure.
5. To ________ this cost, authority should be decentralized wherever feasible.

## Ⅱ. Hospital Story

### Listening Is Powerful Medicine

It was Sunday. I had one last patient to see. I approached her ward ina hurry and stood at the doorway. She was an older woman, sitting at the edge of the bed, struggling to put socks on her swollen feet. I crossed the threshold, spoke quickly to the nurse, scanned her chart noting she was in stable condition. I was almost in the clear.

I leaned on the bedrail looking down at her. She asked if I could help put on her socks. Instead, I launched into a monologue that went something like this: "How are you feeling? Your sugars and blood pressure were high but they're better today. The nurse mentioned you're anxious to see your son who's visiting you today. It's nice to have family visit from far away. I bet you really look forward to seeing him."

She stopped me with a stern, authoritative voice. "Sit down, doctor. This is my story, not your story."

I was surprised and embarrassed. I sat down. I helped her with the socks. She began to tell me that her only son lived around the corner from her, but she had not seen him in five years. She believed that the stress of this contributed greatly to her health problems. After hearing her story and putting on her socks, I asked if there was anything else I could do for her. She shook her head no and smiled. All she wanted me to do was to listen.

Each story is different. Some are detailed; others are vague. Some have a beginning, middle, and end. Others wander without a clear conclusion. Some are true, others not. Yet all those things do not really matter. What matters to the storyteller is that their story is heard—without interruption, assumption, or judgment.

Listening to someone's story costs less than expensive diagnostic testing, but is key to healing and diagnosis.

I often thought of what that woman taught me and reminded myself of the importance of stopping, sitting down, and truly listening. And, not long after, in an unexpected twist, I became the patient with a diagnosis of multiple sclerosis at age 31. Now, 20 years later, I sit all the time—in a wheelchair.

For as long as I could, I continued to see patients from my chair but had to resign when my hands were affected. I still teach med students and other health care professionals, but now from the perspective of physician and patient.

I tell them I believe in the power of listening. I tell them I know first-hand that immeasurable healing takes place within me when someone stops, sits down, and listens to my story.

## New Words & Phrases

ward/wɔːd/*n.* 病房,病室

threshold/ˈθreʃhəuld/*n.* 门槛
bedrail/ˈbedreɪl/*n.* 床的栏杆
monologue/ˈmɒnəlɒg/*n.* 独白，独角戏
vague/veɪg/*adj.* (形状等)模糊不清的，朦胧的，含糊的
sclerosis/sklɪəˈrəusɪs/*n.* 硬化症，硬化

## Exercises

**Task One Translate the following sentences into Chinese.**

1. I was surprised and embarrassed.

2. I often thought of what that woman taught me and reminded myself of the importance of stopping, sitting down, and truly listening.

3. She believed that the stress of this contributed greatly to her health problems.

4. I tell them I know first-hand that immeasurable healing takes place within me when someone stops, sits down, and listens to my story.

5. Listening to someone's story costs less than expensive diagnostic testing, but is key to healing and diagnosis.

# Ⅲ. Human Disease

### Hypertension

High blood pressure, termed "hypertension", is a condition that afflicts almost 1 billion people worldwide and is a leading cause of morbidity and mortality. Many people are not even aware they are hypertensive. Therefore, this disease is sometimes called the "silent killer". This disease is usually asymptomatic until the damaging effects of hypertension (such as stroke, myocardial infarction, renal dysfunction, visual problems, etc.) are observed.

Hypertensive is defined as an abnormal elevation of blood pressure. Both systolic and diastolic pressure values are important to note. According to the latest U. S. national diagnosis guidelines, the following values represent different stages of hypertension:

| Classification | Systolic(mmHg) | Diastolic(mmHg) |
|---|---|---|
| Normal | <120 | <80 |
| Prehypertension | 120-139 | 80-89 |
| Stage 1 | 140-159 | 90-99 |
| Stage 2 | >160 | >100 |

In 90%-95% of patients presenting with hypertension, the cause is unknown. This condition is called primary (or essential) hypertension. The remaining 5%-10% of hypertensive patients have hypertension that results secondarily from renal disease, endocrine disorders, or other identifiable causes. This form of hypertension is called secondary hypertension.

A hypertensive crisis is a severe increase in blood pressure that can lead to a stroke. Extremely high blood pressure—above 180/110 millimeters of mercury (mm Hg)—damages blood vessels. The heart may not be able to maintain adequate circulation of blood. A hypertensive crisis is divided into two categories: urgent and emergency. Signs and symptoms of an urgent hypertensive crisis may include elevated blood pressure, severe headache, severe anxiety, and shortness of breath. During an emergency hypertensive crisis, you may experience life-threatening signs and symptoms, such as pulmonary edema, brain swelling or bleeding, heart attack stroke.

In most cases of hypertension, doctors can't point to the exact cause. But several things are known to raise blood pressure, including being very overweight, drinking too much alcohol, having a family history of high blood pressure, eating too much salt, and getting older. Your blood pressure may also rise if you are not very active, you don't eat enough potassium and calcium.

High blood pressure doesn't usually cause symptoms. Most people don't know they have it until they go to the doctor for some other reason. Without treatment, high blood pressure can damage the heart, brain, kidneys, or eyes. This damage causes problems like coronary artery disease, stroke, and kidney failure. Very high blood pressure can cause headaches, vision problems, nausea, and vomiting.

Treatment depends on how high your blood pressure is, whether you have other health problems such as diabetes, and whether any organs have already been damaged. Your doctor will also consider how likely you are to develop other diseases, especially heart disease. Most people with hypertension are treated with antihypertensive medications. Hypertension is also commonly treated with drugs that decrease cardiac output. Vasodilator drugs, which decrease systemic vascular resistance, are also used to treat hypertension.

You can help lower your blood pressure by making healthy changes in your lifestyle. If those lifestyle changes don't work, you may also need to take pills. Lifestyle changes you can make to help prevent high blood pressure include:

- Lose extra weight.
- Eat less salt.
- Exercise.
- Limit alcohol.
- Get 3,500 mg of potassium in your diet every day. Fresh, unprocessed whole foods have the most potassium. These foods include meat, fish, nonfat and low-fat dairy products, and many fruits and vegetables.

## New Words & Phrases

hypertension/ˌhaɪpəˈtenʃn/*n.* 高血压，过度紧张
mortality/mɔːˈtæləti/*n.* 死亡率
dysfunction/dɪsˈfʌŋkʃn/*n.* 机能不良，功能紊乱，官能障碍
systolic/ˌsɪsˈtɒlɪk/*adj.* 心脏收缩的
diastolic/ˌdaɪəˈstɒlɪk/*adj.* 心脏舒张的
stroke/strəʊk/*n.* 中风
mercury/ˈmɜːkjəri/*n.* 水银，汞
potassium/pəˈtæsɪəm/*n.* 钾
calcium/ˈkælsɪəm/*n.* 钙(元素符号 Ca)
antihypertensive/ˌæntiːhaɪpəˈtensɪv/*adj.* 抗高血压的
vasodilator/ˌvæsəʊdaɪˈleɪtə/*adj.* 血管扩张的 *n.* 血管扩张神经
vascular/ˈvæskjələ(r)/*adj.* 脉管的，有脉管的，血管的
unprocessed/ʌnˈprəʊsest/*adj.* 未被加工的

## Exercises

**Task One Vocabulary Exercise**

**Direction: Match the words or phrases with similar meaning in the two columns.**

| A | B |
|---|---|
| 1. hypertension | a. additional |
| 2. approximately | b. obstruct |
| 3. vision | c. raise |
| 4. systemic | d. trouble |
| 5. elevate | e. fatty deposits |
| 6. category | f. about |
| 7. afflict | g. high blood pressure |
| 8. block | h. sight |
| 9. atheroma | i. all over the body |
| 10. extra | j. kind |

# Part four Practical Writing

## Essay Writing (2)

**Direction: Read the following writing sample carefully. Design and finish an imitated writing task with the similar style.**

解决问题类议论文常为三段：第一段简明扼要地点明要论述的话题，并说明其危害；第二段为中心段，主要分析造成该问题的原因；第三段为结尾段，提出解决的办法。

**【Sample】**

### Reduce the Traffic Accident

**Outline:**

1. 近年来，交通事故的发生呈上升趋势；
2. 交通事故增加的主要原因；
3. 采用相应的措施减少事故。

With the development of society, a growing number of people can afford private cars. Meanwhile, road accidents are often reported in our country and it is amazing that road accidents cause too many deaths, injuries and millions of losses.

Perhaps the key reasons of road accidents are as follows. First, among those accidents, driver's carelessness and lack of the awareness of safety are responsible for most of them. Driving after drinking alcohol, speeding, overloading are the common mistakes that drivers are likely to commit. Second, some people fail to observe traffic regulations, too. They either cross the street with red-light or step on the wrong lane instead of on sidewalks. Last, some roads are in a poor condition. What's worse, there are no traffic signals on some roads.

It is high time we did something to cut the road accidents. On the one hand, people need to be educated to observe the traffic rules. On the other hand, the government should take effective measures, such as "one-way street" or "no left-turn" at certain crossroads to regulate traffic movements. Only in these ways, is it possible to reduce the road accidents in the future.

**【Assignment】**

### Old Men's Problem

**Outline:**

1. 越来越多的老人独居；
2. 老人独居的困难(生活中、经济上、情感上)；
3. 如何解决老人问题。

# Part Five Prefixes, Suffixes & Roots

**Direction: Learn the prefixes, suffixes or roots in the table by heart and then choose the best answers to finish the exercises.**

**Diseases (2)**

| 汉语/英语 | 常用词根 | 例词 |
| --- | --- | --- |
| 肿瘤 tumor | onc(h)/o-<br>-oma | oncogene 致癌或瘤基因 oncology 肿瘤学<br>oncocyte 肿瘤细胞 oncogen 致肿瘤物;<br>myofibroma 肌纤维瘤 melanoma 黑色素瘤 |
| 疾病 disease | path/o-<br>-pathy | pathogen 病原体 histopathology 组织病理学<br>pathoanatomy 病理解剖学;gastropathy 胃病<br>neuropathy 神经病 nephropathy 肾病 |
| 脓 pus | py/o- | pyocyst 脓囊肿 pyorrhea 脓漏(脓溢)<br>pyogenesis 化脓 pyuria 脓尿 |
| 发烧 fever | pyr/o-<br>pyret/o- | pyretic 发热的 pyrexia 发烧(发热) hyperpyrecia 高烧(高热)<br>pyrogenous 高热所产生的;pyretology 热病学 pyretolysis 退烧 |
| 硬化 hardening | scler/o- | sclerosis 硬化症 arteriosclerosis 动脉硬化症<br>sclerometer 硬度计 scleroderma 硬皮病 |
| 软化 softening | malac(i)/o- | malacic 软化的 splenomalacia 脾软化<br>aortomalacia 主动脉软化 cardiomalacia 心肌软化 |
| 狭窄 narrowing | steno/o- | esophagostenosis 食管狭窄 angiostenosis 血管狭窄<br>enterostenosis 肠道狭窄 cardiostenosis 心腔狭窄 |
| 肿大 dilation | -ectasis<br>megalo-<br>megaly- | bronchiectasis 支气管扩张 lymphadenectasis 淋巴结肿大;<br>megalocardia 心肥大 hepatomegaly 肝肿大<br>splenomegaly 脾脏肿大 hepatolienomegaly 肝脾肿大 |

1. The Chinese meaning for "melanoma" is ________.

A. 黑色素瘤 B. 肌纤维瘤 C. 肿瘤细胞 D. 致癌基因

2. Fill in the blank with the combining part for the medical term "神经病":

neuro ________.

A. oma　B. pathy　C. ectasis　D. itis

3. The Chinese meaning for "arteriosclerosis" is ________.

A. 硬皮病　B. 硬化症　C. 主动脉硬化　D. 主动脉软化

4. The English term for "脾软化" is ________.

A. arteriosclerosis　B. cardiomalacia

C. aortomalacia　D. splenomalacia

5. The English term for "肠道狭窄" is ________.

A. angiostenosis　B. cardiostenosis

C. esophagostenosis　D. enterostenosis

6. The word which has nothing to do with "enlargement" is ________.

A. angiostenosis　B. cardiostenosis

C. hepatomegaly　D. enterostenosis

7. To make a word for "支气管扩张",its correct spelling is ________.

A. bronchitis　B. bronchiectasis

C. bronchoscope　D. bronchopneumonia

8. The following words have the meaning of fever except: ________.

A. pathogen　B. pyrexia　C. hyperpyrecia　D. pyretolysis

9. Which word has the meaning of "胆囊切除术"?

A. Hepatolithiasis.　B. Cholecystectomy.

C. Cholecystolithiasis.　D. Cholecystoctomy.

10. The following words have the meaning of disease except ________.

A. gastropathy　B. glucometer　C. neuropathy　D. nephropathy

# Appendix A　Latin Medical Abbreviations

| | |
|---|---|
| aa. | 各 |
| Abs. febr. | 不发热时 |
| Abt. ccen. | 晚饭前 |
| a. c. | 饭前 |
| ad. | 加至 |
| ad lib | 任意 |
| ad us. ext. | 外用 |
| ad us. int. | 内服 |
| Aeros. | 气雾剂 |
| a. h. | 隔一小时 |
| a. j. | 早饭前 |
| alt. die. | 每隔一天 |
| a. m. | 上午 |
| amp. | 安瓿 |
| a. p. | 午饭前 |
| Aq. | 水 |
| Aq. bull. | 开水 |
| Aq. cal. | 热水 |
| Aq. com. | 普通水 |
| Aq. dest. | 蒸馏水 |
| Aq. font. | 泉水 |
| Aq. gel. | 冷水 |
| Aq. steril. | 无菌水 |
| A. S. T. | 皮试后 |
| a. u. a. | 用前振摇 |
| aur. | 耳 |
| Auripil. | 耳丸剂 |
| Auristill. | 滴耳液 |
| b. i. d. | 每日两次 |
| C. | 捣碎,细切 |

| | |
|---|---|
| Caps. | 胶囊 |
| Catapl. | 泥剂 |
| Cit. | 迅速地 |
| Co. | 复方的 |
| Collun. | 洗鼻剂 |
| Collut. | 漱口剂 |
| Collyr. | 洗眼剂 |
| Coq. | 剪,煮 |
| D. | 给予 |
| Dec. | 煎剂 |
| Degl. | 吞服 |
| Dil. | 稀释 |
| D. S. | 给予,标记 |
| D. t. d. | 给予同量 |
| Empl. | 硬膏剂 |
| Emuls. | 乳剂 |
| Enem. | 灌肠剂 |
| Extr. | 浸膏 |
| Filtr. | 过滤 |
| fl. | 花 |
| g. | 克 |
| Garg. | 含漱剂 |
| Gel. | 凝(胶)剂 |
| Gran. | 冲剂,颗粒剂 |
| Gt. | 滴,滴剂 |
| h. | 小时 |
| h. s. | 临睡前 |
| i. h. | 皮下注射 |
| i. m. | 肌肉注射 |
| Inf. | 浸剂 |
| Inhal. | 吸入剂 |
| Inj. | 注射液 |
| i. v. | 静脉注射 |
| L. | 公升 |
| Linim. | 擦剂 |
| Liq. | 溶液 |
| Lot. | 洗剂 |
| M. | 混合 |
| Mag. | 乳胶(剂) |

| | |
|---|---|
| M. D. S. | 混合给予标记 |
| M. f. m. | 混合制成合剂 |
| mg. | 毫克 |
| Mist. Mixt. | 合剂 |
| ml. | 毫升 |
| N. | 数目 |
| Nar. | 滴鼻剂 |
| Neb. | 喷雾剂 |
| Ocul. | 眼膏 |
| Ocus. | 眼药水 |
| O. D. | 右眼 |
| Ol. | 油剂 |
| O. S. | 左眼 |
| O. U. | 双眼 |
| Past. | 糊剂 |
| p. c. | 饭后 |
| Pell. | 膜(剂),薄膜 |
| Pil. | 丸剂 |
| p. m. | 下午 |
| p. o. | 口服 |
| pr. aur. | 耳用 |
| pr. inf. | 婴儿用 |
| pr. nar. | 鼻用 |
| p. r. n | 按情酌定 |
| pr. ocul | 眼用 |
| Pulv. | 粉剂,散剂 |
| q. d. | 每天 |
| q. h. | 每小时 |
| q. i. d. | 每日四次 |
| q. m. | 每天早晨 |
| q. n. | 每天晚上 |
| q. s. | 适量 |
| Rp. | 取 |
| S. | 标记 |
| Serv. | 保存 |
| s. i. d. | 每日 次 |
| Sol. | 溶液 |
| Solv. | 溶解 |
| s. o. s. | 必要时 |

| | |
|---|---|
| Spec. | 搽剂 |
| Spt. | 醑剂 |
| St. | 立即 |
| Supp. | 栓剂 |
| Susp. | 混悬剂 |
| Syr. | 糖浆 |
| Tab. | 片剂 |
| t. i. d. | 每日三次 |
| Tr. | 酊剂 |
| u. | 单位 |
| Ung. | 软膏 |
| ut dict. | 如医师所嘱咐 |
| vesp. | 傍晚,晚间 |

# Appendix B English Medical Abbreviations

| | |
|---|---|
| Ab | antibody 抗体 |
| ABG | arterial blood gas 动脉血气 |
| ACH | adrenal cortical hormone 肾上腺皮质激素 |
| ACTH | adrenocor ticotropic hormone 促肾上腺皮质激素 |
| ADH | antidiuretic hormone 抗利尿激素 |
| adm | admission 入院,接收住院 |
| adm.(admin) | administration 给药 |
| ADR | adverse drug reaction 药物不良反应 |
| A/G ratio | albumin globulin ratio 白球蛋白比 |
| AI | artificial insemination 人工授精 |
| AIDS | acquired immune deficiency syndrome 获得性免疫缺陷综合征 |
| alb | albumin 白蛋白 |
| ALS | advanced life support 进一步生命支持 |
| AMI | acute myocardial infarction 急性心肌梗死 |
| ANS | autonomic nervous system 自主神经系统 |
| APTT | activated partial thromboplastin time 活化部分凝血酶时间 |
| ARDS | acute respiratory distress syndrome 急性呼吸窘迫综合征 |
| ARDS | adult respiratory distress syndrome 成人呼吸窘迫综合征 |
| ARF | acute renal failure 急性肾衰竭 |
| Ba | Barium 钡 |
| BBT | basal body temperature 基础体温 |
| BCG | bacillus Calmette-Guérin 卡介苗 |
| BGL | blood glucose level 血糖水平 |
| bl. cult | blood culture 血液培养 |
| BLS | basic life support 基础生命支持 |
| BMR | basal metabolic rate 基础代谢率 |
| BMT | bone marrow transplantation 骨髓移植 |
| BP | blood pressure 血压 |
| BPD | borderline personality disorder 边缘型人格障碍 |
| BPH | benign prostatic hyperplasia 良性前列腺增生 |

| | |
|---|---|
| BS | blood sugar 血糖 |
| BSL | blood sugar level 血糖水平 |
| BUN | blood urea nitrogen 血尿素氮 |
| C | centigrade 摄氏 |
| CABG | coronary artery bypass grafting 冠状动脉搭桥术 |
| CAD | coronary artery disease 冠心病 |
| CA | carcinoma,cancer 肿瘤 |
| Ca | Calcium 钙 |
| CAH | congenital adrenal hyperplasia 先天性肾上腺增生 |
| Cal | calorie 卡路里 |
| CAT | computed axial tomography 计算机轴向断层成像 |
| cath | catheter 导管 |
| CBC | complete Blood Count 全血细胞计数 |
| CC | cubic centimeter,or chief complaint 立方厘米,主诉 |
| CEA | carcino-embryonic antigen 癌胚抗原 |
| CG | control group 对照组 |
| CHD | coronary heart disease 冠心病 |
| CHF | congestive heart failure 充血性心力衰竭 |
| CK | creatine kinase 肌酸激酶 |
| CKD | chronic kidney disease 慢性肾脏疾病 |
| CLL | chronic lymphocytic leukemia 慢性淋巴细胞白血病 |
| CML | chronic myelogenous leukemia 慢性淋骨髓性白血病 |
| CNS | central nervous system 中枢神经系统 |
| CO | cardiac output 心输出量 |
| CO | carbon monoxide 一氧化碳 |
| $CO_2$ | carbon dioxide 二氧化碳 |
| COAD | chronic obstructive airways disease 慢性阻塞性呼吸道疾病 |
| COPD | chronic obstructive pulmonary disease 慢性阻塞性肺部疾病 |
| CPR | cardiopulmonary resuscitation 心肺复苏 |
| CRF | chronic renal failure 慢性肾脏衰竭 |
| CS | Caesarean section 剖腹产 |
| CSF | cerebrospinal fluid 脑脊液 |
| CT | computed tomography 计算机断层扫描 |
| CVA | cerebrovascular accident 脑血管意外 |
| CVC | central venous catheter 中心静脉插管 |
| CVD | cardiovascular disease 心血管疾病 |
| CVP | central venous pressure 中心静脉压 |
| Cx | microbiological culture 微生物培养 |
| CXR | chest X-ray 胸部透视 |

| | |
|---|---|
| DBP | diastolic blood pressure 舒张压 |
| DDD | daily defined doses 每日规定剂量 |
| DD | differential diagnosis 鉴别诊断 |
| DIC | disseminated intravascular coagulation 弥散性血管内凝血 |
| DJD | degenerative joint disease 退行性关节疾病 |
| DM | diabetes mellitus 糖尿病 |
| DNA | deoxyribonucleic acid 脱氧核糖核酸 |
| DOA | dead on arrival 到达时已死 |
| DOB | date of birth 出生日期 |
| DIW | dextrose in water 葡萄糖液 |
| DU | duodenal ulcer 十二指肠溃疡 |
| ECG/EKG | electrocardiogram 心电图 |
| ED | emergency department 急诊科 |
| EDD | estimated date of delivery 预产期 |
| EDD | estimated date of discharge 预计出院日期 |
| EEG | electroencephalogram 脑电图 |
| ELISA | enzyme-linked immunosorbent assay 酶连接免疫吸附剂测定 |
| ENT | ear nose and throat (otolaryngology)耳鼻喉 |
| ER | emergency room 急诊室 |
| F | fahrenheit 华氏 |
| FBC | full blood count 全血计数 |
| FBG | fasting blood glucose 空腹血糖 |
| FFA | free fatty acid 游离脂肪酸 |
| FHR | fetal heart rate 胎儿心率 |
| ft. | foot or feet 英尺 |
| FUO | fever of unknown origin 不明原因发热 |
| g | gram 克 |
| GA | general anaesthesia 全身麻醉 |
| gal. | gallon 加仑 |
| GH | growth hormone 生长激素 |
| GI | gastrointestinal 胃肠道的 |
| GU | gastric ulcer 胃溃疡 |
| H/A | headache 头痛 |
| HAV | hepatitis A virus 甲型肝炎病毒 |
| Hb | hemoglobin 血色素/血红蛋白 |
| HBV | hcpatitis B virus 乙型肝炎病毒 |
| Hct | hematocrit 血细胞压积 |
| HCV | hepatitis C virus 丙型肝炎病毒 |
| HDL | high-density lipoprotein 高密度脂蛋白 |

| | |
|---|---|
| HDL-Ch | high density lipoprotein cholesterol 高密度脂蛋白胆固醇 |
| HDV | hepatitis D virus 丁型肝炎病毒 |
| HEV | hepatitis E virus 戊型肝炎病毒 |
| HGB | hemoglobin 血色素/血红蛋白 |
| HIV | human immunodeficiency virus 人类免疫缺陷病毒 |
| HLA | human leukocyte antigen 人类白细胞抗原 |
| HR | heart rate 心率 |
| HT | hypertension 高血压 |
| IA | intra-arterial 动脉内的 |
| IC | intracardiac 心脏内的 |
| ICD | International Classification of Diseases 国际疾病分类 |
| ICP | intracranial pressure 颅内压 |
| ICU | intensive care unit 重症监护病房 |
| I&D | incision and drainage 切割和引流 |
| IDA | iron deficiency anemia 缺铁性贫血 |
| IDL | intermediate density lipoprotein 中等密度脂蛋白 |
| Ig | immunoglobulin 免疫球蛋白 |
| IGT | impaired glucose tolerance 糖耐量受损 |
| i. m. | intramuscular 肌内 |
| IMI | intramuscular injection 肌内注射 |
| INF | interferon 干扰素 |
| I&O | inputs and outputs 输入和输出 |
| IOP | intraocular pressure 眼内压 |
| IQ | intelligence quotient 智力商数 |
| IUCD | intrauterine contraceptive device 子宫内避孕器 |
| i. v. | intravenous 静脉内 |
| IVDU | intravenous drug user 静脉注射吸毒者 |
| IVP | intravenous pyelogram 静脉注射肾盂造影 |
| kg | kilogram 千克 |
| LDH | lactate dehydrogenase 乳酸盐脱氢酶 |
| LDL | low density lipoprotein 低密度脂蛋白 |
| LDL-C | low density lipoprotein cholesterol 低密度脂蛋白胆固醇 |
| Leu | leukocyte(in Greek, *leuko*)白细胞 |
| LFT | liver function test 肝功能测试 |
| LMP | last menstrual period 末次月经 |
| Lp | lipoprotein 脂蛋白 |
| LP | lumbar puncture 腰椎穿刺 |
| LPL | lipoprotein lipase 脂蛋白脂肪酶 |
| LUL | left upper lobe 左上叶 |

| | |
|---|---|
| Ly | lymphocyte 淋巴细胞 |
| MAP | mean artery pressure 平均动脉压 |
| MCD | mean corpuscular diameter 平均红细胞直径 |
| MCH | mean cell hemoglobin 红细胞平均血红蛋白 |
| MCHC | mean cell hemoglobin concentration 红细胞平均血红蛋白浓度 |
| MCV | mean cell volume 平均细胞容积 |
| Mg | Magnesium 镁 |
| MI | myocardial infarction 心肌梗死 |
| Mod | moderate 中等的 |
| Mo | monocyte 单核细胞 |
| MPV | mean platelet volume 平均血小板容积 |
| MRA | magnetic resonance angiogram or angiography 磁共振血管造影 |
| MRI | magnetic resonance imaging 磁共振成像 |
| NA | nursing assistant 护理员 |
| NAD | no abnormality detected 未见异常 |
| NBM | nothing by mouth 禁食 |
| NE | norepinephrine 去甲肾上腺素 |
| Neo | neoplasm 肿瘤 |
| NIDDM | non-insulin-dependent diabetes mellitus Ⅱ型糖尿病 |
| NREM | non-rapid eye movement 非快速眼动 |
| NS | normal saline 生理盐水 |
| NTG | nitroglycerin 硝化甘油 |
| N&V | nausea & vomiting 恶心和呕吐 |
| NVD | nausea, vomiting & diarrhea 恶心、呕吐和腹泻 |
| NVD | normal vaginal delivery 正常阴道分娩 |
| $O_2$ | oxygen 氧 |
| OA | osteoarthritis 骨关节炎 |
| OB-GYN | obstetrics and gynecology 产科与妇科 |
| OD | overdose 剂量过多 |
| OGTT | oral glucose tolerance test 口服葡萄糖耐量实验 |
| OP | outpatient department 门诊部 |
| OS | orthopedic surgery 整形外科 |
| OR | operating room 手术室 |
| OTC | over-the-counter drug 非处方药 |
| PA | pulmonary artery 肺动脉 |
| PAH | pulmonary arterial hypertension 肺动脉高压 |
| PE | pulmonary embolism 肺栓塞 |
| PE | physical examination 体格检查 |

| | |
|---|---|
| PLT | platelet 血小板 |
| Post-op | postoperative 手术后 |
| PPH | post partum haemorrhage 产后出血 |
| PPH | primary pulmonary hypertension 原发性肺动脉高压 |
| Pre-op | preoperative 术前 |
| PT | physical therapy 体疗 |
| PVD | peripheral vascular disease 外周血管疾病 |
| PVR | pulmonary vascular resistance 肺血管阻力 |
| Px | physical examination 体格检查 |
| Prog | prognosis 预后 |
| RA | refractory anaemia 难治性贫血 |
| RA | rheumatoid arthritis 风湿性关节炎 |
| RAI | radioactive iodine 放射性碘 |
| RBC | red blood cell 红细胞 |
| REM | rapid eye movement 眼速动 |
| RF | rheumatoid factor 类风湿因子 |
| RFT | renal function test 肾脏功能测试 |
| RhF | rheumatoid factor 风湿因子 |
| RI | regular insulin 普通胰岛素 |
| RLQ | right lower quadrant 右下腹部 |
| ROM | range of motion 环绕关节地运动,全关节运动图 |
| RR | respiratory rate 呼吸率 |
| RT | radiotherapy 放射治疗 |
| RUQ | right upper quadrant 右上腹部 |
| RV | right ventricle 右心室 |
| RVF | right ventricular failure 右心室衰竭 |
| RVSP | right ventricular systolic pressure 右心室收缩压 |
| SARS | severe acute respiratory syndrome 严重急性呼吸道综合征 |
| SBE | subacute bacterial endocarditis 亚急性感染性心内膜炎 |
| SBP | systolic blood pressure 收缩压 |
| SBP | spontaneous bacterial peritonitis 自发性细菌腹膜炎 |
| SHx | surgical history 手术史 |
| SLE | systemic lupus erythematosus 系统性红斑狼疮 |
| SOB | shortness of breath 气促 |
| SOS | save our souls,meaning “in case of emergency” 急救 |
| ST | skin test 皮试 |
| STD | sexually transmitted disease 性传播疾病 |
| STI | soft tissue injury 软组织损伤 |
| Subq | subcutaneous 皮下 |

| | |
|---|---|
| SVI | systemic viral infection 系统性病毒感染 |
| Syr | syrup 糖浆 |
| TB | tuberculosis 肺结核 |
| TF | transfer 转院，转科 |
| THR | total hip replacement 全髋关节置换术 |
| TIA | transient ischemic attack 短暂性脑缺血发作 |
| TKR | total knee replacement 全膝关节置换 |
| TLC | total lung capacity 肺总容量 |
| TOP | termination of pregnancy 妊娠终止 |
| TPN | total parenteral nutrition 全胃肠道外营养 |
| TSH | thyroid stimulating hormone 促甲状腺激素 |
| TT | thrombin time 凝血酶时间 |
| TTE | transthoracic echocardiogram 经胸廓心回波图 |
| Tu | tumor 肿瘤 |
| TUR | transurethral resection 经尿道切除术 |
| Tx | transplant 移植 |
| UBT | urea breath test 尿素呼气实验 |
| URTI | upper respiratory tract infection 上呼吸道感染 |
| US | ultrasound 超声 |
| USG | ultrasonography 超声波检查法 |
| USS | ultrasound scan 超声波扫描 |
| UTI | urinary tract infection 尿道感染 |
| VA | visual acuity 视觉敏度 |
| VC | vital capacity 肺活量 |
| VD | vaginal delivery 产道分娩 |
| VE | vaginal examination (manual examination)阴道检查 |
| VF | ventricular fibrillation 心室纤维性颤动 |
| VLDL | very low density lipoprotein 极低密度脂蛋白 |
| WBC | white blood cell 白细胞 |

# Appendix C Medical Word-Building Elements

| | |
|---|---|
| adeno-腺体 | adenoma 腺瘤；adenoid 腺的，淋巴组织的 |
| an-无，没有，缺乏 | analgesic 止痛的；anemia 贫血 |
| anti-对抗 | antibody 抗体；antibiotics 抗生素 |
| auto-自己，自体 | autograft 自体移植物；autopsy 尸检 |
| arthr(o)-关节 | arthritis 关节炎；arthralgia 关节痛；arthropod 节肢动物 |
| arteri-动脉 | arteriotomy 动脉切开术；arteriography 动脉 X 线摄影法 |
| -ase 酶 | lipase 脂肪酶；transaminase 转氨酶 |
| audi-听 | auditory 听觉的；audiometer 听力计 |
| bi-两，双 | bipolar 双极的；bilateral 双侧的 |
| brady-缓慢的 | bradypnea 呼吸过慢；bradycardia 心动过缓 |
| bronch(o)-气管 | bronchitis 气管炎；bronchodilator 气管扩张剂 |
| carbo-碳 | carbonate 碳酸盐；carbohydrate 碳水化合物 |
| cardi(o)-心脏 | cardiovascular 心血管的；cardialgia 胃灼痛 |
| chemo-化学的 | chemoanalysis 化学分析；chemotherapy 化疗 |
| circum-周围，环 | circumcorneal 角膜周围；circumcision 包皮环切术 |
| cranio-颅(骨)的 | craniofacial 颅面的；craniology 头骨学 |
| cortico-皮，皮质 | corticose 皮层的；corticosteroid 皮质激素 |
| cyst-囊，胞 膀胱 | cystectomy 胆囊切除术；cystitis 膀胱炎 |
| -cyte 细胞 | erythrocyte 红细胞；thrombocyte 血小板 |
| de-脱离，去除，剥夺 | degeneration 恶化；decongestant：解充血药 |
| dermat(o)-皮肤 | dermatopathy 皮肤病；dermatalgia 皮痛 |
| dys-困难 | dyskinesia 运动障碍；dyspnea 呼吸困难 |
| electro-电 | electrocardiogram 心电图；electrolyte 电解质 |
| -emia 同-hemia，血 | leukemia 白血病 |
| -esthe-感觉 | esthesia 感觉，感知；anesthetics 麻醉剂 |
| encephal(o)脑 | encephalopathy 脑病；encephalitis 脑炎 |
| endo-内，内部 | endocrine 内分泌；endotrachea 气管内 |
| epi-在……之上 | epinephrine 肾上腺素；epicardium 心外膜 |
| epiglott-会厌 | epiglottitis 会厌炎；epiglottidectomy 会厌切除术 |
| erythro-红，红色 | erythromycin 红霉素；erythroderma 红皮病 |

| | |
|---|---|
| -esia 疾病 | amnesia 健忘症；agennesia 无生殖力 |
| -esis 疾病 | tyremesis 吐乳症；diuresis 利尿 |
| ex-自……出来，排出 | excrete 排泄；expectorant 化痰的，化痰剂 |
| exo-外部的 | exotoxin 外毒素；exocrine 外分泌 |
| febri-发烧 | febricide:退热剂 |
| fibr(o)-纤维 | fibrocyte 纤维细胞；fibrosis 纤维化 |
| -fus-合并，注入 | infusion 灌输，输液；transfusion 输液 |
| gastr(o)-胃 | gastrointestinal 胃肠道的；gastritis 胃炎 |
| gene-基因 | generation 产生；genetic 遗传的 |
| genit(o)-生殖，生殖器 | genitourinary 泌尿生殖的；genitalcoelom 生殖腔 |
| -gia 疼痛 | neuralgia 神经痛；arthralgia 关节痛 |
| globul-球 | globulin 球蛋白；globulimeter 血球计算器 |
| hemo-血，血液 | hemoglobin 血红蛋白；hemorrhage 出血 |
| histo-组织 | histocyte 组织细胞；histology 组织学 |
| -hydrat-水化物 | hydratase 水和酶；dehydrate 脱水 |
| hyper-高，过多 | hypertension 高血压；hyperinflation 过度膨胀 |
| hypo-低于，不足 | hypotrophy 不足生长；hypotonic 张力下降 |
| -ia 疾病 | dyspepsia 消化不良；aphasia 失语症 |
| -iasis 疾病 | elephantiasis 象皮病；siriasis 中暑 |
| idio-特殊的，自己的 | idiopathy 特发病，自发病；idioparasite 自体寄生物 |
| -igo 疾病 | vertigo 晕眩；porrigo 头癣 |
| -ism 疾病 | deaf-mutism 聋哑症；nicotinism 尼古丁中毒症 |
| -itis 炎症 | meningitis 脑膜炎；bronchiolitis 细支气管炎 |
| intra-内，内部 | intracellular 细胞内的；intracranial 颅内的 |
| -kine-运动 | kinesimeter 运动测量计；akinesia 运动不能 |
| lacer-撕裂 | lacerant 令人痛苦的；laceration 伤口 |
| -lateral 侧边 | unilateral 单侧的；trilateral 三边的 |
| leuk-同 leuc-，白 | leucocyte 白细胞；leukemia 白血病 |
| litho-结石，石 | lithotomy 结石切除术；lithotrity 碎石术 |
| lymph-淋巴 | lymphadenopathy 淋巴腺疾病；lymphangitis 淋巴管炎 |
| -ma 斑，瘤 | myoma 肌瘤；sarcoma 肉瘤，恶性毒瘤 |
| mal-坏，错误，疾病 | malignant 恶性的；malabsorption(营养)吸收不良 |
| -mening(o)脑膜 | meningitis 脑膜炎；meningioma 脑(脊)膜瘤；meningococcal 脑膜炎球菌的 |
| -meter 测量 | audiometer 听力计；kinesimeter 运动测量计 |
| muco-黏膜，黏液 | mucosa 黏膜；mucoid 黏液样的 |
| multi-多 | multisystem 多系统的；multiple 多样的 |
| myxo-黏，黏液 | myxocyte:黏液细胞；myxocoel 黏液腔 |
| -natal-出生 | prenatal 产前的；出生前的；natality 出生率 |

| | |
|---|---|
| neutro-中 | neutrocyte 中性粒细胞;neutropenia 中性粒细胞减少症 |
| neo-新 | neomycin 新霉素;neonate 新生儿;neonatal 新生期的 |
| nephro-肾 | nephrocyte 肾原细胞;nephrotoxicity 肾毒性;nephrosis 肾病 |
| non-非,不,无 | nonabsorbable 不能被吸收的;noninfectious 非传染的 |
| -ology 学 | biology 生物学;psychology 心理学 |
| -oma 疾病 | neuroma 神经病;xanthoma 黄色瘤 |
| -ostomy 切开术,造瘘术 | tracheostomy 气管切开术;colostomy 结肠造瘘术 |
| orch(o)-睾丸 | orchotomy 睾丸切开术;orchitis 睾丸炎 |
| or(o)-口 | oral 口头的;oronasal 口鼻的 |
| -osis 疾病 | tuberculosis 结核病;necrosis 坏死 |
| ot(o)-耳 | otitis media 中耳炎;otitis 耳炎;otophone 助听器 |
| ox(ygen)氧气 | hypoxia 低氧血症;oxygenic 含氧的 |
| para-副,侧面 | parablast 副胚层;paramyxovirus 副黏病毒 |
| -path(y)-疾病 | neuropathy 神经病;nephropathy 肾病;pathogenetic 发病的 |
| -penia 血细胞减少 | thrombocytopenia 血小板减少症;neutropenia 中性粒细胞减少症 |
| per-通,穿透 | perfusion 灌注;perforate 打孔 |
| pharyng(o)-咽 | pharyngitis 咽炎;pharyngalgia 咽痛;pharyngoscope 咽镜 |
| -phil 亲,嗜 | neutrophil 中性白细胞;hemophilia 血友病 |
| -phag(o)-吞咽,吞噬 | phagocyte 吞噬细胞;dysphagia 吞咽困难 |
| photo-光,相片 | photophobia 畏光;photoactive 光(激)活的 |
| -phobia 恐惧症 | acrophobia 恐高症;basophobia 步行恐惧症 |
| pneumo-肺,气 | pneumonia 肺炎;pneumococcus 肺炎球菌 |
| -pnea 气体,呼吸 | apnea 呼吸停止;dyspnea 呼吸困难 |
| poly-多 | polycyte 多形核细胞;polyphagia 多食 |
| pro-居前,领先 | proenzyme 酶原;prodromal 前驱的,有前驱症状的 |
| psycho-心理,精神 | psychopathy 心理病态;psychology 心理学 |
| pulmo-肺 | pulmometer 肺量计;pulmonary 肺的 |
| reticul(o)-网状的 | reticular 网状组织;reticuloendothelium 网状内皮组织 |
| rheumat(o)-风湿 | rheumatoid 类风湿的;rheumatic 风湿性的 |
| -rrhea 大量流出 | diarrhea 腹泻;steatorrhea 脂肪泻 |
| soma-体 | somatic 肉体的;somasthenia 体无力,疲惫 |
| -spir(o)-通气 | respiration 呼吸;inspire 吸气;spirography 呼吸描记法 |
| steato-脂肪 | steatoma 脂肪瘤;steatorrhea 脂肪泻 |
| steno-狭窄 | stenocephaly 头狭窄,小头;stenosis 狭窄 |
| strepto-链状 | streptomycin 链霉素;streptococcus 链球菌 |
| sub-下,亚,次 | subcutenous 皮下;submaxillary 下颌的 |
| syn-共同,联合 | synkinesia 协同性运动,辅助运动;syncytial 合胞病毒的 |
| -therm(o)-体温,热度 | thermometer 体温计;hyperthermia 高热 |

| | |
|---|---|
| tracheo-气管 | tracheotomy 气管切开术；tracheobronchial 气管支气管的 |
| tachy-快，迅速 | tachypnea 呼吸过快；tachycardia 心动过速 |
| -tension 压力，张力 | hypertension 高血压；hypotension 低血压 |
| thrombo-血小板，血栓 | thrombosis 血栓症；thrombocytopenia 血小板减少症 |
| trans-转移 | transfusion 输血；transfer 转移，传递 |
| -tomy 切 | anatomy 解剖学；appendectomy 阑尾切除术 |
| -tonic-强身的（药） | cardiotonic 强心的，强心剂；tonicity 肌肉弹性 |
| umbil-脐 | umbilectomy 脐切除术；umbilical cord 脐带 |
| -uria 尿 | oliguria 少尿；hematuria 血尿 |
| vaso-血管，输精管 | vasodilation 血管扩张；vasoactive 血管活性的 |
| vascul-血管 | vasculitis 血管炎；vascularity 血管分布 |

# Appendix D　Transcripts of Dialogues

## Unit One

### Dialogue 1　Receiving a Patient (1)

Doctor: Good morning. I am Doctor Sterling. How can I help you?

Patient: Good morning, doctor. I am Emily. I have a fever and sore throat since yesterday.

Doctor: Oh, did you take your temperature?

Patient: Yes, I did. The highest temperature was 39.8 ℃ at 11pm last night. I took one pill of aspirin and feel much better.

Doctor: Any other symptoms?

Patient: I have a runny nose and headache, too.

Doctor: OK, let me take your temperature first. Please keep this thermometer under your armpit for 5 minutes. Open your mouth and say "Ah", please. Your tonsils and larynx are red and swollen. Your temperature is 38.5 ℃. Your breathing sounds are normal and there is no problem with your lungs. You'd better take the blood test, OK? This paper is for the lab test.

Patient: Sure. I really hope I get better as soon as possible. See you later.

### New Words & Phrases

sore　*adj.* 疼痛的
sore throat　*n.* 咽喉痛
aspirin　*n.* 阿司匹林
thermometer　*n.* 温度计，体温表
tonsil　*n.* 扁桃体
larynx　*n.* 咽喉
blood test　*n.* 血液检查

### Dialogue 2　Receiving a Patient (2)

(30 *minutes later, the patient comes back*)

Patient: Excuse me, doctor. Here's the result of my blood test.

Doctor: OK. The blood routine shows that your WBC is 12,000/$mm^3$, N 80%, L 20%. It indicates that you have an upper respiratory tract infection. Are you allergic to any drugs or foods?

Patient: No. I don't think so.

Doctor: I'll prescribe Amoxicillin for you. It's an oral medicine. Take 2 tablets 3 times a day around the clock. You can take aspirin if fever persists. You'd better take vitamin C—2 tablets 3 times a day, too. And drink a lot of liquids and have plenty of rest.

Patient: How long should I take the medicine?

Doctor: Take it for 5 days, and come back for a follow-up check up. Don't hesitate to call me if you have any problems.

Patient: Thank you so much. I really appreciate your help.

## New Words & Phrases

blood routine 血常规

WBC (abbr. white blood cell) 白细胞

upper respiratory tract infection 上呼吸道感染

Amoxicillin *n.* 阿莫西林

follow-up 后续的

# Unit Two

### Dialogue 3 Consulting a Doctor (1)

Doctor: Hi, I am Doctor Susan. How can I help you?

Patient: Hi, doctor. I am Mary. Would you please take a look at my lab result?

Doctor: Sure. Take a seat please.

Patient: Thank you. This is the blood result of my kidney function, and the other is the liver function.

Doctor: I see. I'd like to know your medical history first. Have you had any problems with your kidney or liver?

Patient: Yes. I was told I have IgA nephropathy 5 years ago because both my uric acid and creatinine were too high. My urine has been tea-colored for almost 5 years.

Doctor: Did you have a biopsy?

Patient: No. The doctor suggested the biopsy but I am really afraid of that. So they haven't been able to diagnose the IgA until now.

Doctor: What kind of symptom do you have now?

Patient: Oh, I have had a gout for a week, and my left foot is still painful and swollen.

## New words & phrases

lab result　实验室检查结果
kidney function　肾功能
liver function　肝功能
IgA(abbr. immunoglobulin A)nephropathy　免疫球蛋白 A 肾病
urine acid　尿酸
creatinine　*n.* 肌酐
biopsy　*n.*（活组织）切片检查法
gout　*n.* 痛风

### Dialogue 4　Consulting a Doctor（2）

Doctor: May I take a look of your foot? Ah, I see. Are you taking any medication?

Patient: Yes. I am taking a pain killer for my gout these days. But I don't remember the name of the medication.

Doctor: Your present lab results are good; the urine acid and creatinine are normal. You'd better avoid the pain killers since they affect kidney function.

Patient: Good. Your instructions are really helpful. Do I need any other medications for my gout?

Doctor: You could try some Chinese traditional herbs, such as notoginseng, to enhance your blood circulation.

Patient: Oh, really? I haven't heard that before. But I have heard that Chinese traditional medicine does cure some sicknesses. I'd like to try.

Doctor: OK, you can buy some from the drug store.

Patient: Thank you so much. I really appreciate your instructions. Have a good day!

Doctor: You're welcome. Have a good day!

## New Words & Phrases

pain killer　止痛药物
herb　*n.* 中草药
notoginseng　*n.* 三七
enhance　*v.* 提高，增强
blood circulation　血液循环

# Unit Three

### Dialogue 5　Admitting a Patient(1)

Nurse: Good morning, Mrs. Wilson. I am the nurse of the GI department. My name is

Emily. I'll be admitting you to the ward today.

Patient: Good morning, Emily. What should I do now?

Nurse: Would you please come with me to the nurses' office so I can finish the paperwork first?

Patient: Sure. May I sit down?

Nurse: Yes, of course. Please sit down and make yourself comfortable, OK? Can you tell me your full name and your date of birth?

Patient: My full name is Rose Wilson. And I was born on Nov. 15th, 1968.

Nurse: Can you tell me why you are here today?

Patient: Well, um. I've had a duodenal ulcer for about five years. My stools have been black for the past two days. I feel weak, too. My occult blood test is positive, so my doctor suggested for me to come here.

## New Words & Phrases

admit *v.* 许可进入，承认

GI (gastrointestinal) *adj.* 胃肠的

duodenal *adj.* 十二指肠的

ulcer *n.* 溃疡

stool *n.* 大便

admit a patient 收病人入院

GI department 消化科

### Dialogue 6 Admitting a Patient (2)

Nurse: OK. Would you please give me your past results, such as the barium X rays and gastrointestinal endoscopy? We need to make a copy and put it into your chart.

Patient: Sure. I'll give them to you later.

Nurse: By the way, I'd like to know your past medical history. Have you had any serious illnesses in the past besides the duodenal ulcer?

Patient: No. I think my duodenal ulcer came from too much pressure in my job. I am busy with my work every day, so I can't take good care of myself.

Nurse: Mm, that's reasonable. I'll take the BP for you now. I'd like you to sit a little closer to this desk and roll up your sleeve. OK, it's one ten over 70, that's good. I'd also like to take your pulse rate.

Patient: Is my pulse too fast? I always feel palpitations these days.

Nurse: Mm, a little bit fast. It's one fifteen. And please put this thermometer under your tongue. You can take it out when you hear the beep. OK, it's 37.0 ℃. Thank you very much for your cooperation, Mrs. Wilson. Now please follow me, and I will show you around the ward.

## New Words & Phrases

Barium *n.* 钡

endoscopy *n.* 内视镜检查法

chart *n.* 病历

palpitation *n.* 心悸

ward *n.* 病房，病区

barium X rays X线钡餐检查

BP (blood pressure) 血压

gastrointestinal endoscopy 胃肠道内镜

pulse rate *n.* 脉率

# Unit Four

### Dialogue 7 In the Nurses' Office (1)

Doctor: Hello. Mary, are you looking after Mr. John today?

Nurse: Yes. Any questions?

Doctor: Oh, can we take a few minutes to talk about his situation?

Nurse: Sure. Have a seat, please.

Doctor: Thank you. He was back from the OR an hour ago and there are a lot of orders for him. Let's make sure they are clear.

Nurse: OK. Let me see. Blood pressure, pulse rate, breathing rate every 30 minutes, temperature every 4 hours. And monitor the GCS every 4 hours.

Doctor: And also monitor his I & O, OK?

Nurse: Sure. How about his fluids?

Doctor: Now his potassium levels are very low according to his blood result. Would you please give him a liter of normal saline with 20 millimoles of KCL?

Nurse: Sure. Please fill out the patient's chart first.

## New Words & Phrases

order *n.* 医嘱

liter *n.* 升

potassium *n.* 钾

millimole *n.* [医]毫克分子，毫摩尔

OR(operation room) 手术室

GCS(Glasgow Coma Scale) 格拉斯哥昏迷评分量表

I&O(intake and output) 出入量

normal saline 生理盐水

### Dialogue 8 In the Nurses' Office (2)

Doctor: No problem. Thanks for your reminder. The normal saline with 20 millimoles of KCL should be given over 4 hours, OK?

Nurse: I see. Any other fluids?

Doctor: Yes. I will prescribe some antibiotics for him. I'd prefer you to run them through a secondary line(第二条静脉通路).

Nurse: OK. May I run them through the cannula?

Doctor: Right. Make sure the cannula is still working because we didn't use it yesterday. And I want to give him some nutrients with the fluids. These nutrients are sticky, so you can't run them through the cannula in case of blockage.

Nurse: I understand.

Doctor: Furthermore, start him on some oxygen at 2 liter per minute for 3 hours because his oxygen saturation is 90. We also need to monitor his oxygen saturation, OK?

Nurse: Of course. Don't forget to fill out all these orders, doctor.

## New Words & Phrases

fluid *n.* 液体
cannula *n.* 导管、套管
blockage *n.* 堵塞
nutrient *n.* 营养物, 营养品
saturation *n.* 饱和度
oxygen saturation 血氧饱和度

# Unit Five

### Dialogue 9 Administering Medications (1)

Nurse: Hi, Janice, Good to see you again.

Patient: Thank you and me too. You look so nice today.

Nurse: How are you doing today?

Patient: Not good, I have a headache and feel dizzy today. My blood pressure was one eighty over one ten (180/110) this morning. That's really high, isn't it?

Nurse: Oh, I see. That's the reason why Dr. Peter prescribed two new medications for you. One is Metoprolol, to lower your BP. And another is Lasix, a diuretic.

Patient: Oh, I can't remember the names. Would you please repeat them?

Nurse: Sure, and I'll tell more about them. Metoprolol is in the green box, and I already wrote down the instructions for you. You take this 2 pills once, twice a day; that's 8am before your breakfast and 8pm before your bedtime. Got it?

Patient: Mm, but I have a very poor memory. Instructions on the box are good for me.

## New Words & Phrases

dizzy *adj*. 头晕眼花的，眩晕的
diuretic *n*. 利尿剂
Metoprolol *n*. 美托洛尔
Lasix *n*. 速尿(呋喃苯胺酸制剂的商品名)

### Dialogue 10 Administering Medications (2)

Nurse: OK, let's continue. You have to put this medicine in a cool place because it would be melt at 45 ℃, Another one, Lasix, is in the white box. It's a diuretic (water pill) that prevents your body from absorbing too much salt, allowing the salt to instead be eliminated through the urine. This medication is also used to treat hypertension.

Patient: Does that mean I will pass more urine after I take this medication?

Nurse: Yes, absolutely. The frequency and amount of your urine will be increased. But don't worry, that's the normal effect of the medication. Please let us know if you aren't comfortable or have any problems, OK?

Patient: Thank you. Any other instructions?

Nurse: Oh, by the way, you'd better eat a the low-cholesterol, low-fat, low-sodium diet with more dietary fiber. That means that you'd better eat more fresh vegetables and fruits, less salt and meat. That's good for both your hypertension and heart.

Patient: That's really very hard for me. Anyway, I'll try my best to follow your guidance. You are a great nurse.

## New Words & Phrases

hypertension *n*. 高血压
fat *n*. 脂肪
dietary *adj*. 与饮食有关的，饮食的
fiber *n*. 纤维

# Unit Six

### Dialogue 11 Preoperative Nursing (1)

Nurse: Morning, Mrs. Peter. I am Cathy. Did you sleep well last night?

Patient: Morning, Cathy. I was a little nervous about the surgery, so I didn't sleep that well.

Nurse: Yes, it's hard for everyone at this point. Do you have any questions about the surgery?

Patient: Mm, I signed the consent form two days ago, and I saw the risks of the operation in the form, such as the complications from the anesthesia, the bleeding, and even death. I am a little afraid of these things.

Nurse: (smiles and touches the patient's hand) I understand it's not easy for you. Actually the consent form tells us all kinds of the possibilities during the surgery, but these risks are very small and not likely to happen to you. It's just standard hospital procedure.

Patient: I see. I hope my surgery is successful, especially my child is only five years old.

Nurse: (smiles) It will be fine. You should trust the doctors. And you have been on a low-residue diet for 3 days, right?

Patient: Yes. May I eat today?

Nurse: Yes, but only clear fluids for today. Then you'll start NPO after midnight.

## New Words & Phrases

preoperative *adj.* 手术前的

consent form 知情同意书

anesthesia *n.* 麻醉

bleeding *n.* 出血

low-residue diet 少渣饮食

NPO (abbr. nothing per mouth) 禁食

### Dialogue 12 Preoperative Nursing (2)

Patient: Does that mean I won't be able to eat or drink anything after midnight?

Nurse: No, you won't. And you will be given an enema tonight around 8 pm.

Patient: For what? Is it painful?

Nurse: The enema causes you to have a bowel movement and then lower the risk of contamination from the bowel contents. It won't be painful; I am sure you can handle it.

Patient: OK. If I have to, I will.

Nurse: There are two more things before the surgery. Tomorrow morning you'll be given a nasogastric tube to keep the stomach empty. You'll keep the tube for a few days for gastric decompression. It will also lower the pressure of the incision.

Patient: Oh, my goodness! I hope that's all.

Nurse: It's good for you to know all the details of your procedure. The other tube you'll have is an indwelling catheter, which can be taken out when you can void by yourself. I'll take care of you before and after the operation tomorrow. You'll be just fine.

## New Words & Phrases

enema *n.* 灌肠
bowel *n.* 肠
bowel movement 大便，排便
contamination *n.* 污染
nasogastric tube 鼻胃管
decompression *n.* 减压
incision *n.* 切口
indwelling catheter 留置尿管
void *v.* 排空

# Unit Seven

### Dialogue 13 Postoperative Nursing Discussion (1)

Head Nurse: Hello, everyone. Let's start with Mrs. John. Mrs. John is a 40-year-old American lady and was admitted last Friday. From her biopsy she was diagnosed with rectum cancer 6 months ago in our hospital. A colostomy was performed on her at 10am yesterday. She is fully awake and recovered from the procedure. We are going to talk about her nursing implementations, especially the stoma care after the surgery.

Nurse 1: Mm, I examined her yesterday after she came back from the OR. I feel that she's doing well. Her vital signs are good, except for a slight fever. But that's normal after the surgery. The stoma is swollen, but the blood circulation around the stoma is good.

Nurse 2: Yes, we need to pay close attention to the stoma.

Head Nurse: What kind of stoma is normal, post-op?

Nurse 1: Stoma is initially edematous and shrinks over the next 4 to 6 weeks. A normal stoma is moist and reddish pink. I think Mrs. John's is a standard.

Head Nurse: Any other signs? How about the skin?

## New Words & Phrases

rectum cancer 直肠癌
colostomy *n.* 结肠造口术
nursing implementations 护理措施
stoma *n.* 造口
post-op 手术后

edematous *adj*. 水肿的
shrink *v*. 收缩，退缩

### Dialogue 14 Postoperative Nursing Discussion (2)

Nurse 2: The skin is intact and free of irritation. And we should continue to monitor the condition of the stoma.

Head Nurse: Good. Sounds that you know everything of the observation. Let's move on. How about the application of the pouching system? We should talk about the steps of the pouching system.

Nurse 1: The first step is to wash our hands and apply clean gloves. And then place a towel across the patient's lower abdomen to protect bed linen. Remove the used pouch and skin barrier gently.

Head Nurse: Mary, do you want to follow? You must have some ideas.

Nurse 2: Mm, the skin around the stoma should be cleaned with warm water using a washcloth. Measure the stoma before cutting an opening on skin barrier. After that, the protective backing will be removed. Then apply pouch over stoma.

Head Nurse: Perfect! By the way, don't forget to close the end of pouch if it is open. You guys did a wonderful job with the discussion. Thank you. Have a good day!

Nurses: You, too.

## New Words & Phrases

intact *adj*. 完整无缺的，未经触动的，未受损伤的
irritation *n*. 刺激
pouching system 造瘘袋
skin barrier 皮肤黏着物
washcloth *n*. 擦洗布
protective backing 保护层

# Unit Eight

### Dialogue 15 Enema (1)

Nurse: Hi, Mrs John. How are you today?

Patient: Not bad. How are you?

Nurse: Good. I hear you've been constipated for a few days.

Patient: Yes. I haven't had bowel movement at least 4 days, so my abdomen feels distended and painful. I took some medicine but it doesn't work.

Nurse: That must be uncomfortable. Dr. Peter ordered an enema for you.

Patient: Oh, what is enema? Will it hurt?

Nurse: An enema is a tube of liquid inserted into the rectum through the anus to help your bowel movements. It won't hurt. I am sure you can handle it.

Patient: OK, I hope so. What should I do now?

Nurse: You should go to the bathroom first. I'll go to prepare the stuff and come back later.

## New Words & Phrases

constipation *n.* 便秘

distend *v.* 膨胀，肿胀

rectum *n.* 直肠

anus *n.* 肛门

stuff *n.* 东西

### Dialogue 16 Enema (2)

(*The nurse comes back a few minutes later*)

Nurse: Mrs. John. Are you ready?

Patient: Yes.

Nurse: OK, would you please show me your identification bracelet? OK, thanks. Now take off your pants to the knees and lie on your left side. Good, bend your knees, please.

Patient: Could you let me know when you start?

Nurse: Sure. Now take deep breaths. Good. Now there we go. How are you feeling now?

Patient: Is it done? I feel very uncomfortable.

Nurse: Please keep this position for 5～10 minutes and then you can go to the bathroom. Please ring the bell if you need me.

Patient: Thank you so much. I appreciate your help.

## New Words & Phrases

identification bracelet *n.* 腕带识别卡

pants *n.* 长裤

lie on one's left side 左侧卧位

bend the knees 屈膝

take deep breath 深呼吸

# Unit Nine

### Dialogue 17 Health Education (1)

Nurse: Hi, Mrs. Peter. How are you today?

Patient: Good. How are you?

Nurse: Very good. Thank you. I'd like to talk about your diabetes management before your discharge.

Patient: Oh, thanks. I am really worrying about the complications of the diabetes after I go back home.

Nurse: I understand it's not easy for you to manage it now, so we need to educate you first.

Patient: I think so.

Nurse: OK, let's start. There are two types of diabetes, type 1 and type 2. Do you know what type you have?

Patient: Type 2. It's also called the non-insulin-dependent diabetes. And the doctor suggested that I take the insulin injections.

Nurse: Good. Can you tell me how many units have been prescribed for you?

Patient: 4 units of regular insulin. But I am not sure.

## New Words & Phrases

non-insulin-dependent diabetes　非胰岛素依赖型糖尿病
regular insulin　普通胰岛素

### Dialogue 18　Health education (2)

Nurse: That's correct. 4 units of insulin marks 0.1 millimole for the 1ml syringe. Remember to inject the insulin 30 minutes before your meal. It'll be more convenient for you if you can afford the insulin pen. Most diabetics use insulin pen because its prefilled devices are disposable and easy for them.

Patient: Oh, I've heard that before. I hope I can.

Nurse: OK. You need to control your weight and nutrition, too. Some regular physical activities are good for you but do not try to exercise too much at one time. Always bring some snacks with you to prevent hypoglycemia.

Patient: OK, I see. But it's more difficult for me to control the nutrition because I am always hungry.

Nurse: I understand. But you must control your food according to doctors' orders in case of hyperglycemia.

Patient: My husband is always talking about that, too. I will try.

Nurse: Good. Here is a pocket booklet of diabetes management. Bring it with you.

## New Words & Phrases

diabetic　*n.* 糖尿病患者
disposable　*adj.* 一次性的
hypoglycemia　*n.* 低血糖
hyperglycemia　*n.* 高血糖

# Unit Ten

## Dialogue 19 Intravenous Therapy (1)

Nurse: Morning, Miss Susan. I am Mary. I will be looking after you today.

Patient: Morning, Mary. Pleased to meet you. How does my urine culture look? I can't handle the pain any more. Today I have to go to bathroom more often(今天我上卫生间的次数越来越多).

Nurse: Your urine culture indicated you have a urinary tract infection. And Doctor Wilson prescribed intravenous antibiotics according to your sensitivity test.

Patient: You mean you will give me an IV right now?

Nurse: Yes, if you are ready.

Patient: OK. Do I need to take the skin test first?

Nurse: No need. But you can go to the bathroom first and I will come back later.

Patient: Sure. See you later.

## New Words & Phrases

urine culture 尿培养

urinary tract infection 尿路感染

IV 静脉输液

sensitivity test 药敏试验

skin test 皮试

## Dialogue 20 Intravenous Therapy (2)

(*A few minutes later, the nurse comes back*)

Nurse: Susan, are you ready?

Patient: Yes. Will it hurt?

Nurse: Mm, just a little bit. Not much. May I check your identification bracelet first?

Patient: Sure, here you are.

Nurse: OK, thanks. Please lie down and make yourself comfortable. Hold your hand for a minute. Good. Now relax your hand. There we go.

Patient: Oh, that wasn't bad. You did a good job.

Nurse: Thank you. You'd better not to change the dripping rate. Keep your hand in whenever you move.

Patient: Alright.

Nurse: Please ring the call bell if you need help.

## New Words & Phrases

identification bracelet 腕带识别卡
dripping rate 滴速
call bell 呼叫铃

# Appendix E　Translation for Texts

## Unit one

### 甲型流感疫苗

现已有疫苗可用来预防 H1N1 流感。这些疫苗就像季节性流感疫苗一样。人们认为它们是安全和有效的。

2～49 岁年龄的人，除了孕妇和有特定健康问题的人，均可以使用该疫苗。如果使用者对鸡蛋出现严重过敏，或对该疫苗所含其他物质严重过敏，则不能使用该疫苗。

本疫苗不能用于下列人群：

- 2 岁以下儿童和 50 岁以上成年人
- 孕妇
- 免疫系统薄弱的人群
- 有心、肾、肝、肺部疾病和其他血液疾病等长期健康问题的人群
- 5 岁以下患哮喘的儿童或过去一年里发作一次或多次哮鸣的人群
- 患肌肉疾病和神经紊乱可能导致呼吸或吞咽问题的人群
- 与免疫系统严重削弱人群亲密接触的人群
- 长期服用阿司匹林的儿童或青少年

如患中度或严重疾病，建议等到疾病恢复时再使用该疫苗。如果只是轻微感冒或其他疾病，则通常没有必要等到恢复便可以使用。

该疫苗的预期风险类似季节性疫苗：

轻微问题(2 至 17 岁儿童及青少年)：

- 流鼻涕、鼻塞或咳嗽
- 头痛和肌肉酸痛
- 发热
- 哮鸣
- 腹痛或偶尔呕吐或腹泻

轻微问题(18 岁至 49 岁成年人)：

- 流鼻涕或鼻塞
- 咳嗽、畏寒、疲劳/身体虚弱
- 喉咙痛
- 头痛

严重问题：

· 使用本疫苗后出现危及生命的过敏反应非常罕见。如果确有发生，通常出现在使用该疫苗后几分钟到几个小时内。

## 叙利亚医院里的生与死

一位父亲冲开医院大门，怀里的孩子浑身是血。后面紧跟着一名年青男人，他的脸在最近的空袭中被炸开了花。在医院的接待区，医生正在给一名哭泣的小女孩缝合着撕裂开的脚。一名年仅 11 岁的男孩静静地离开了这个世界，他的父亲在旁边悄悄哭泣。一位护士推开拥挤的人群，鲜血溅满了她白色的大褂和头巾。

这是位于阿勒波（叙利亚的一个城市）中心区域的一间医院最普通的一天。每天 70 到 100 名病人进入医院，其中 80％是平民。

24 岁的医疗志愿者哈勒格在革命爆发前是一名学习兽医的学生，而如今成为医院的顶梁柱。当阿勒波的街道爆发冲突的时候，成百上千的医生逃离了该地，只剩下少数训练有素的专业人员来应对这场医疗危机。

“这些医生赚人民的钱致富，但在人民最需要他们的时候，他们却跑开了。他们的人性在哪？”他发问道。

大多数病人被皮卡车送入医院。虽然这种方式运送病人路途折腾且有可能致命，但却无法避免。医院的五辆救护车仅仅只剩下了一辆。唯一的救护车驾驶员沙丁，以前是一名婚纱设计师，他说道：“以前我专为女士工作，而现在我为所有人工作。”医院外，一场爆炸晃动了街道，民众纷纷跑向掩体，而一些医生则奔向了发出爆炸声响的地方寻找幸存者，沙丁冲向了他的救护车。

“我的家人不得不离开这个城市，但是我却不能离开我的岗位。”其中的一名护士说道。像许多其他的医生一样，这些女士们以前都没有医学方面的经验。然而，现在她们俨然已成为救治创伤病人的好手。

坐在医院的大街上，哈勒格从忙碌中抽身休息。在他的右边，蓝色的布覆盖着一具男人和一具男孩的尸体，他们在等待着人认领。“最后，当死亡成为常态的时候”，他说道，看了看四周，“也许我们已经丧失了感知的能力，……也许”。

## 普通感冒

普通感冒，亦称上呼吸道感染，是一种由诸多不同类型病毒所致的传染性疾病。由于导致感冒的病毒数量众多，新的感冒病毒不断出现，人体不能对所有感冒病毒产生抵抗力，因此，感冒易频发和复发。

普通感冒的症状有鼻塞、流鼻涕、咽喉痛、声音嘶哑、咳嗽，还有可能发热和头痛。许多感冒患者感到疲倦和疼痛。这些症状一般会持续 3 到 10 天。

无论患者是否服药，感冒经常在几天到数周时间里好转。但是，感冒病毒会引起其他感染侵袭人体，这些感染包括鼻窦感染、耳部感染和支气管炎。哮喘、慢性支气管炎或肺气肿患者即使在感冒消失后，其症状也可能在数周里加剧。

普通感冒大多通过手部接触传染。例如，感冒患者流鼻涕，用手接触鼻子，然后接触其他人，其他人就会被感冒病毒感染。此外，人们还可能被钢笔、书籍、咖啡杯子等物体上的感冒病毒感染。尽管常识认为咳嗽和打喷嚏传染感冒，但事实上这些并非传播感冒的常见方式。

一般说来,治疗感冒时抗生素药物并无疗效。抗生素药物只是对细菌所致疾病有疗效,而感冒通常由病毒所致。抗生素药物不仅没有帮助,而且可能导致致命的过敏性反应。还有,不必要地使用抗生素药物已经导致几株常见细菌对抗生素药物产生耐药性。由于上述及其他原因,将抗生素药物的使用限于必要情形显得十分重要。有时,感冒病毒之后会出现细菌感染。普通感冒产生的细菌性并发症可用抗生素药物治疗。

有几种缓解感冒症状的疗法。解充血药和鼻用喷剂有助于缓解症状。心脏病患者、高血压控制不良者和患有其他疾病的人在使用这些药物之前应该与医生联系。而且,鼻用喷剂非处方药的使用不应超过3天,原因是鼻部可能对它们产生依赖性,这些药物一旦中止使用会产生更严重的鼻塞。

## Unit Two

### OTC药品的说明标签

当你使用OTC药品时,阅读药品标签对照顾自己和家人非常重要。标签能告诉你该药品的作用、适宜及不适宜人群以及服用方法。OTC药品的标签通常都为消费者提供了使用和安全注意事项的信息。在1999年3月的《联邦公报》上,FDA公布了有关OTC药品标签的规定。该项标签的规定将运用于10万多种OTC药品。

在简化OTC药品标签之前,FDA就消费者如何利用(阅读)标签进行了广泛的研究。主要问题之一是标签的可读性,尤其是对于上了年纪的美国人,这一人群购买(消费)了美国市场上约30%的OTC药品。FDA同时还发现:消费者认为,像"适应证""注意事项"及"禁忌证"等词汇过于令人困惑,同时也不易理解。

对于那些可能对药品成分过敏的人群来说,查找药品的非活性成分也成了一个难题。

仿照营养食品的标签,药品标签使用简明的语言和易于阅读的格式来帮助人们比较及选择OTC药品,并依照药品剂量说明服用药品。药品的各项信息应按下列顺序排列。

· 药品的活性成分,包括每次剂量。

· 药品的使用目的。

· 药品的使用(适应证)。

· 具体的警告(事项),包括不可使用该药品的任何情况及何时适合咨询医师或药师。

· 剂量说明——何时如何服用药品及服用次数。

· 药品所含的非活性成分,该信息对于帮助消费者避免可能引起过敏反应的药品成分是非常重要的。

除了使用标准化的格式外,标签应使用简明易懂的文字描述每一种OTC药品的各项内容。

如果你阅读了OTC药品的说明书,但对药品仍然有疑问,请咨询你的医师、药师或是其他专业保健人员。

### 患病见真情

只有区区三天!仅仅三次旅程!开车在路上,我想到了自己这些时间起早驱车去市区,在医生办公室候诊,接收放射治疗的事情。我会记住那个候诊室——正是在那里我认识了四位好女人。我们之间已经形成了一种特别的东西——建立于清晨一起焦虑候诊的情谊。

其中一个女人患宫颈癌，她母亲最近刚死于这种癌症。另一个女人来自百慕大，和她姐姐住在一起以便能在医院接受子宫癌治疗。我的第三个朋友是乳腺癌晚期，虽然她必须使用助步车而且疼痛不断，但总是面带笑容。第四个女人，虽然不是病人，但是让我最想念。导医玛丽有办法使每个人都感到轻松自在，让每个人觉得都受到了关怀——她会用甜美的声音问候每个人。

当我第一次来接受放射治疗时，我感到紧张、焦虑、害怕。但是玛丽能看出我眼里的恐惧。她暖人的语言和温柔的微笑消解了我心中的恐惧，燃起了我向候诊室其他女士敞开心扉、结下情谊的渴望。玛丽影响着每个人。我们不再阅读杂志，而是分享我们的故事。我们不再目光茫然，而是表达出我们的恐惧和希望。我们不再盯着钟表，而是心心相连，结下情谊，共渡难关。

虽然这样说也许听起来有些怪异，但是我觉得我很荣幸能有这样的经历，有幸能感受到玛丽温暖的笑。

## 生命过程

生命的基本过程包括组织协作、新陈代谢、反应、运动和繁殖。对人类而言，生命过程还要包括生长、分化、呼吸、消化和排泄。所有这些过程相互关联，一起维持着个体生命。疾病和死亡代表着对生命过程平衡的破坏。以下是对生命过程的简要介绍。

**组织协作**　在人体所有层次的组织安排上都存在分工。人体每一个组成部分都有自己特定的任务，并与其他部分合作。如果失去完整性或组织性，即使单个细胞也会死去。

**新陈代谢**　新陈代谢包括身体内发生的所有化学反应。新陈代谢的一个阶段叫做分解代谢。分解代谢时，复杂的物质分解成更简单的组成材料，能量被释放。

**反应**　反应也叫兴奋，即对内外环境变化的觉察并对该变化做出反应，也可以说是对刺激的觉察和反应。

**运动**　身体内有许多类型的运动。在细胞层面，分子在运动。血液在身体各处运动。每次呼吸，横膈膜会运动。

**繁殖**　生命通过生物体的繁殖代代相传。从广义上讲，繁殖还指为了生长以及为了替换和修复老细胞的新细胞形成。

**生长**　生长指由于细胞数量增加或个体细胞增大而形成的增大。机体为了生长，合成代谢的速度一定要高于分解代谢的速度。

**分化**　分化是一种发育过程，在这个过程中，未分化细胞转化成具有独特结构和功能特征的专门化细胞。通过分化，细胞发育成组织和器官。

**呼吸**　呼吸指在细胞和外部环境间氧气和二氧化碳交换的所有过程。

**消化**　消化指个体摄取的复杂物质分解成可被血液吸收和机体利用的简单分子的过程。

**排泄**　排泄指从身体排除消化和新陈代谢产生的废物的过程。排泄过程排除身体不能利用的副产物，其中有很多有毒和与生命不相容的物质。

除了上述十种生命过程之外，生命还依赖环境中的某些物理因素，包括水、氧气、营养物、热量和压力等。

# Unit Three

## 医生手脏　病人死亡

美国一项研究发现，医护人员不洗手的频率惊人，这些本可以预防的医院内感染每天导致 247 例病人死亡。

某机构联合八大医院来处理全国范围内的低洗手频率问题。该活动始于春天，医院对医护人员的洗手情况进行了严格的评估。他们发现只有 30%～70%的医生和护士在进入或退出病房的情况下会洗手。

进出病房应洗手为(对医生、护士)要求的关键内容，同时该行为也受到了疾病预防和控制中心以及世界卫生组织的推崇。

医院随后评估了妨碍医护人员充分洗手的原因。某些情况下，问题出自后勤部门，这些问题可以通过将洗手台移动到更方便的位置或在洗手台增设台架方便搁放医护人员随身携带的物品等措施轻易解决。至于其他一些情况，问题似乎则是来自于人们的态度，解决起来要难得多。

医院尝试通过持续监控等方法解决这些问题。从开始实施纠正策略以来，参与该项活动医院的洗手率已经上升到 74%，但仍低于 90%的长期目标。

## 音符与生命

每个人都有自己最喜欢的歌曲，不管它出自后街男孩、贝多芬还是甲壳虫乐队。音乐能激发你、安抚你，也可以唤起许多情感。现在它正被用来治疗焦虑症、减轻疼痛和改善沟通技巧。

帕特里夏·特思深知音乐的功用。作为有执业资格的音乐治疗师，帕特里夏的工作是使孩子们待在医院的时候不害怕，并且感觉更舒适。

音乐一直是她生命的一部分，她想用她的天赋做一点特别的事。

“我想帮助人们，音乐对我来说总是有益的。我确信它在很多方面都有帮助，”帕特里夏说。

帕特里夏目前的工作对象是儿童，但她也治疗精神疾病和化学物质成瘾的成年人。她每天要看 10～15 个孩子，一个一个地处理，因为每个孩子需要解决的问题不同。

“我帮助他们缓解疼痛、孤独或焦虑。有时候在某个孩子出院回家前，我只有一天时间去了解和评估他，”帕特里夏说。

“我觉得我能为人们做点什么，利用音乐使患者冷静，用音乐治愈患者。”帕特里夏会为他们弹竖琴，教他们调节呼吸的技巧，帮助他们渡过难关。“有时，我们会一起唱歌，我们也一起写歌，”帕特里夏说。

她回忆起对一个患自闭症的五岁女孩的治疗。

“她爱敲鼓，所以我们一整天唱歌敲鼓。治疗结束后，她仍不想停止敲鼓。我真的很喜欢她。音乐疗法可以帮助提高孩子的沟通技巧和社交技能，”帕特里夏指出。

显然，在帕特里夏的帮助下，这些孩子们的生活增添了美丽的音符。

## 禽 流 感

禽流感也称 H5N1。这种疾病与猪流感、犬流感、马流感和人类流感相似，由已适应某特定物种的不同株系流感病毒所致。

禽类像人类一样会染上流感。禽流感病毒感染包括鸡、鸭、其他家禽和野鸟等禽类。然而，禽流感会对人类的健康产生威胁。1997 年在中国香港出现第一例直接感染人类的禽流感病毒，H5N1。然后，禽流感病毒传播到亚洲、非洲和欧洲的许多国家。

禽流感病毒对人类的感染虽然少，但是导致鸟类感染的病毒会变化，或变异，然后更容易感染人类。这样会导致禽流感大范围流行，或在全世界爆发。

在禽流感爆发期间，与感染禽类接触过的人群会生病。吃没有煮熟的家禽或通过接触已感染人群也可能使人致病。禽流感会使人重病甚至会致人死亡。目前还没有出现能预防该疾病的疫苗。

禽流感病毒在禽类中自然发生。全世界的野禽在肠道中都存在这种病毒，但它们一般不会因此生病。然而，禽流感病毒在禽类中传染性很强，会使鸡、鸭、火鸡等家禽患病身亡。

被禽流感病毒感染的禽类，在它们的唾液、鼻涕和粪便中含有病毒。易感禽类在接触含病毒的分泌物或排泄物时，或接触被此类分泌物或排泄物污染的物体表面时，就会感染禽流感病毒。家禽感染禽流感病毒的途径有直接接触已感染水禽或其他已感染家禽，或通过接触被禽流感病毒污染的表面（如尘土或鸟笼）或物质（如水或饲料）。

人类禽流感的症状包括典型的人类流感样症状（如发热、咳嗽、咽喉痛和肌肉疼痛）、眼睛感染、肺炎、严重呼吸道疾病（如急性呼吸道窘迫），以及其他严重威胁生命的并发症。禽流感的症状取决于导致感染的病毒类型。

实验室已有研究表明，一些处方药在治疗人类禽流感感染方面应该有效。但是，流感病毒会对这些药物产生耐药性，因此这些药物并非总是有效。人们需要更多的研究来证实这些药物的有效性。

# Unit Four

## 学生意识与心理健康

美国有一千六百多万年轻人在大学里学习。据自杀预防资源中心的统计，五分之一的大学生患有精神疾病，现今，越来越多的学生在进入校园开始大学生活前就已接受过心理健康服务。同时，越来越多的大学生正寻求帮助来解决进入大学之后产生的情感问题。临床上的第一次抑郁症往往出现在青春期。

自杀，全美第八大死因，是大学生这个年龄段个体死亡的第二大原因。大学生年龄段的成年人最易出现心理健康问题，在一定程度上是因为许多心理卫生问题最初出现二十岁左右。总的来说，年龄在 18 岁至 24 岁之间的年轻人中，估计有 27% 患有可诊断的心理疾病。

通过结合学校校园咨询服务、心理学俱乐部、残障人士办公室、学生处、多元文化办公室或其他组织的服务工作，学生可以提高心理健康的意识，使自己认识到良好心理健康的重要性——特别是在五月（心理健康月）和十月的第一个星期（心理疾病意识周）。

此外，全国各地大学校园已在尝试以下这些做法：

· 在校园繁华地段增加招贴广告进行宣传。
· 在心理学课堂上做演示。
· 把心理健康纳入新生入学适应教育。
· 写信给校报编辑。
· 请校园电台突出宣传精神健康问题。
· 训练这方面的校园领导。
· 播放电影,探讨该电影在精神健康方面的启示。
· 提供免费的心理健康筛查。
· 组织一次跑步/步行。
· 组织一场慈善演出。
· 组织一次"减压活动"。
· 建立你自己的小组。

让活动参与过程令人享受,做好相关宣传活动,招录其他人帮忙等,对有效开展活动至关重要。

## 面对 H1N1

十岁的本杰明·欧巴克脸部呈现猪流感加重期的典型脸色。他躺在戴维斯儿童医院的重症监护病房,他父母在祈祷。近两个星期来,他们的儿子一直为活下来而挣扎着。

"我感觉糟透了。我感到我的部分灵魂已被轧碎。"本杰明的父亲伊礼克·欧巴克说。

刚开始一切都像普通流感。7 月 4 日是星期天,本杰明了骑自行车后,感到喘不过气来。

"星期天的时候,他抱怨胸痛。我们以为他得了轻微流感,"他母亲朱莉·欧巴克说,儿科医生听了听他的肺部,说他的肺部呼吸音清晰。我问要不要让孩子吃点特敏福。他说,"不用,他病得没那么严重。到了周末他就会好起来的。"九小时后,孩子病情恶化。

本杰明不省人事,立即被送往医院。

"所以那天晚上、周二晚、周三上午是最糟糕的,"朱莉·欧巴克说,"这不是普通的发病过程。大多数 H1N1 患者都没事,但是大家都不知道哪些患者的病情会恶化,而事情的可怕之处就在于此。"

"就本杰明的病例来说,主要症状是体液聚集在他的肺外而不是肺内。我想这就是为什么儿科医生没能用听诊器听出来的原因。"本杰明的爸爸说。

现已证明,与季节性流感相比较,H1N1 对儿童更致命。

"当本杰明最初到医院的时候,他已经病得很严重了,"本杰明的主治医生乔安妮·纳塔乐说:"他当时已失去意识,现在他康复得很快。"

大难不死的本杰明病后恢复良好。他妈妈说她得到了很有价值的教训。现在,本杰明是幸运的,因为他赢得了这场夺去了很多人甚至是许多年轻人的疾病的战争。

## 糖 尿 病

糖尿病是一系列以高血糖为标志的代谢性疾病,由胰岛素分泌不足或功能降低引起,或二者兼而有之。

糖尿病可能导致失明、肾衰竭和神经损伤。以上病症是由于微小血管受损,即微血管病变造成的。糖尿病也是加快动脉硬化和变窄(动脉粥样硬化)的重要因素,从而导致中风、冠心病和其他大血管病变。

未经治疗的糖尿病早期症状与升高的血糖水平和葡萄糖在尿液中的流失有关。尿液中葡萄糖过多可造成尿量增加,并导致脱水。脱水引起的口渴会导致摄水量增多。胰岛素不能正常发挥作用会影响蛋白质、脂肪和碳水化合物的代谢。胰岛素是促进合成代谢的一种激素,能促进脂肪和蛋白质的贮存。患者虽然食欲增大,但胰岛素的相对或绝对不足最终会导致体重减轻。一些未经治疗的糖尿病患者也会出现疲劳、恶心和呕吐等症状。糖尿病患者易发生膀胱、皮肤和会阴部感染。血糖波动可导致视力模糊。血糖太高可导致嗜睡和昏迷。

糖尿病主要有两种,即 1 型和 2 型。1 型糖尿病也称为胰岛素依赖型糖尿病,或青少年发病型糖尿病。在 1 型糖尿病中,胰腺受到自身免疫系统的攻击而不能产生胰岛素。2 型糖尿病也称为非胰岛素依赖型糖尿病(非胰岛素依赖型糖尿病),或成人发病型糖尿病。2 型糖尿病患者仍可以产生胰岛素,但相对而言不能满足身体的需要,尤其是在面对胰岛素耐受性时。

积极加强对 1 型和 2 型糖尿病患者体内高血糖的控制,可以减少肾病、神经病变和视网膜病变的并发症,并有可能减少大血管病变的发生和恶化。积极控制和强化治疗可使空腹血糖水平达到 70～120 mg/dL,饭后血糖水平低于 160 mg/dL。

糖尿病治疗的目标是使血糖水平接近正常,达到尽可能安全的水平。此外,由于糖尿病有可能极大地增加病人患心脏病的危险,积极控制血压和胆固醇的预防性措施,也是目前糖尿病治疗的重要部分。

# Unit Five

## 抗生素耐药问题与人类健康

专家担心抗生素的耐药性会把人类置于危险之中,致使人类在某些细菌感染时几乎毫无抵抗之力。世界卫生组织称抗生素耐药性是人类健康的三大威胁之一。

不当使用抗生素导致了对抗生素具有耐药性的细菌群的出现。专家说如果现在不开始着手解决这个问题,本可治愈的感染可能会再度成为危险的疾病。美国疾病控制与预防中心的负责人托马斯 · 弗莱登博士呼吁美国立法者解决这一问题。

"如果我们不改善针对抗生素耐药性这个公共卫生问题的应对机制,我们可能会进入一个后抗生素世界,对某些感染,我们几乎无法进行临床干预,"他说。

专家担心,一种抗生素被使用得越多,它的药效就越低。细菌的遗传突变是一个自然过程,能使细菌对抗生素产生耐药性,但是药物过量使用加速了这个过程。

"最终,泌尿道的细菌将非常具有耐药性。这只是一个例子。还有不同细菌引起的皮肤感染、肺部感染,由于这些细菌的耐药性越来越强,你遇到的疾病问题也越严峻,就像世界上许多地方的肺结核一样。"一位传染性疾病专家唐纳德 · 坡汝博士说,"人们为了治疗结核病,这样的抗生素用一点,那样的也用一点,结果结核杆菌产生了抗药性。"

"全世界范围内我们都能遇到耐药性问题,可能在世界不同地方不同药物有不同的耐药性,"他说,"通过快捷的旅游,人们能把这些耐药性细菌传给任何地方的任何人。"

专家说解决办法在于教育病人和医生在没有必要用抗生素时，避免抗生素的使用。

## 护理行业的真相

雷丽是约翰霍普金斯医院的护士，她回想起带侄女去看的一部电影，其中的一名角色是护士。

“在电影中，有个小女孩快死了。这是一个令人悲哀的场景，护士很突然地走进来对全家人说，‘你们现在都得回去，探视时间结束了，’然后这个护士走出了房间，”雷丽说。

“我在心里对自己说，‘天啊！我侄女会不会认为这就是真正发生着的事情呢？所有护士都是这样吗？这就是我们如何对待病人的吗？’这太让我伤心了。这件事情让我在侄女面前很难堪！”

雷丽在医院的同事内萨·恩斯特说，电视上刻画的护士好不了多少。

“在美国有 290 万名护士和 79 万名医生，而当你看电视节目时，你看到的是医生做完所有护士通常会做的工作，”恩斯特说。

“做心电图的人是护士，把病人送来送去做检查的是护士，确保正确实施医疗步骤的是护士。电视上可没表现出这些。”

九年前一群护士学生成立了一个叫护理真相的组织，鼓励媒体展现出护理行业真实的一面。今年，该组织发布了它的“十年奖”——一个自 2000 年以来对护理行业进行最佳和最差描绘的媒体清单。

NBC 新上演的以医院为背景的系列剧《仁慈》获最佳奖。一些最流行的以医院为背景的电视剧——如 ABC 播出的《实习医生格蕾》——被评为“十年最差”。这些剧中表现的护理工作往往不能反映出当今护士接受的教育及其专业化程度。她说，除非这种情况能改变，否则护理行业将无法够吸引那些想把护理作为自己事业的人才。

## 急性肾衰

急性肾衰是肾的重要功能（即从血液中排除过多的体液和废物的功能）突然消失。当肾丧失了过滤功能时，你体内就会出现体液失衡和废物聚集的症状。

在就医的肾病人群中，急性肾衰的症状最普遍。特殊人群甚至需要重症护理。急性肾衰趋向于发生在复杂的手术后，或者严重受伤等导致的对肾的血液供应中断时。

肾功能的衰竭也会随着时间的推移发展逐步发展，疾病早期的临床表现及症状并不多。在这种情况下，通常会被认为是一种慢性肾衰。高血压和糖尿病是引起慢性肾衰的主要原因。

急性肾衰是很严重的，不同于慢性形态，通常需要精心护理。尽管如此，急性肾衰是可逆的，如果你身体很健康，几周内就可以自动恢复，如果急性肾衰发生在慢性病过程中，如心脏病的发作、阵痛、急性感染等，结果就会很严重。

急性肾衰的临床表现和症状包括：

· 尿量减少；

· 体液潴留，导致大腿、踝部或脚部水肿；

· 气促；

· 疲劳；

· 代谢紊乱；

· 重症患者可出现谵妄或昏迷；

· 心包炎(囊状膜的发炎包围心脏)引起的胸痛。

很多人在早期症状出现的时候没有足够重视，或者被导致突发肾衰的潜在问题所干扰。

肾是两个蚕豆形的器官，有人的拳头那么大，位于脊柱两侧，紧贴腹后壁，居腹膜后方。它们分泌尿液，排出血液中的代谢废物。最初，血液通过肾动脉进入肾，肾动脉是身体大动脉的分支，然后血液从肾动脉流向每个肾单位。

每一个肾脏大约包含 100 万个肾单位。每个肾单位都含有大量的毛细血管和与众多大的集流管道相通的大量肾小管。毛细血管能过滤血流中的体液。

被滤掉的物质既有废物，也有于身体健康有益的物质，都进入肾小管，在那里，尿素、尿酸、肌氨酸酐等代谢废物形成尿液，身体的必需物如糖、氨基酸、钙、盐被重新吸收回血液中。

# Unit Six

## 儿童癌症发病率持续上升

卫生专家已警告公众，污染和环境恶化导致中国 14 岁以下儿童癌症发病率上升。

据中国抗癌协会一名秘书说，中国大陆现有 32 000 多名 14 岁以下的儿童患有各类癌症，换句话说，发病率达到万分之一点零四。

“引人注目的是，一直被人们认为在高年龄段才出现的致命疾病正爆发在越来越多的孩子身上。主要的危险因素包括污染和不健康的生活方式。儿童中最常见的肿瘤类型有白血病、淋巴瘤和脑癌。13 到 19 岁的年轻人骨癌发病率比年龄较小的儿童要高。我亲眼看到了多例儿童在房屋装修后患白血病。长期暴露在装饰材料有害化学物质中会显著增加患肿瘤的风险，尤其是对孩子们而言，”他说。

专家说，同样，研究发现父母职业也有关联。例如，司机和油漆工人更有可能接触铅，这就意味着他们的孩子面临着更高的患癌风险。

儿童癌症患者有相同的症状，包括持续低热、不明原因体重减轻和鼻出血。

同时，不健康的生活方式大大增加了患癌的风险，这就是“生活方式慢性病”。科学已经证明如肥胖、锻炼不足的生活方式和高热量饮食等也是影响儿童癌症形成的因素。

“对孩子不健康的生活方式进行早期干预将大大降低儿童期及成人期的患癌风险。例如，没有外界干预，偏好吃肉的超重儿童通常会长成肥胖的成年人，这些成年人患乳腺癌和肠癌的风险更高。与肺癌和肝癌相比，乳房、皮肤和结肠部位的癌症和不健康的生活方式关联更大。”这位秘书说。

“这些癌症的发病率在中国人群中迅速上升，因为最近几十年里这些人变得更加富有并且采取了西方生活方式。”他补充说。

## 从病人到护士

说到医院护理，乔迪·贝克可有独到见解——不管是从护士还是从病人的角度。

二十三年前，那时乔迪·贝克 24 岁，下班途中发生的一件事永远改变了她的命运。一次车祸让她多处受伤，包括骨折和脑外伤。

在埃迪森市的一家医疗中心，人们都以为乔迪活不了了。她在重症监护室昏迷了一个月。尽管她已记不得那场事故，也记不清在医院的情况，但是有一点她深信不疑，那里精湛的医疗护理技术挽救了她的生命。

当她的病情稳定到了可以移动的时候，乔迪就转到了离家不远的伍德伯里的昂德伍德医院继续进行康复治疗。她在昂德伍德坚持了几个月痛苦的康复治疗和理疗。

"昂德伍德的护理人员真体贴细致，能及时悉心照料我这位卧床不起的脑外伤病人。"乔迪说。

乔迪在灾难之后迎来成功。当她终于回到工作岗位之后，她意识到自己想用这个重生的机会做一些有意义的事：她想当护士。

她在格罗斯特郡学院获得护理学专科学位。后来一直在一家医疗中心担任急救护理的临床护士工作，最近她获得该中心 CT 心血管造影室的注册护士职位。

乔迪觉得那场车祸是注定的。她相信她是有福之人，能帮助其他人也获得重生。当病人家属的挚爱带着尊严离开尘世的时候，乔迪会握住他们的手，她会安慰局促不安的病人使之平静。她会在病人万念俱灰的时候支持他们。

"种瓜得瓜，种豆得豆"，乔迪说，"说不定哪天我又会生病。我深信那时某位好护士也会成为我的保护神。"

## 便　秘

便秘是消化系统常见的健康问题之一，其表现为排便次数减少，粪便干结，或者说排便困难，有时甚至好几天都不排便。

即使不是天天都排便，也不能就此下结论说明就是便秘。判断便秘，还应该有以下表现：

- 便干结且一周内排便次数少于 3 次；
- 排便困难经常发作；
- 腹胀或其他腹部不适。

要进一步理解便秘，就要了解结肠或者说大肠的运转。当食物残渣随着肠蠕动进入大肠时，其中一部分水分被大肠吸收后形成粪便。粪便随着肠蠕动到达直肠。当粪便到达直肠后就变成了固体，因为大部分的水被吸收了。

当大肠吸收的水分过多或者肠蠕动减慢使粪便在肠道中停留时间过长时，就导致了便秘。结果是大便变得干燥坚硬。通常情况下，引起便秘的原因有：

- 水分摄入不足；
- 食物中缺少纤维；
- 没有养成良好的排便习惯；
- 年龄；
- 缺乏运动；
- 怀孕；
- 疾病。

当发生便秘时，你会感觉到排便比平时更困难。有各种原因会导致排便困难。例如，排便的次数减少，或者无效(感觉排便不尽)。

大多数患有便秘的人不用过多担心，只有少数便秘的人存在严重的医学问题。如果你已经有两个星期以上都没有大便了，那就要去医院就诊，以确诊病因，及时治疗。如果便秘是由于结肠癌引起的，早诊断、早治疗就显得非常关键。

便秘的诊断通常依赖于你的病史和物理检查。医生首先会想办法确定你的小肠或者直肠有没有阻塞(肠梗阻)，然后是激素水平，比如说甲状腺功能减退或者电解质失衡。医生还会核实你的药物治疗情况，这些药物可能是引起你便秘的原因。

如果便秘不是由医学问题引起的，可以通过饮食来调节，例如，多喝水，多吃一些纤维素含量高的食物(可以从大量的蔬菜、水果、面食中获得)，以及增加饮食中亚麻油的含量。除非医学上确有必要，不要长期使用泻药，因为这会导致肠蠕动对泻药产生依赖性。灌肠可作为一种医学治疗方法来解除便秘，然而，灌肠常常只用于由于直肠原因引起的便秘，而非整个肠道系统。

# Unit Seven

## 同仁堂在西方

中药制造商北京同仁堂集团有限公司一位总裁说，该公司计划在欧洲增开三家药店，并正在寻找合作伙伴以在美国建立自己的店铺。

同仁堂起源于大约两百年前一家中国皇室药房，该公司今年将在欧洲开设三家药店，分别位于德国、波兰和匈牙利。

该公司的海外扩展开始于 1993 年，现公司在 16 个国家和地区拥有 45 家合资或全资药店。

公司大多数海外药店设在亚洲，因为在这些地方中国文化和中医非常流行，还有，在一定程度上是因为这些地方有大型华人社区。

同仁堂在西方开设的店则少得多。它在英国伦敦开设了一家药店，在加拿大开了两家，同时在澳大利亚也开设了两家药店。

同仁堂正在美国寻找合作伙伴以建立第一家药店。“我们在美国已有经销商，也十分关注美国市场。我们下一发展阶段就是在那里建立一个药店。”这位管理人员说。

非华人客户也在增长。在加拿大，约 10%的客户都是当地人，这个比例在澳大利亚是百分之二十。

但是专家称，在西方拓展业务面临很多挑战。

“中医在全球的拓展从来都不顺利，随着全球药物监管更加严格，情况更加严峻。”一名专家说。

“西方社会有一些人是承认中医的，但是西医和中医的原理是完全不同的，所以中医很难适应西方医学的情况。”北京中医药大学一位教授说。

## 我在北京看中医

我去中国北京时，打算做的最主要的事情是让一位中医医生做身体检查。不用脱衣服，不用血液检查，不用 X 光片，真的就能诊断吗？

我报名去参观北京一所中医院。和我一起去的还有导游和另外 9 人。

据说中医包括草药、针灸、按摩和艾灸。非常迷人的导游告诉我们一个真正的中医医生应该长什么样。首先，中医医生应该很老，因为需要多年时间才能学好中医。随后，她告诉我们，一头灰白的头发是(中医)年纪最好的证明。最有趣的一个特征就是腹部——好中医应该有小肚子，这能证明他知道如何正确吐纳。

轮到我了。医生诊断花了不到五分钟。

首先，他摸了我的脉。陪同护士告诉我说，从历史渊源看，古时有钱人家的妇女不愿意在看病时脱下衣服，因此医生只有通过外显的体征来形成诊断。

其次，医生看了看我的舌头，上面有点饼干，但是这没关系。护士解释说，摸脉为主，舌苔诊断为次。舌头的不同地方与身体的不同部位相关联。例如，舌根与肾脏和膀胱有关。

我的诊断结果？医生说，我后背和肩膀疼痛，头脑恍惚比较严重。这是真的。事实上我身上一直痛，特别是我的右肩，因为时间太长了，所以我没有在意它。然而，我还是买够了足用一两个月的中草药。那么结果呢？服用草药后，多年的肩膀疼痛还有头脑恍惚都一去不返了。

## 骨　折

当施加外力在骨骼上时，骨骼便有可能出问题。如果骨骼不能承受这些外力，就会发生骨折。骨折发生时，骨骼将失去完整性，骨骼结构被破坏。

根据骨折发生的部位和外观等特点，骨折可分为许多类。如果骨折周围的皮肤没有破损，为闭合骨折。开放骨折皮肤破损，暴露骨头，使伤口更易于感染。如果骨骼完全折断，称为完全骨折；如果是部分折断则称为非完全骨折或青枝骨折。由于骨骼承受长期重复活动带来的压力而破裂，称为压力性骨折。根据骨折线形状，有横形骨折、斜形骨折、螺旋形骨折。如果骨折成许多片，称为粉碎性骨折。事实上，骨折发生时可能只有一种情况，也可能同时发生多种骨折。

一般说来，骨折会导致疼痛、肿大，有时因内出血会出现淤伤。由于受伤区域不能承受重力或压力，移动时会产生剧烈疼痛。折骨周围的软组织也可能受伤。由于患处脉搏丧失，骨折周围或以下部位会出现麻木、瘫痪。

可通过患处体格检查和放射检查对骨折进行诊断。然而，某些类型骨折很难通过放射检查发现。在这种情况下，医生会让病人做其他的影像诊断，如计算机断层扫描、磁共振成像或骨骼扫描。开放骨折需要做另外的医学化验检查，以确定是否有失血和存在感染。

对手、臂、足、腿部位的骨折进行的初步治疗包括在肢体原位上夹板、抬高受伤肢体、对受伤区域冰敷。固定患处对最初疼痛控制极有帮助。对于颈部和背部损伤，最先参与处理的急救人员或护理人员可以将伤员置于长形木板上，带上项领，以保护脊髓免受潜在的损伤。

骨折手术在很大程度上取决于骨折类型和骨折部位。外科医生对骨折进行处理，使骨头位置复原，再安上石膏等固定位置。有时，骨折需要用插入金属来固定位置。根据骨折情况的不同，有时这些金属是永久安放不再取出的；有时只是暂时安放，在骨折完全愈合后一段时间通过手术取出。

# Unit Eight

## 孤独症是一种传染病吗?

孤独一直与抑郁和其他健康问题相关。现有一项研究表明它还能传染。一个孤独者的朋友染上孤独情绪的可能性会增加52%。一个孤独者的朋友的朋友染上孤独情绪的可能性也会增加25%。

早期研究结果表明在社会群体内部,幸福感、肥胖和戒烟的能力都像传染病一样是可以传染的,这些发现来自于美国马萨诸塞州小镇弗莱明翰的一项大型健康研究。

这项始于1948年的研究起初调查心脏病病因。自那时起,研究已增加了更多的测试项目,包括评估孤独症和抑郁症。

新发现调查了5千多名曾参与过弗莱明翰心脏研究的人的后代,研究人员调查了交友历史以及孤独情绪主诉。

例如,孤独症能影响邻里关系。邻居曾是亲密的朋友,但现在待在一起的时间变少时,孤独情绪就开始传播。研究还发现,孤独情绪在女性中比在男性中更容易传染。

这些发现发表在上个月的《人格与社会心理学》杂志上。

据说,一般的人每年感到孤独的平均天数是48天。研究发现,如有一个孤独的朋友,时间可以增加约17天。但每增加一个朋友可以降低孤独感天数,约5%,或两天半的时间。

孤独的人变得越来越不相信别人。这使得他们结交朋友越来越困难——更有可能的是社会将排斥他们。

芝加哥大学的一位专家主持了这次研究。他说识别和处理孤独情绪很重要。他说那些已经被推到社会边缘的人应该有人来帮助他们修复社会网络。

目标应该是积极建立起一种他称为“保护屏障”的东西来对抗孤独。他说这一屏障可以阻止患者的整个社会网络瓦解。

## 特别的礼物

安东尼·墨菲得到了一份他终生难忘的礼物——妻子丁娜为他捐献的肾脏。

安东尼生下来只有一个无法正常运转的肾脏。两年前,医生惊恐地发现他的血压异常偏高。后来到2008年年底,血液检查结果已表明他需要做移植手术。很快,他就开始寻找匹配的供体。

最初,由于健康原因或无肾脏组织匹配,许多潜在的肾脏捐献者都被排除掉了。接着,奇迹发生了。检查发现,丁娜竟然成为她丈夫的匹配捐献者。

“我当时很惊讶,但知道将是我自己为丈夫捐肾又让我十分宽慰。”丁娜说。

考虑到孩子,想到两个大人同时要接受手术,问题变得有些复杂。孩子科林和凯尔还小,但他们似乎明白这次手术对父亲来说很重要。

“我们对他们说,妈妈要把身体很重要的一部分给爸爸,爸爸的身体要好起来就得需要这个。他们认为父母能这样做简直太棒了。”安东尼说。

“大家都体贴谅解,”丁娜补充说,“医护人员对我和安东尼都很好。他们鼓励我们,告诉我们一切都会正常起来,没事。”

移植手术在2009年1月进行。大约六个月后安东尼才恢复元气,不过肾脏功能正常了，两个人都恢复了健康。

“我从爱人那里得到了世界上最好的礼物，现在我又能与丁娜和孩子们在一起了。能看见这一切都变成现实，这种感觉真是美妙。”安东尼说。

“的确有一种喜出望外的感觉，”丁娜补充道，“我们从家人、朋友和陌生人那里得到了爱和支持，这一切都是战胜疾病的最好方式。安东尼和我能一起看着我们年轻的家庭茁壮成长，这种感觉对我而言非常特别。这就是爱。”

## 艾 滋 病

人们受到艾滋病毒的威胁已经超过二十年，已经有成千上万人死于艾滋病。艾滋病是当今世界面临的一个巨大问题。大家都应该了解有关艾滋病的基本知识。

**2007 年 12 月全球艾滋病流行概况**

| | | |
|---|---|---|
| 2007 年艾滋病病毒感染者人数 | 共计 | 3 320 万(3 060 万～3 610 万) |
| | 成人 | 3 080 万(2 820 万～3 360 万) |
| | 妇女 | 1 540 万(1 390 万～1 660 万) |
| | 15 岁以下儿童 | 250 万(220 万～260 万) |
| 2007 年新感染艾滋病病毒人数 | 共计 | 250 万(180 万～410 万) |
| | 成人 | 210 万(140 万～360 万) |
| | 15 岁以下儿童 | 42 万(35 万～54 万) |
| 2007 年艾滋病死亡人数 | 共计 | 210 万(190 万～240 万) |
| | 成人 | 170 万(160 万～210 万) |
| | 15 岁以下儿童 | 33 万(31 万～38 万) |

艾滋病(AIDS)是获得性免疫缺陷综合征的简称，是由免疫缺陷病毒(HIV)所引起的致命性慢性传染病。该病主要通过性接触和血液传播，病毒主要侵犯和破坏辅助性 T 淋巴细胞，这些细胞是身体免疫系统的一部分，能对抗感染和各种癌症。

艾滋病的症状由于内脏机能和肿瘤部位的不同而有不同的表现。常见的艾滋病症状有以下几个方面：一般症状包括持续发热、虚弱、盗汗、全身浅表淋巴结肿大、体重下降；呼吸道症状包括长期咳嗽、胸痛、呼吸困难，严重时痰中带血；消化道症状有厌食、恶心、呕吐、腹泻，严重时可便血；神经系统症状包括头晕、头痛、反应迟钝、智力减退、精神失常、抽搐、偏瘫、痴呆等；皮肤和黏膜损害包括弥漫性丘疹、带状疱疹、口腔和咽部黏膜炎症及溃烂；还有可能出现多种恶性肿瘤，位于体表的卡波西氏肉瘤可见红色或紫红色的斑疹、丘疹和浸润性肿块。由此可见，艾滋病的症状非常复杂。

诊断艾滋病病毒感染者可以通过检定抗疾病蛋白或血液里抗体的表现来确认。两种不同类型的抗体试验，即酶联免疫分析(ELISA)和免疫着色，可供选择。

避免某些高危险性行为及采取以下措施可减少感染 HIV 的风险：

· 避免性滥交。

· 每次性行为使用安全套。

· 使用静脉注射时，不要与其他人共用针头。

· 医疗保健工作者应严格遵循预防措施(建立感染控制程序避免接触体液)。

· 想怀孕的女性最好预先做一个 HIV 测试，特别是有感染史者。孕妇艾滋病病毒阳性者需要特别的产前护理和药物，以减少将艾滋病病毒传给自己的新生婴儿的风险。

自 90 年代中期以来，对艾滋病的防治已经有很大改善，但到目前为止仍然无法治愈艾滋病。总的治疗原则为抗感染、抗肿瘤、杀灭或抑止 HIV 病毒、增强机体免疫机能。

# Unit Nine

## 少 吃 盐

少吃盐可以降低血压，但是也能减少心脏病吗？

一些科学家说，这项减少美国人食盐用量的运动是一种用数百万人的健康来做的实验。

上个月我们报道了一项研究，该研究表明即使少吃一点点盐也会极大地有利于心脏。这项研究发表在《新英格兰医学杂志》上。在美国，科学家们使用了一种计算机模型来预测每天少吃 3 克盐会如何影响心脏疾病。

科学家说，研究的结果是心脏病发作将减少 13%，中风将减少 8%，死亡率将减少 4%，新发心脏病将减少 11%。研究人员说，这样做每年可以减少十万人次心脏病发作和 9 200 例病人死亡。

研究人员来自旧金山的加利福尼亚大学、斯坦福大学和哥伦比亚大学。

这些研究人员和美国公共卫生专家热衷于开展一个全国性的活动来说服人们少吃盐。类似活动在英国、日本和芬兰等地已在进行。

但是，一些科学家指出，这一活动是用数百万人的健康在做实验。

迈克尔 · 艾德曼就是批评者之一。这位高血压专家说，少吃盐会导致低血压。他说研究并没有明确地表明降低用盐会减少心脏病或中风的发作。

他同时说到盐还有其他的生物作用。他说，呼吁全国饮食减少用盐可能有良好的效果，但也可能有不良后果。他说两者都没有足够的证据。

另一个批评者是营养和肾病专家戴维 · 麦卡伦。他说，一个人的大脑可以决定吃多少盐，这一点全世界相似。

麦卡伦和艾德曼医生都与盐业协会，即制盐产业的贸易集团有密切联系。艾德曼医生是顾问委员会成员，然而他表明他没有收过集团的钱。麦卡伦医生向盐业协会提供科学建议则是有薪资的。

## 医 院 窗 户

两个人，身患重病，住在同一间病房里。

一个人可以每天下午在床上坐一个小时进行肺部液体引流。

他的床紧挨着这个病房唯一的一扇窗户。

另一个人则只能全天平躺在床上度日。

他们能连续谈上几个小时。他们聊到了自己的妻子和家人、他们的家、他们的工作以及他们曾经度假的地方。

每天下午，当窗边的人坐起来时，他就会向室友描述他所看到的窗外的一切来打发时间。

终日与床为伴的室友开始企盼每天的这一小时。外面多彩的世界和各种活动开阔了他的视野，让他的生命更加鲜活。

透过窗户可俯瞰一个有着美丽湖泊的花园。鸭子和天鹅在水上嬉戏，孩子们操纵着模型船。年轻的情侣们在色彩缤纷的花丛中手挽着手走过，远处可以看到城市轮廓的美丽风景。

当窗旁的那个人详尽地描述这一切时，房间另一边的病友就会闭上眼睛想象着这如画的风景。

一天一天过去了，一周一周过去了。

一个早上，值班护士打来水到病房为他们洗浴，却发现了窗旁那个人已经毫无生气，他已经在睡梦中安然去世。护士很悲伤地叫来医院的护理人员抬走了尸体。

似乎合适的时机到了，卧床的病友问护士他是否可以搬到挨着窗户的床位。护士很高兴地给他换了床，确信他已经安顿舒适后，就离开了。

他慢慢地、痛苦地用一只胳膊撑起身体，想第一次看看外面真实的世界。他慢慢地、费劲地转过身，向床边的窗外望去。

是一面空荡荡的墙壁！

这个人问护士是什么促使他已逝的室友描绘出那么丰富的窗外世界。

护士回答说，那个人是个盲人，甚至连墙都看不见。

## 压　力

一位衣着讲究的白领对她的朋友说："这些日子我觉得很压抑，因为工作让我很有压力。"这让她的朋友很吃惊。

关于压力的调查有很多。那么究竟什么是压力？Hans Selye 在 1936 年第一次使用了这个词语。Hans 把 "stress" 定义为"机体对变化的不明确的反应"。也有人把"stress" 定义为"当机体应对变化时产生的一种情感"。字典上把"stress" 定义为"一种生理、心理和情绪的张力"或"当个体意识到需求超出了个人和社会的能力范围时产生的情况或情感"。医学上认为压力会从生理上和心理上破坏体内平衡。

因此，当人应对压力时，情绪、心理和生理都会产生变化。医学通过对神经系统和激素的刺激研究可以解释压力产生的基本原因。下丘脑发出信号，使得肾上腺产生更多的肾上腺激素和皮质激素进入血液，而这些激素会加快心跳、呼吸，增高血压，加快新陈代谢。血管进一步扩张，瞳孔增大，肝脏释放更多储存的血糖进入血液，汗液分泌增多。短时间的轻微压力有助于人处理紧急事件，使人表现得更好。然而，过多的压力如果处理不当，或者不能很快恢复，就会引起很多问题。

人们无法避免现代社会快速的工作、生活产生的压力，但是可以学会接受压力，在压力下生活。

首先，要学会辨认压力产生的症状。压力最先影响的是内心情绪。压力使人们觉得焦急、恐慌、压抑，甚至特别忧虑，然后人们对一切事物变得很敏感，容易从工作中分心，以自我为重心。若果压力没能得到控制，日益累积，人们会觉得乏力、胃部不适、胸闷、失眠，甚至恶心呕吐。

其次，应该了解怎样控制压力。压力伴随着变化和挑战发生。重新看看日程安排，放弃不太重要的事件,做出最优的选择。对工作成绩要有比较现实的预期。要有充足的高质量的睡眠。

最后,要尽量多了解产生压力的原因。好不好的事件都可能引起压力,一旦出现压力的征兆,尽量找出是由什么引起的:工作、学习、家庭、社会、生活习惯还是环境。如果不能完全放弃某事,至少也应在处理事情时放慢节奏。

人们都知道在巨大压力下生活的人容易有不利于健康的行为和形成不利于健康的习惯。因此,压力会损害健康。压力有多种表现形式,也会影响各个年龄段的人。时间和空间是治疗压力最好的良药。

# Unit Ten

## 医生和头痛

很多头痛病人没有去看医生。美国最近一项研究表明,50%的偏头痛病人没有寻求医疗建议,且未被诊断为偏头痛,所以他们并没有接受偏头痛的治疗。

许多病人因头痛而丧失活动能力,亲戚、朋友和同事对他们报以同情,但这却无法减轻疼痛。他们可能会服用多种药物进行治疗,但这些药物却起不了什么作用。他们可能已经去看过一次医生,医生也为他们开了药,但也没有太大的效果。

让医生对头痛进行诊断非常重要。如果突然出现严重或持续性头痛,伴随着乏力、头晕、麻木或其他奇怪的生理感觉,应当立即告知医生。

如果经常出现使人虚弱的头痛或者服用了过多的止痛药,也应该咨询医生。与医生的约诊应主要用来谈论头痛的情况。

医生的角色在于准确诊断头痛,并帮助减少头痛对病人及其生活方式的影响。推荐药物是这个过程的一部分。如同任何医学问题一样,得到最好的医疗建议是重要的。病人可能会发现,当地医生也许没有有关头痛的足够的专业知识,或者可能不把头痛当回事。病人一定要让医生意识到头痛对生活品质的破坏,以及它对病人伴侣、孩子、雇主、同事和朋友的影响。

控制头痛是一个巨大的挑战。每个病人可能不得不尝试大量的治疗方案,进行大量的准备,采取不同的服药方式,来找出对他最有效的方法。医生的角色在这个过程中至关重要。一旦医生对头痛作出了正确的诊断,那么就可以制定治疗头痛方案。这个方案应当定期进行评价和更新。

医患沟通对取得最好的(医疗)效果非常重要。双方有效的沟通能产生一个试误过程,这样才能进行有效治疗,从而最大限度地减少疼痛和由头痛引起的丧失活动能力的风险。

## 倾听是良药

这是一个周日,我还要看最后一位病人。我匆匆走向她的病房,停在了门口。她是一位年迈的妇女,坐在病床的一角,正费劲地把袜子穿上她水肿的双脚。我跨过门槛,快速对护士嘱咐了几句,浏览了病人的病历记录,记录显示她病情稳定。我差不多清楚了她的情况。

我靠着床栏低头看着她。她问我能否帮她穿上袜子。然而,我却开始自言自语说了下面这番话:“你今天感觉怎么样?你的血糖和血压还是挺高,但今天好点了。护士说你迫不及待地想去看今天来探望你的儿子。家里人从那么远的地方来看你，真好！我敢肯定你早就期待看到他了。”

她用坚决而毋庸置疑的声音打断了我：“请坐，医生。这是我的事，与你无关。”

我很惊讶，也很尴尬。我坐了下来，帮她穿袜子。她开始告诉我，她唯一的儿子其实就住在不远的地方，但她已经五年没有看到他了。她觉得这事极大地影响了她的健康。在听完她的故事，给她穿上袜子后，我询问她还有什么可以帮忙的，她微笑着摇了摇头。她要我做的只是去倾听她。

每个故事都不同。有些细节丰富，有些则较为模糊；有些有开头、中间和结尾，有些则洋洋洒洒没有结尾；有的真，有的假。但这一切都没有关系。对述说者来说，最重要的是，他们的故事有人听，没有被打断、妄加猜测或是评判。

倾听一个人的故事，不像做昂贵的医学诊断检查那样花费巨大，但却是治疗和诊断的关键。

我常常思考那位女士让我学到的东西，而我也总是提醒自己不要忽略停下来、坐下来和专心倾听的重要性。在那以后不久，一次意想不到的角色转换，我成了病人，在 31 岁的时候被确诊为多发性硬化症。现在，20 年后，我仍旧终日坐在轮椅里。

只要情况允许的话，我坚持在轮椅上给病人看病，但当病情影响到我的双手时，我不得不辞职了。我仍在给医学院学生和其他医务专业人员上课，只不过是从医生和病人的双重角度。

我告诉他们我相信倾听的力量。我还以自己的亲身经历告诉他们，当有人停下来、坐下来倾听我的故事的时候，就会在我体内产生不可估量的康复力量。

## 高 血 压

全世界约有 10 亿人患有高血压，它是发病和死亡的一个主要原因。许多人并没有意识到他们患有高血压，因此，这种疾病有时被称为“无声杀手”。在人们能观察到高血压的损害后果（如中风、心肌梗死、肾脏功能紊乱、视力问题等）之前，高血压往往是没有症状的。

高血压被定义为血压的异常升高。收缩压和舒张压数值都应被注意。根据最近的美国全国诊断指南，可用下表数值描述高血压的不同阶段。

| 分　类 | 收缩压（mmHg） | 舒张压（mmHg） |
|---|---|---|
| 正常 | <120 | <80 |
| 临界 | 120～139 | 80～89 |
| 第一阶段 | 140～159 | 90～99 |
| 第二阶段 | >160 | >100 |

对于 90%～95% 的高血压患者而言，病因尚不清楚，这种情况称为原发性高血压。其余 5%～10%的患者的高血压是由于肾病、内分泌疾病或其他可确认病因而继发的，这种高血压称为继发性高血压。

高血压危象指可能导致中风的血压急剧升高。血压过度增高（超过 180/110mm Hg）将损害血管。心脏可能无法维持足够的血液循环。高血压危象分为高血压急症和高血压危症两类。高血压急症的体征和症状包括血压升高、严重头痛、严重焦虑和呼吸短促。高血压危症病人会出现肺水肿、脑水肿或脑出血、心脏病发作、中风等威胁生命的体征和症状。

医生还不能确定大多数高血压病例的病因,但是人们现已公认有几种情况会提高血压,如肥胖、酗酒、有高血压家族史、盐摄入过多、衰老等。体力锻炼过少、钾和钙摄取不足也可能会使血压升高。

高血压一般不会产生症状。大多数人因其他原因就医时才被告知他们患有高血压。如果不经治疗,高血压会损害心脏、大脑、肾或眼睛。其损害会导致冠心病、中风和肾脏衰竭等问题。非常高的血压会导致头痛、视力问题、恶心和呕吐。

高血压的治疗取决于病人血压的高度、病人是否有糖尿病等其他健康问题以及病人是否已有任何器官被损伤。医生也会考虑病人患上其他疾病,特别是心脏病的可能性。大多数高血压病人用抗高血压药物治疗。高血压还通常用降低心脏输出量的药物治疗。血管扩张药物会降低全身血管阻力,也被用来治疗高血压。

人们可以通过采用健康的生活方式来降低血压。如果这些方式不起作用,则可能需要服用药物。有助于预防高血压的生活方式包括:

· 减肥。

· 减少盐的摄入量。

· 锻炼。

· 限制酒精摄入量。

· 每天从饮食中摄入 3 500 mg 钾。新鲜的、未被加工的完整食物中钾含量最高,如肉、鱼、无脂或低脂奶制品、许多水果和蔬菜。

# Appendix F　Keys to the Exercises

## Unit One

## Part One　Picture & Chart

**Ⅰ. Medical Instrument**

1. stomach irrigator　2. sputum aspirator　3. respirator　4. simple respirator

**Ⅱ. External Human Organs**

1. 脐　2. 腹部　3. 腹股沟　4. 小腿　5. 脚踝

**Ⅲ. First Aid (CPR)**

4,2,3,1

## Part Two　Listening Comprehension

**Task One**

fever　sore throat　runny nose　headache　blood test

**Task Two**

1. upper　2. take aspirin　3. three times

## Part Three　Reading Comprehension

**Ⅰ. Medical Horizon**

**Task One**

1. C　2. D　3. D　4. B　5. D

**Task Two**

1. pregnancy　2. allergic　3. approved　4. wheezing　5. expect

**Ⅱ. Hospital Story**

**Task One**

1. 一位护士推开拥挤的人群，鲜血溅满了她白色的大褂和头巾。

2. “这些医生赚人民的钱致富，但在人民最需要他们的时候，他们却跑开了。他们的人性在哪？”他发问道。

3. 医院外，一场爆炸晃动了街道，民众纷纷跑向掩体，而一些医生则奔向了发出爆炸声响的地方寻找幸存者，沙丁冲向了他的救护车。

**Ⅲ. Human Disease**

**Task One**

1. d 2. h 3. e 4. a 5. i 6. c 7. j 8. f 9. b 10. g

## Part Four Practical Writing

**Reference Sample:**

Birth Certificate

This is to certify that Liu Yang (female) was born on May 1, 2008 in Shanghai, China, to Liu Hongwei, father, and Jiang Lihong, mother. Weight: 3.1 kg. Length: 48 cm.

The First People's Hospital of Shanghai
(sealed)
Signature: (sealed)
Dated the 20th day of May, 2008

注:每单元 Part Five 答案略。

# Unit Two

## Part One Picture & Chart

**Ⅰ. Medical Instruments**

1. pulse oximeter 2. thermometer 3. blood pressure cuff
4. digital blood pressure monitor 5. electric thermometer
6. blood pressure monitor 7. ID bracelet 8. stethoscope

**Ⅱ. Internal Human Organs**

1. 胰腺 2. 胆囊 3. 十二指肠 4. 结肠 5. 阑尾 6. 咽 7. 食管,食道 8. 空肠

**Ⅲ. First Aid**

Method One: 4, 2, 1, 3 Method Two: 1, 3, 2, 5, 4

## Part Two Listening Comprehension

**Task One**

kidney function liver function biopsy painful swollen

**Task Two**

1. pain killer 2. kidney function 3. Chinese traditional herbs

## Part Three Reading Comprehension

**Ⅰ. Medical Horizon**

**Task One**

1. B 2. D 3. B 4. C 5. D

**Task Two**

1. comply 2. content 3. simplify 4. specific 5. dosage

**Ⅱ. Hospital Story**

**Task One**

1. 我们之间已经形成了一种特别的东西——建立于清晨一起焦虑候诊的情谊。

2. 当我第一次来接受放射治疗时，我感到紧张、焦虑、害怕。

3. 她暖人的语言和温柔的微笑消解了我心中的恐惧，燃起了我心中向候诊室其他女士敞开心扉，结下情谊的渴望。

**Ⅲ. Human Disease**

**Task One**

1. digested 2. excreted 3. toxic 4. malnutrition 5. cellular

6. matured 7. fertilized 8. respiration 9. component 10. irritable

## Part Four Practical Writing

**Reference Sample:**

Doctor's Certificate

March 11th, 2012

This is to certify that the patient, Zhang Ming, male, aged 21, was admitted into our hospital on March 5th, 2012 for suffering from diarrhea. After a week of treatment, he has got complete recovery and will be discharged on March 12th, 2012. It is suggested that he rest for one week at home before returning to his study.

(Signature) Li Wei

Physician-in-chief

# Unit Three

## Part One Picture & Chart

**Ⅰ. Medical Instrument**

1. dressing 2. drain tube 3. oxygen mask 4. syringe driver 5. ice pack

6. heat pack

**Ⅱ. Human Skeleton**

1. 椎骨，脊椎 2. 锁骨 3. 肱上膊，肱部 4. 桡骨 5. 尺骨 6. 股骨

7. <解>胫骨 8. 腓骨

**Ⅲ. First Aid**

2,1,4,3,5,6,8,7

## Part Two Listening Comprehension

**Task One**

GI department admitting Nov. 15th stools positive

**Task Two**

1. pressure 2. good 3. palpitations

## Part Three Reading Comprehension

Ⅰ. **Medical Horizon**

**Task One**

1. B 2. D 3. A 4. D 5. D

**Task Two**

1. obstacle 2. rigorous 3. preventable 4. stem from 5. compliance

Ⅱ. **Hospital Story**

**Task One**

1. 现在它正被用来治疗焦虑症、减轻疼痛和改善沟通技巧。

2. 帕特里夏目前的工作对象是儿童,但也治疗精神疾病和化学物质成瘾的成年人。

3. 帕特里夏会为他们弹竖琴,教他们调节呼吸的技巧,帮助他们渡过难关。

Ⅲ. **Human Disease**

**Task One**

1. g 2. e 3. f 4. h 5. b 6. a 7. i 8. d 9. j 10. c

## Part Four Practical Writing

**Reference Sample:**

Mrs. Martha was born on 17 September, 1921. She was admitted on 23, April, 2009 and discharged on 10 May, 2009. There are still some problems to be solved after discharge. For example, she has been suffering from hypertension and degenerative bone disease. She needs to urinate frequently and is diagnosed with left pneumonia and urinary tract infection. Since she has no family members, she needs a bath seat and safety rails in the bathroom. She needs a nurse to visit her twice a week to monitor the medications. Finally she needs physiotherapy 3 times a week. By the way, she is a very independent-minded woman who is fully alert and articulate.

# Unit Four

## Part One Picture & Chart

Ⅰ. **Medical Instrument**

1. nebulizer 2. air sterilization machine 3. ultraviolet sterilizer

4. hypodermic syringe 5. scales 6. air tank

Ⅱ. **Brain Cross-Sections**

1. 横断面;横截面图 2.(大脑)回间沟 3. 脑回 4. 脑室

Ⅲ. **First Aid**

1,4,3,2

# Part Two Listening Comprehension

**Task One**

Blood pressure pulse rate breathing rate fluids chart

**Task Two**

1. secondary line 2. nutrients 3. sticky, blockage

# Part Three Reading Comprehension

Ⅰ. **Medical Horizon**

**Task One**

1. B 2. D 3. A 4. C 5. B

**Task Two**

1. vulnerable 2. aware 3. teamed up with 4. emerged 5. adolescent

Ⅱ. **Hospital Story**

**Task One**

1. 本杰明不省人事,立即被送往医院。

2. 就本杰明的病例来说,主要症状是体液聚集在他的肺外而不是肺内。

3. 现已证明,和季节性流感相比较,H1N1 对儿童更致命。

Ⅲ. **Human Disease**

**Task One**

1. e 2. g 3. a 4. b 5. h 6. i 7. c 8. d 9. j 10. f

# Part Four Practical Writing

**Reference Sample:**

**THE INPATIENT OFFICE OF CHINA NUMBER ONE HOSPITAL**

**PATIENT'S NAME:** Johnson

**CHART NUMBER:** 15672

**DATE OF BIRTH:** 06/4/1993

**PLACE OF BIRTH:** New York, America

**SEX:** Male

**DATE OF ADMISSION:** 06/7/2006

**CHIEF COMPLAINT:** Coughing, wheezing with difficult respiration.

**PRESENT ILLNESS:** This is the first admission for this thirteen-year-old boy with a history of asthma since the age of 3 who had never been hospitalized for asthma before and had been perfectly well since he came to China until the touring the Great Wall prior to admission when the patient developed shortness of breath and was unresponsive to cough medicine. The wheezing progressed and the child was taken to the Emergency Room of Chinese Number One Hospital, Beijing, where the child was given epinephrine and oxygen. Then he was sent back to Hilton Hotel. The patient was brought back to the ER three hours later and admitted.

**PAST HISTORY:** The child was a product of an eight and half month's gestation. Immunization: All. Allergies: Dust and onions.

**FAMILY HISTORY:** The mother is 37 and father is 45, all alive and well. Two siblings, one elder brother and one younger sister, are healthy. The family history was not positive for asthma and diabetes.

**REVIEW OF SYSTEMS:** Negative except for occasional conjunctivitis and asthma.

**IMPRESSIONS:** asthma.

# Unit Five

## Part One Picture & Chart

**Ⅰ. Medical Instrument**

1. roller clamp 2. IV solution bag 3. IV stand 4. catheter

**Ⅱ. Oral Cavity**

1. 牙龈 2. 悬雍垂,小舌 3. 乳头,小乳头状突起 4. 上颚的 5. 前臼齿 6. 臼齿
7. 犬齿 8. 门牙

**Ⅲ. First Aid**

3,1,2

## Part Two Listening Comprehension

**Task One**

headache dizzy prescribed lower instructions

**Task Two**

1. melt 2. absorbing, salt 3. dietary fiber

## Part Three Reading Comprehension

**Ⅰ. Medical Horizon**

**Task One**

1. C 2. A 3. B 4. C 5. D

**Task Two**

1. intervene 2. resistant 3. severe 4. end up with 5. launching

Ⅱ. **Hospital Story**

**Task One**

1. 把病人送来送去做检查的是护士，确保正确实施医疗步骤的是护士。

2. 九年前一群护士学生成立了一个叫护理真相的组织，鼓励媒体展现出护理行业真实的一面。

3. 她说，除非这种情况能改变，否则护理将无法吸引那些想把护理作为自己事业的人才。

Ⅲ. **Human Disease**

**Task One**

1. f 2. e 3. h 4. g 5. b 6. a 7. d 8. c

## Part Four Practical Writing

**Reference Sample:**

Name: Jenny Duncun Age: 35 Date: 07/28/2009

Address: 5th Ave., New York

Rx.: Aspirin 0.5gram/tab; Throat lozenge 100mg/tab

Sig.: Aspirin: Three tabs. daily, t. i. d. p. c.; Throat lozenge: Six tabs. daily, Q4h

Disp.: Aspirin: 8 tabs.; Throat lozenge: 30 tabs.

Name of Doctor: Kate Longley

Signature: *Kate Longley*

# Unit Six

## Part One Picture & Chart

Ⅰ. **Medical Instrument**

1. commode chair 2. shower chair 3. walking frame 4. walking stick 5. crutches 6. wheelchair

Ⅱ. **Respiratory System**

1. 鼻孔，鼻孔内壁 2. 会厌 3. 咽 4. 喉 5. 气管 6. 肋膜的，胸膜的 7. 支气管 8. 横隔膜

Ⅲ. **First Aid**

1, 5, 2, 4, 3, 6, 7

## Part Two Listening Comprehension

**Task One**

surgery risks anesthesia bleeding standard low-residue fluids

**Task Two**

1. around 8 pm  2. bowel movement  3. stomach

# Part Three  Reading Comprehension

## Ⅰ. Medical Horizon

**Task One**

1. C  2. D  3. A  4. D  5. B

**Task Two**

1. prevalence  2. lymphoma  3. obesity  4. symptom  5. Chronic

## Ⅱ. Hospital Story

**Task One**

1. 说到医院护理，乔迪·贝克可有独到见解——不管是从护士还是从病人的角度。

2. 昂德伍德的护理人员真体贴细致，能及时悉心照料我这位卧床不起的脑外伤病人。

3. 当他们的挚爱带着尊严离开尘世的时候，乔迪会握住病人家属的手；她会安慰局促不安的病人使之平静；她会在病人万念俱灰的时候支持他们。

## Ⅲ. Human Disease

**Task One**

1. A  2. D  3. B  4. C  5. A  6. C  7. D  8. B  9. A  10. D

# Part Four  Practical Writing

| Patient: | Sex: Male  Age: 15 |
|---|---|
| HOD (hospital day): | 15 days |
| DOA (date of admission): | April 5, 2008 |
| Attending Physician: | Dr. John |
| Conditions on Admission: | High fever, dry cough, no appetite |
| AD (admitting diagnosis): | Pneumonia |
| Hospital Course: | The patient was admitted and placed on erythromycin |
| DOD (date of discharge): | April 20, 2008 |
| Conditions on Discharge: | The patient improved, showing general state of health. And the patient had good appetite. The patient was discharged in stable condition. |
| DD (discharge diagnosis): | Pneumonia |
| Prognosis: | Good. No medications needed after discharge. |

The patient is to follow up with Dr. John in one week.

______________________________

John  D: 20/04/2008

# Unit Seven

## Part One　Picture & Chart

**Ⅰ. Medical Instrument**

1. alcohol wipe　2. acupuncture　3. cotton swab　4. glucometer　5. lancet
6. medical rubber gloves

**Ⅱ. Digestive System**

1. 食管，食道　2. 胆囊　3. 十二指肠　4. 空肠　5. 结肠　6. 盲肠　7. 回肠　8. 直肠

**Ⅲ. First Aid**

1,3,2,4,5

## Part Two　Listening Comprehension

**Task One**

admitted　recovered　vital　normal　blood circulation

**Task Two**

1. wash，clean gloves　2. over　stoma　3. close

## Part Three　Reading Comprehension

**Ⅰ. Medical Horizon**

**Task One**

1. A　2. D　3. C　4. B　5. D

**Task Two**

1. overseas　2. wholly-owned　3. presence　4. pharmacy　5. executive

**Ⅱ. Hospital Story**

**Task One**

1. 医生说，我后背和肩膀疼痛，头脑恍惚比较严重。

2. 不用脱衣服，不用血液检查，不用 X 光片，真的就能诊断吗？

3. 医生诊断花了不到五分钟。

4. 医生看了看我的舌头，上面有点饼干，但是这没关系。

5. 陪伴护士告诉我说，从历史渊源看，古时有钱人家的妇女不愿意在看病时脱下衣服，因此医生只能通过外显的体征来形成诊断结果。

**Ⅲ. Human Disease**

**Task One**

1. e　2. f　3. g　4. i　5. j　6. a　7. b　8. c　9. d　10. h

## Part Four Practical Writing

May 5th,2008

Dear Mr. /Ms. ,

We are pleased to introduce Ms. Xu Hua, our head nurse from the Department of Pediatrics who will be on business for three weeks in Hilton Hospital in New York.

We shall be most grateful that you give her any help or advice she may need.

Yours faithfully,

Qiu Yang Medical University

# Unit Eight

## Part One Picture & Chart

**Ⅰ. Medical Instrument**

1. grab bar 2. vomit bowl 3. light 4. non-slip mat 5. slide sheet 6. non-tip cup

**Ⅱ. Blood Circulatory System**

1. 小静脉 2. 静脉 3. 毛细血管 4. 小动脉 5. 主动脉 6. 动脉 7. 肺的,肺部的

**Ⅲ. First Aid**

1,3,2,4,6,5

## Part Two Listening Comprehension

**Task One**

took some medicine ordered an enema handle

**Task Two**

1. identification 2. on her left side 3. five to ten

## Part Three Reading Comprehension

**Ⅰ. Medical Horizon**

**Task One**

1. B 2. D 3. C 4. A 5. B

**Task Two**

1. infection 2. spread 3. loneliness 4. Obesity 5. barrier

**Ⅱ. Hospital Story**

**Task One**

1. 最初,由于健康原因或无肾脏组织匹配,许多潜在的肾脏捐献者都被排除掉了。
2. 检查发现,丁娜竟然成为她丈夫的匹配捐献者。
3. 考虑到孩子,想到两个大人同时要接受手术,问题变得有些复杂。
4. 我从爱人那里得到了世界上最好的礼物,现在我又能与丁娜和孩子们在一起了。

5. 安东尼和我能一起看着我们年轻的家庭茁壮成长，这种感觉对我而言非常特别。这就是爱。

**Ⅲ. Human Disease**

**Task One**

1. i 2. g 3. f 4. a 5. c 6. e 7. b 8. j 9. d 10. h

## Part Four Practical Writing

May 10,2010

Mr. Li,

How do you do? My name is Wang Lu and I get the latest information from the local newspaper that you need some nurses. I am very interested in the job. So I am writing to you to apply for the nurse position in the surgical department of your hospital.

I graduated from the Nursing Department of East Medical College. After three years of work, including ten-month clinical practice in various departments in Southwest Hospital, I have acquired sound knowledge and core competencies of nursing. Besides, I worked as a volunteer in a hospital near our college and obtained some experience caring senior citizens. I passed the national exam for nurse license last year and worked as a registered nurse in a private clinic in the last half year. I am now confident that I am well prepared to be a qualified nurse in a general hospital likes yours.

I enclose a resume, some copies of my qualifications and certificates, as well as a personal reference from my college teacher.

Thank you for reading my letter. I am looking forward to your reply.

Sincerely your,

Wang Lu

# Unit Nine

## Part One Picture & Chart

**Ⅰ. Medical Instrument**

1. scalpel 2. bandage 3. forceps 4. stretcher 5. first-aid kit 6. scissors

**Ⅱ. Hospital Departments**

1. 早产的，早产儿的 2. 修复，(病残人的)康复 3. 精神病学，精神病治疗

4. 消化(食物)的 5. 整形手术，矫形术 6. 新生的，初生的

7. 神经学的，神经病学的 8. 内镜检查术

**Ⅲ. First Aid**

1,4,3,2

## Part Two Listening Comprehension

**Task One**

diabetes educate you insulin prescribed regular

**Task Two**

1. before his meal 2. disposable and easy 3. snacks

## Part Three Reading Comprehension

### Ⅰ. Medical Horizon

**Task One**

1. C 2. D 3. A 4. C 5. D

**Task Two**

1. heart attack 2. Biological 3. harmful 4. kidney 5. nutrition

### Ⅱ. Hospital Story

**Task One**

1. 一个人可以每天下午在床上坐一个小时进行肺部液体引流。
2. 外面多彩的世界和各种活动开阔了他的视野,让他的生命更加鲜活。
3. 透过窗户可俯瞰一个有着美丽湖泊的花园。
4. 护士很高兴地给他换了床,确信他已经安顿舒适后,就离开了。
5. 护士回答说,那个人是个盲人,甚至连墙都看不见。

### Ⅲ. Human Disease

**Task One**

1. d 2. f 3. a 4. b 5. j 6. e 7. c 8. i 9. g 10. h

## Part Four Practical Writing

At present, blood donation has aroused considerable concern. In other words, blood donation is widely advocated in many countries including China. More and more people gather together in different areas to donate their blood without repayment.

It is a noble action for a person to donate blood without repayment. The action shows his love to his country and people, because the blood transfusion is saving thousands dying men every day. We firmly believe that it won't be the problem to keep adequate store of blood if more people join in as voluntary donators. On the other hand, blood donation does no harm to the donator's health. As we know, only health people are allowed to donate blood. After blood donation, his body will make a quick adjustment to let mechanism operate in its normal way.

Generally speaking, blood donation is a meaningful and selfless deed; it's unnecessary for people to be afraid of blood donation and blood donation should be encouraged.

# Unit Ten

## Part One Picture & Chart

**Ⅰ. Medical Instrument**

1. filiform needle 2. cupping jar 3. moxa stick

**Ⅱ. ICU**

1. 气管内的 2.(人工)呼吸机 3. 导管 4. 气管内导管 5. 鼻胃管吸出 6. 集尿袋 7. 集尿 8. 胸腔引流器

**Ⅲ. First Aid**

1,4,2,3,6,5

## Part Two Listening Comprehension

**Task One**

urine bathroom infection antibiotics skin test

**Task Two**

1. identification bracelet 2. relax 3. call bell

## Part Three Reading Comprehension

**Ⅰ. Medical Horizon**

**Task One**

1. A 2. D 3. A 4. D 5. A

**Task Two**

1. migraine 2. headache 3. prescribe 4. affect 5. minimize

**Ⅱ. Hospital Story**

**Task One**

1. 我很惊讶,也很尴尬。

2. 我常常思考那位女士让我学到的东西,而我也总是提醒自己不要忽略停下来、坐下来和专心倾听的重要性。

3. 她觉得这事的压力极大地影响了她的健康。

4. 我还以自己的亲身经历告诉他们,当有人停下来、坐下来倾听我的故事的时候,就会在我体内产生不可估量的康复力量。

5. 倾听一个人的故事,不像做昂贵的医学诊断检查那样花费巨大,但却是治疗和诊断的关键。

**Ⅲ. Human Disease**

**Task One**

1. g 2. f 3. h 4. i 5. c 6. j 7. d 8. b 9. e 10. a

## Part Four Practical Writing

Nowadays, with the emergence of the nuclear family, more and more old men no longer live with their children. Instead, most of the old couples live by themselves. Most old people think they have different style from their children and would like to live respectively. However, the happiness of several generations living together has been lost; meanwhile, they will feel isolated from the family. What's worse, if something unfortunate happens to them, nobody is close to offer help. Another problem is that old men, despite their pensions, can hardly support themselves sufficiently. They need financial help from their grown-up children in order to live comfortably. However, the middle-aged people care more about their careers and their children than the parents. Therefore, old people become a forgotten group.

How can we solve old men's problem, then? In my opinion, we should take up the duty of taking care of them and respect them. As for those old men without sons or daughters, such institutions as Old People's Home should be set up to give the helpless old men good care.

# Appendix G  Sample Tests for METS

# 医护英语水平考试
# Medical English Test System (METS)
# Model Test 1

姓名________  准考证号________  时间:120 分钟

## 考生须知

1. 严格遵守考场规则,考生得到监考人员指令后方可开始答题。

2. 答题前考生须将自己的姓名和准考证号写在试卷和答题卡上。

3. 答客观题时,一律用 2B 铅笔,按照答题卡上的要求答题。如要改动答案,必须用橡皮擦干净。

4. 答写作题时,必须用黑色签字笔在答题卡上答题。

5. 注意字迹清楚,保持卷面整洁。

6. 考试结束时将试卷和答题卡放在桌上,不得带走。待监考人员收毕清点后,考生方可离场。

※ 未经批准,本试卷任何单位或个人不得保留、复制和出版,违者必究。

# I Listening

## Part 1

**Questions 1—5**

- You will hear five patients describing their pain to the nurse.
- Where does each patient have pain?
- For questions 1—5, mark the correct letter A—H on your answer sheet.
- You will hear each conversation twice.

Example:

0 Heath

| 0 | A | B | C | D | E | F | G | H |
|---|---|---|---|---|---|---|---|---|
| | ☐ | ☐ | ☐ | ☐ | ☐ | ■ | ☐ | ☐ |

1 Hales

2 Ian

3 Jack

4 Swift

5 Bloomfield

A In the eye.

B In the stomach.

C In the leg.

D In the back.

E In the chest.

F In the hands.

G In the forehead.

H In the throat.

## Part 2

**Questions 6—10**

- You will hear a conversation between Dr Davis and Miles, the Ward Nurse, about his patient's IV infusion regimes.
- For questions 6—10, decide if each sentence is correct or incorrect.
- If it is correct, put a tick (√) in the box next to A for Yes. If it is not correct, put a tick (√) in the box next to B for No.
- You will hear the conversation twice.

**Example:**

0 Doctor Davis wants to review Mrs Miles' IV fluids. A Yes ☑ B No ☐

6 Miles is looking after Mrs Cohen all day today. A Yes ☐

B No ☐

7 Mrs Smith's potassium levels are above average. A Yes ☐

B No ☐

8 Mrs Smith has been started on one litre of Normal Saline for more than eight hours. A Yes ☐

B No ☐

9 Her antibiotics are to be given through a separate line. A Yes ☐

B No ☐

10 Mr Clark's cannula is going to be removed. A Yes ☐

B No ☐

# Part 3

**Questions 11—15**

- You will hear a conversation between Louisa, the Ward Nurse, and Gina about her operation.
- For questions 11—15, choose the correct answer A, B or C. Put a tick (√) in the box.
- You will hear the conversation twice.

---

11 How was Gina feeling about her coming operation?

A Very anxious. ☐

B More excited. ☐

C Much confident. ☐

12 What kind of operation is she going to have?

A Transplant surgery. ☐

B Keyhole surgery. ☐

C Emergency surgery. ☐

13 The surgeon carries out the operation with

A a plastic container. ☐

B a laparoscope. ☐

C a light cover. ☐

14 How long will the plastic mini-drain remain inside after the operation?

A Two or three hours. ☐

B Three or four days. ☐

C A week. ☐

15 Louisa will ask someone to cover the drain because Gina is

A afraid of seeing the blood. ☐

B worried about the blood's smell. ☐

C not allowed to see its contents. ☐

## Part 4

**Questions 16—20**

- You will hear a nurse getting personal details from a patient.
- Listen and complete questions 16—20 on your answer sheet.
- You will hear the conversation twice.

---

SURNAME Green FIRST NAME (16) ……………

---

AGE 42 SEX M MARITAL STATUS M

---

OCCUPATION Salesman

---

PRESENT COMPLAINT

(17) ……………chest pain started with severe attack. Pain lasted

(18) …………… mins relieved by rest. Has occurred when shopping.

---

O/E

General Condition

ENT

RS Chest (19) ……………

CVS P 70/min (20) …………… 130/80

HS normal

---

POINTS TO NOTE

---

# Ⅲ Reading and Writing

## Part 1

**Questions 1—5**

- Look at the medicine labels on the right.
- Match the reassurance and explanations(A—F) to the suggested actions (1—5) on the left.
- Mark the correct letter A—F on your answer sheet.

---

1 Donna had better not drive her car to school when she is taking the medicine.

2 Julie should take the medicine with meals.

3 Ted should not drink beer while he is taking the medicine.

4 John should take the medicine between meals.

5 Having a baby, Lucy should ask a health professional before taking the medicine.

A CONSULT A DOCTOR OR PHARMACIST BEFORE USE IF PREGNANT OR BREASTFEEDING.

B TAKE MEDICATION ON AN EMPTY STOMACH 1 OR 2 HOURS BEFORE OR AFTER A MEAL.

C EXCITABILITY MAY OCCUR, ESPECIALLY IN CHILDREN.

D AVOID ALCOHOLIC BEVERAGES WHEN TAKING THIS MEDICATION.

E TAKE WITH FOOD OR MILK.

F MAY CAUSE DIZZINESS OR DROWSINESS. BE CAREFUL WHEN DRIVING A MOTOR VEHICLE OR OPERATING MACHINERY.

## Part 2

**Questions 6—15**

- Read the descriptions of six cases on the next page.
- Which case (A—F) mentions this (6—15)? The cases may be chosen more than once. There is an example at the beginning (0).
- Mark the correct letter A—F on your answer sheet.

---

**Which case(s) mention(s) someone who**

| | | | |
|---|---|---|---|
| had his teeth broken? | 0 | A | |
| suffered from loss of hearing? | 6 | | |
| was weak in fingers? | 7 | | |
| had a fever? | 8 | | 9 |
| suffered from weight loss? | 10 | | 11 |
| was diagnosed with pericarditis? | 12 | | |
| lost hair? | 13 | | |
| could not distinguish hot from cold? | 14 | | |
| had night sweats? | 15 | | |

**CASE A**

**Name:** James Fox

**Age:** 6

**Occupation:** Pupil

**Chief complaint:** Hit in face by swing at school.

**Other symptoms:** Blooding, no significant fever.

**Physical examination:** One tooth knocked out, one broken. Missing tooth replaced and splinted. Temporary crown put on broken tooth. No other injuries besides teeth.

**CASE B**

**Name:** Art Halamka

**Age:** 45

**Occupation:** Housewife

**Chief complaint:** Chest pain at work.

**Other symptoms:** Fever

**Physical examination:** ECG shows generalized ST segment elevation and there is some pericardial fluid around the heart as shown by echo. The cardiologist diagnosed pericarditis and is going to drain the fluid.

**CASE C**

**Name:** Charmine Plantz

**Age:** 31

**Occupation:** Sales Manager

**Chief complaint:** Lump on front of neck for one month.

**Other symptoms:** Palpitations, heat intolerance, nervousness, insomnia, breathlessness.

**Physical examination**: Enlarged thyroid. Tachycardia. Slight hypertension. Warm, moist, smooth skin. Exophthalmus. Tremor. Weight loss. Muscle weakness. Hair loss.

**CASE D**

**Name**: Selina Burton

**Age**: 37

**Occupation**: Typist

**Chief complaint**: Tingling of first three fingers and thumb that gets worse at night.

**Other symptoms**: Weakness of fingers (has difficulty buttoning clothes).

**Physical examination**: Muscle wasting at base of thumb. Unable to distinguish hot from cold.

**CASE E**

**Name**: Bob Smithson

**Age**: 50

**Occupation**: Construction worker

**Chief complaint**: Attacks of dizziness with nausea and vomiting. During attack, high pulse rate and rapid breathing. No pattern to attacks.

**Other symptoms**: Hissing or ringing in ears (on both sides), loss of hearing.

**Physical examination**: Vital signs normal. Nystagmus. Positive Romberg test.

**CASE F**

**Name**: Chuck Talavera

**Age**: 38

**Occupation**: Farmer

**Chief complaint**: Low subjective fever, cough with bad tasting phlegm, night sweats, and weight loss getting worse over the last four months.

**Physical examination**: Temperature of 38 centigrade, gingival disease, dullness to percussion and absent breath sounds in lower right lobe of lung. Clubbing of fingers.

## Part 3

**Questions 16—25**

- Read the following passage.
- Are sentences 16—25 on the next page "Right" or "Wrong"? If there is not enough information to answer "Right" or "Wrong", choose "Doesn't Say".
- For each sentence 16—25, mark one letter A—C on your answer sheet.

---

### Being a midwife

In Malawi, all hospitals, especially government hospitals, are greatly understaffed. For example, one qualified nurse with the assistance of a patient attendee (similar to the nursing assistants in the UK) looks after a 75-bed tuberculosis ward in a busy city hospital.

Poor pay drives the qualified nurses out of government hospitals to work in the private sector or to take their skills to other countries. Here at St Luke's, we are a mission hospital and it's difficult to keep staff, for similar reasons of a poor wage and allowances package.

I am a nurse tutor and work 50% in the classroom and 50% in the clinical area. My role incorporates the task of teaching in the classroom and also following the students into the clinical area to carry out the teaching of skills, general supervision, and performing assessments of competency. In the UK, tutors very rarely go into the clinical area, as there are always plenty of members of staff to mentor students while they are on their practical placements. This is not the case in Malawi; you will often find students on their own in a ward full of very sick patients.

Through training I try to emphasize the importance of ensuring individualized care is carried out. I also stress that nursing is a partnership between the nurse, patient, their friends and family, and that good nursing care is achieved in collaboration with these individuals, and other health professionals in the multi-disciplinary team.

Ensuring that patients are cared for with respect, in a non-judgemental manner, is a very important aspect of my job here in sub-Saharan Africa, where a high percentage of patients on the wards are HIV positive.

I have learnt to cope in a clinical area that is very poorly resourced. I have had to become very inventive and utilize everyday items in an attempt to solve the problems that I come up against. I have also learnt to appreciate the NHS in the UK, and hopefully I will never complain about the lack of resources again!

16 The hospitals in Malawi have plenty of qualified nurses.

A Right B Wrong C Doesn't Say

17 The qualified nurses in Malawi prefer to work in private hospitals.

A Right B Wrong C Doesn't Say

18 Nurse tutors in Malawi need to mentor students in the clinical area.

A Right B Wrong C Doesn't Say

19 Nurse tutors in the UK also supervise the students in the clinical area.

A Right B Wrong C Doesn't Say

20 Nurse students in the UK seldom take care of sick patients on their own in the hospital.

A Right B Wrong C Doesn't Say

21 The author teaches her students to collaborate with the patients, their friends and family.

A Right B Wrong C Doesn't Say

22 There are many patients with HIV positive in the suburb London hospitals.

A Right B Wrong C Doesn't Say

23 The author has had to become inventive in the clinical area in Malawi.

A Right B Wrong C Doesn't Say

24 The clinical area in Malawi is well resourced.

A Right B Wrong C Doesn't Say

25 The qualified nurses are well paid in government hospitals in Malawi.

A Right B Wrong C Doesn't Say

## Part 4

**Questions 26—30**

- Read the text on the new treatment for asthma sufferers.
- For questions 26—30, choose the answer (A, B or C) which you think fits best according to the text.
- Mark the correct letter A, B or C on your answer sheet.

---

### New Treatment for Asthma Sufferers

A new technology that uses radio waves to burn off overgrown muscle in the airways of asthma sufferers helps them breathe better, have fewer symptoms and use less medication, researchers report. The technique, called bronchial thermoplasty, is now being tested in a larger trial that could lead to its approval by the US Food and Drug Administration.

With thermoplasty, doctors snake wires that can emit radio waves into the lungs. These radio waves emit heat that can burn off some smooth muscle in the airways. The basic idea behind thermoplasty is that smooth muscle sits around the airway, and when it contracts, it makes the airway narrower. When the amount of muscle is reduced, and it is triggered to contract, there is nothing to contract.

The trial included 112 people with moderate to severe asthma. Half underwent three sessions of thermoplasty; the other half had their usual drug treatment. One year later, air flow was much better in patients receiving thermoplasty—39 liters per minute compared to 8.5 liters per minute for those getting standard treatment.

The thermoplasty group also reported an average of 40 symptom-free days, compared to 17 for the others, with fewer asthma symptoms and less medication used. The therapy may also produce other beneficial effects besides just giving air more space to move in. Living muscle cells produce chemicals and biological signals that increase inflammation. It may also change some of the dynamics of connective tissue in the airway. Thermoplasty ultimately may be especially useful for asthma sufferers whose problem is severe enough to bring them to the emergency room, though they may probably spend a little bit more for this treatment.

26 The passage is mainly about a new technology which helps asthma patients ________

A to emit waves into the lungs.

B not to take any medicine.

C to breathe better.

27 How is the new treatment administered?

A Wires are inserted into the lungs.

B Muscles are removed by surgery.

C Airways are dilated through drugs.

28 Which statement about the treatment is NOT true?

A Radio waves burn off some muscle inside the airways.

B Thermoplasty has some advantage over drug treatment.

C The therapy may also increase inflammation.

29 Which of the following could be the disadvantage of the new treatment?

A Cost. B Effectiveness. C Side effect.

30 What is the key benefit of this treatment?

A More air flow moving into the body.

B More days without asthma symptoms.

C More dynamics of connective tissues.

# Part 5

**Questions 31—35**

- Read the following text about pain assessment with some sentences left out.
- Choose from the procedures A—F the one which fits each space (31—35). There is one extra procedure which you do not need to use.
- For each space (31—35), mark one letter A—F on your Answer Sheet.

---

## Pain assessment

Assessing pain can be complicated as the physical and physiological aspects of the patient all need to be considered. Because the experience of pain is very subjective, the nurse needs to be able to use some objective criteria to evaluate the location, nature and intensity of the pain so that a diagnosis can be made. (31) ………………… He suggests that pain is "whatever the experiencing person says it is and exists whenever he says it does".

**Assessments of the patient's pain experience**

When identifying the characteristics of the patient's pain it is essential the nurse consider the following:

√***The type of pain***: Is it crampy, stabbing, sharp? The patient's description of the pain may help in diagnosing its cause. (32)………………

√ ***Its intensity***: Is it mild, severe or excruciating? This can be described by using a pain assessment scale. (33)……………… With children, a range of pictures showing a child changing from happy to sad can be used. Colour charts with a series of colours from black through grey to yellow and orange can be used, especially with patients who have difficulty grasping numbers or articulating exactly what their pain is like.

√ ***The onset***: Was it sudden or gradual? Find out when it started and in what circumstances. What makes it worse? What makes it better? What was the patient doing immediately before it happened?

√ ***Its duration***: Is it persistent, constant or intermittent?

√ ***Its location***: (34)………………

√ ***Changes in the site***: There may be tenderness, swelling, discolouration, firmness or rigidity. (35)……………… In a myocardial infarction (a heart attack), pain classically radiates down the arm, and with liver pain it can radiate to the shoulder.

√ ***Any associated symptoms***: Some of the common symptoms of disease that can influence the response to pain are anorexia, constipation, cough, inflammation, anxiety and fear, dryness of the mouth.

A With appendicitis, a classic sign is the movement of pain to the right and downwards.

B Ask the patient to be as specific as possible, for example, indicating the site by pointing.

C Myocardial (heart) pain is often described as stabbing, but liver pain as cramping or aching.

D The nurse asks the patients to rate the pain on a scale of 0 to 10; zero being no pain and 10 being excruciating pain.

E Being objective means relying on facts, rather than personal beliefs or feelings.

F One of the most widely accepted definitions of pain was put forward by McCaffery.

# Part 6

**Questions 36—45**

- Read the following passage.
- Choose the best word (A, B or C) for each space.
- For each space 36—45, mark one letter A—C on your answer sheet.

# Ways to Prevent Osteoporosis

Even if you feel as strong as an ox, you may still be at risk for osteoporosis. This condition develops when your bones lose mass and density, (36) ……………them to become porous (多孔的), weak and brittle (脆的). As the bones weaken, they become more (37) ……………to fractures that can cause serious health consequences.

Although osteoporosis tends to affect older people—especially women after menopause—you can lower the risk of this disease significantly (38) ……………taking certain actions when you are younger.

Perform weight-bearing exercise. The risk of osteoporosis for both men and women depends largely on the(39) ……………of bone mass attained between the age of 25 and 35. Developing a peak store of bone mass will help protect you when your bones (40) ……………begin to thin. Weight-bearing exercise is one of the best ways to increase bone mass because bone responds to exercise by becoming denser. (41) ……………it is important to build as much bone mass as possible when you are younger, exercise at all ages helps the bones. Examples of weight-bearing activities include lifting weights, walking or running, tennis, and dancing.

Get adequate(42) ……………of calcium and vitamin D. Eating foods high in calcium helps strengthen bones. Obtaining adequate levels of calcium is particularly important while the skeleton is growing in childhood and adolescence and during pregnancy and breastfeeding. (43) ……………sufficient levels of vitamin D also is crucial to keeping bones healthy because this mineral is essential for helping the body to absorb calcium.

Do not smoke. Smoking increases bone loss, although scientists aren't exactly sure why. Many experts believe this(44) ……………because smoking decreases a woman's production of estrogen and reduces the absorption of calcium in the intestine. It is not known whether or not (45) ……………to secondhand smoke can affect a person's bone mass.

36 A to cause B cause C causing
37 A accessible B susceptible C sensitive
38 A in B with C by
39 A amount B range C extent
40 A possibly B quickly C inevitably
41 A Because B Although C Since
42 A content B volume C intake
43 A Consuming B Containing C Conducting
44 A begins B stops C occurs
45 A contact B exposure C excess

# Ⅲ Writing

**Directions:**

***Read the patient discharge summary. Use the information in the summary to write a report in about* 100 *words.***

46.

DISCHARGE SUMMARY

**Patient:** Mrs Martha　　**D. O. B.** 17/9/1921

**Date of Discharge:** 10 May, 2009　　**Date of Admission:** 23 April, 2009

**Problems:**

1. Has been suffering from hypertension & degenerative bone disease.
2. Needs to urinate frequently.
3. Diagnosed—left pneumonia & urinary tract infection.

**Next of Kin:**

4. No immediate family.

**Needs:**

5. Bath seat and safety rails in bathroom.
6. Nurse to visit 2 x week to monitor medications.
7. Physiotherapy 3 x week.

**Strengths and Resources:**

8. Independent-minded woman, fully alert and articulate, can cook.

# Model Test 1 参考答案

## 听力部分录音稿

**This is METS listening test.**

**There are four parts to the test. Part 1, 2, 3, and 4.**

**You will hear each part twice.**

**We will now stop for a moment before we start the test.**

**Please ask any questions now because you must not speak during the test.**

*Pause*(10 seconds)

**Now, look at the instructions for Part One.**

*Pause*(5 seconds)

**You will hear five patients describing their pain to the nurse.**
**Where does each patient have pain?**
**For questions 1—5, mark the correct letter A—H on your answer sheet.**
**You will hear each conversation twice.**

**Here is an example:**
**Nurse (Woman):** Are you feeling better today, Mr Heath?
**Patient (Man):** Not really. My hands ache a lot.
**Nurse (Woman):** Would you like some pain relief?
**Patient (Man):** Yes, please. My hands ache more in the mornings.

*Pause*(5 seconds)

**The answer is *In the hands*, so mark letter F in the box.**
**Now we are ready to start.**

*Pause*(5 seconds)

**Conversation 1**

**Nurse (Woman):** Are you all right, Mr Hales?
**Patient (Man):** No. I've got a really bad stomach ache.
**Nurse (Woman):** Sit down on the bed and I'll get you some pain relief.
**Patient (Man):** Thanks.
**Nurse (Woman):** When did you last have some tablets?
**Patient (Man):** I'm not sure. I think it was a few hours ago.

*Pause*(5 seconds)
*Repeat*
*Pause*(5 seconds)

**Conversation 2**

**Nurse (Woman)**: How are you feeling, Mr Ian?
**Patient (Man)**: Not very well. Can I have some painkillers, please?
**Nurse (Woman)**: Sure. Where does it hurt?
**Patient (Man)**: My lower back's really aching.
**Nurse (Woman)**: OK, I'll get the tablets and a heat pack, too.

*Pause*(5 seconds)
*Repeat*
*Pause*(5 seconds)

**Conversation 3**

**Nurse (Woman)**: Hello, Jack. How do you feel today?
**Patient (Man)**: Well, I've got a bit of a sore throat.
**Nurse (Woman)**: I'll get you some pain relief for that.
**Patient (Man)**: Thanks, it's really painful. Can I have a cold drink too, please?
**Nurse (Woman)**: Sure. I'll get some iced water for you.

*Pause*(5 seconds)
*Repeat*
*Pause*(5 seconds)

**Conversation 4**

**Nurse (Woman)**: So, what brings you here today, Mr Swift?
**Patient (Man)**: Um, I've been having these really bad headaches.
**Nurse (Woman)**: Go on...
**Patient (Man)**: Well, I keep getting them.
**Nurse (Woman)**: Ah-huh? Can you describe them?
**Patient (Man)**: Um, it's quite a dull pain, but there's a constant throbbing pain as well—it builds up.
**Nurse (Woman)**: Mm. Whereabouts do you get these headaches?
**Patient (Man)**: Here, around the front, around the forehead.

*Pause*(5 seconds)
*Repeat*
*Pause*(5 seconds)

**Conversation 5**

**Nurse (Woman)**: Good morning, Mr Bloomfield. What can I do for you?

**Patient (Man)**: I've been having some problems with my breathing.

**Nurse (Woman)**: Mm-hmm. Can you tell me a little bit more about it?

**Patient (Man)**: Well, I keep getting breathlessness and wheezing in my chest. It all started about three weeks ago, and I've been coughing a lot with it. I thought it might be a cold coming on, but then after about another week I started finding it more and more difficult to catch my breath.

**Nurse (Woman)**: Right, so you've had the wheezing and the breathlessness for roughly three weeks.

**Patient (Man)**: Yes, give or take a day.

*Pause*(5 seconds)

*Repeat*

*Pause*(5 seconds)

**This is the end of Part 1.**

*Pause*(5 seconds)

**Now look at Part 2.**

*Pause*(5 seconds)

**Look at the six sentences for this part.**

**You will hear a conversation between Dr Davis and Miles, the Ward Nurse, about his patient's IV infusion regimes.**

**For questions 6—10, decide if each sentence is correct or incorrect.**

**If it is correct, put a tick (√) in the box next to A for YES. If is not correct, put a tick (√) in the box next to B for No.**

**You will hear the conversation twice.**

**Doctor (Man)**: Hello, Miles. Are you looking after Mrs Cohen today?

**Nurse (Woman)**: No, that's Jane, but she's just gone down to X-ray with a patient.

**Doctor (Man)**: Oh, I wanted to review Mrs Cohen's IV fluids.

**Nurse (Woman)**: I'm looking after Jane's patients while she's away. Do you want me to pass on any updates?

**Doctor (Man)**: Yeah, thanks. Could you take down Mrs Cohen's IV when it's finished, please?

**Nurse (Woman):** Sure. I'll just write a note about it for Jane. What about the cannula? Do you want it left in?

**Doctor (Man):** I think so. Leave it for another day in case she needs some more fluids.

**Nurse (Woman):** OK. Do you want to see Mrs Smith in the next room, too?

**Doctor (Man):** Yes, I need to see her. According to her blood results her potassium levels are quite low. I'll put in a cannula when I finish my rounds. Could you start her on a litre of Normal Saline with 40 millimole of KCL?

**Nurse (Woman):** OK. Here's the Prescription Chart for you to fill out.

**Doctor (Man):** Thanks. That saves me a bit of leg work. Can you run it over eight hours, please?

**Nurse (Woman):** Sure. One litre of Normal Saline with 40 millimole KCL over eight hours.

**Doctor (Man):** Oh, I'll have to order her some IV antibiotics, too?

**Nurse (Woman):** Yeah, OK. We'll run them through a secondary line. The primary line will have the KCL running through, so we won't mix the solutions in the same line.

**Doctor (Man):** Great. Now there's just Mr Clark left. How is he?

**Nurse (Woman):** He's one the Jane's patients, too. He's pretty good. He's going home today, I think.

**Doctor (Man):** Yes, that's right. He's ready for discharge. Can you take out his cannula before he goes home, please?

**Nurse (Woman):** Yes, sure, we can do that. I'll pass on your instructions to Jane when she gets back.

*Pause*(5 seconds)

*Repeat*

*Pause*(5 seconds)

**This is the end of Part 2.**

*Pause*(5 seconds)

**Now look at Part 3.**

**You will hear a conversation between Louisa, the Ward Nurse, and Gina about her operation.**

**For questions 11—15, choose the correct answer A, B or C. Put a tick (√) in the box.**

**You will hear the conversation twice.**

*Pause*(5 seconds)

**Nurse (Woman)**: Hello, Gina. I'll be looking after you today. I want to have a talk about your operation tomorrow.

**Patient (Woman)**: Oh. Is everything all right?

**Nurse (Woman)**: Yes, everything's fine. There are no problems. I just want to go through what will happen when you come back to the ward after the operation. People always feel better when they know what to expect.

**Patient (Woman)**: Oh, yes, you're right. I'm so nervous about the operation. I haven't been in a hospital since I was a kid, when I broke my leg. Things have probably changed a lot since then.

**Nurse (Woman)**: Well, hospitals have changed a bit, but don't worry. I'll go through it all now, and you'll have the opportunity to ask as many questions as you like.

**Patient (Woman)**: Thanks. I feel silly being so worried. I'm not normally like this.

**Nurse (Woman)**: That's OK, Gina. It's quite normal to feel a bit worried. Um, I'll try and cover everything so you're prepared for what'll happen after the operation. Um, I see you've brought the leaflet about keyhole surgery.

**Patient (Woman)**: Yes, um, it was sent to me at home last week. The only thing I know is that I won't have a big cut so the operation won't leave a big scar.

**Nurse (Woman)**: That's right. Um, keyhole surgery is also called minimally invasive surgery because it's performed with the use of a laparoscope, using small incisions or surgical cuts. They are just small holes made near your navel. And you'll have a small dressing covering the holes made during surgery. It's just a light covering to keep the area clean until it heals.

**Patient (Woman)**: Oh.

**Nurse (Woman)**: During the operation, the surgeon uses a laparoscope, which is passed through the holes to visualize your gallbladder. The infected gallbladder is removed through the largest puncture site. You'll have a mini-drain which will only stay in for a couple of hours. It's a small plastic container attached to some tubing which takes away any excess blood from your wound.

**Patient (Woman)**: Ah-hah. There won't be lots of blood, will there? I can't stand the sight of blood.

**Nurse (Woman)**: No, not much, but I can make a note for the rest of the staff to cover the drain for you so you don't see any of it.

**Patient (Woman)**: Thanks. Um.

*Pause* (5 seconds)

*Repeat*

*Pause*(5 seconds)

**Now look at Part 4.**

**You will hear a nurse getting personal details from a patient.**

**Listen and complete questions 16—20 on your answer sheet.**

**You will hear the conversation twice.**

**Nurse:** Come in, Mr Green. Come and sit down here. So, what's your name?

**Green:** It's Peter.

**Nurse:** That's P-E-T-E-R. Is that right?

**Green:** Yes.

**Nurse:** Well, how are you feeling, Mr Green?

**Green:** I've been having pain, pain in my chest.

**Nurse:** Yes, now when did you first notice this pain?

**Green:** Er, well, I suppose about six months ago.

**Nurse:** And can you remember when it first came on?

**Green:** Yes, well I remember, I got a bad pain in my chest when I was shopping. It was so bad I couldn't breathe and...

**Nurse:** And where, in which part of your chest did you feel the pain?

**Green:** Well, right across my chest.

**Nurse:** And how long did it last?

**Green:** Oh, about ten minutes.

**Nurse:** And what did you do when it happened?

**Green:** I had to stop and wait for it to go away.

**Nurse:** So, have you had this, the pain again since then?

**Green:** Yes, I often get it when I overdo things, and when I...

**Nurse:** Well, I think at this stage I'd like to examine you, your chest. So if you could strip to your waist?

**Green:** Right. There we go.

**Nurse:** That's fine. I'll just check your pulse first of all. Fine. That's fine. It's quite normal, seventy per minute.

**Green:** Er, right.

**Nurse:** Now your blood pressure. Fine. That's quite normal too. 130 over 80.

**Green:** Oh, I'm pleased to hear it.

**Nurse:** Now you're going to take deep breaths in and out while I check your lungs. In. Out. In. Out. Fine. They're completely clear. Well, Mr Green, the pain you've been having sounds very much like the pain of what we call angina, and this, well, this occurs when not enough oxygen is getting to the heart. Now I'd like to check a few tests, and, following that I'll be able to advise some treatment for you...

*Pause*(5 seconds)
*Repeat*
*Pause*(5 seconds)

**This is the end of Part 4.**

**You now have five minutes to write your answers on the answer sheet.**

*Pause*(4 minutes)

**You have one more minute.**

*Pause*(60 seconds)

**This is the end of the listening test.**

# 参考答案

## Ⅰ Listening

**Part 1** 1. B 2. D 3. H 4. G 5. E
**Part 2** 6. B 7. B 8. B 9. A 10. A
**Part 3** 11. A 12. B 13. B 14. A 15. A
**Part 4** 16. Peter 17. Central 18. 10 19. clear/normal 20. BP/blood pressure

## Ⅱ Reading and Writing

**Part 1** 1. F 2. E 3. D 4. B 5. A
**Part 2** 6. E 7. D 8. B 9. F 10. F/C 11. C/F 12. B 13. C 14. D 15. F
**Part 3** 16. B 17. A 18. A 19. B 20. A 21. A 22. C 23. A 24. B 25. B
**Part 4** 26. C 27. A 28. C 29. A 30. B
**Part 5** 31. F 32. C 33. D 34. B 35. A
**Part 6** 36. C 37. B 38. C 39. A 40. C 41. B 42. C 43. A 44. C 45. B

## Ⅲ Writing

46.

Mrs. Martha was born on 17 September, 1921. She was admitted on 23, April, 2009 and discharged on 10 May, 2009. There are still some problems to be solved after discharge. For example, she has been suffering from hypertension and degenerative bone disease. She needs to urinate frequently and is diagnosed with left pneumonia and urinary tract infection. Since she has no family members, she needs a bath seat and safety rails in the bathroom. She needs a nurse to visit her twice a week to monitor the medications. Finally she needs physiotherapy 3 times a week. By the way, she is a very independent-minded woman who is fully alert and articulate.

# 医护英语水平考试
# Medical English Test System（METS）
# Model Test2

姓名________　　准考证号________　　时间：120 分钟

## 考生须知

1. 严格遵守考场规则，考生得到监考人员指令后方可开始答题。

2. 答题前考生须将自己的姓名和准考证号写在试卷和答题卡上。

3. 答客观题时，一律用 2B 铅笔，按照答题卡上的要求答题。如要改动答案，必须用橡皮擦干净。

4. 答写作题时，必须用黑色签字笔在答题卡上答题。

5. 注意字迹清楚，保持卷面整洁。

6. 考试结束时将试卷和答题卡放在桌上，不得带走。待监考人员收毕清点后，考生方可离场。

※ 未经批准，本试卷任何单位或个人不得保留、复制和出版，违者必究。

# Ⅰ Listening

## Part 1

**Questions 1—5**

- You will hear five extracts from conversations on a ward.
- For questions 1—5, choose from the list A—F to show which case each intern is talking about. Use the letters only once. There is one extra letter which you do not need to use.
- You will hear each recording twice.

---

| | |
|---|---|
| Intern 1 | 1 |
| Intern 2 | 2 |
| Intern 3 | 3 |
| Intern 4 | 4 |
| Intern 5 | 5 |

A The little girl has symptoms such as fever, cough, sneezing, stuffed nose and sore throat.

B The patient's tachypnea was caused by a lung infection.

C The patient suffers from orthopnea.

D The patient is suffering from severe episodic headaches which are not relieved by aspirin or rest.

E There is a mass in the left breast of the patient.

F The patient is in coma several hours after a head trauma.

## Part 2

**Questions 6—13**

- You will hear a conversation between the patient and the doctor.
- Are the following statements "Right" or "Wrong"? If there is not enough information to answer "Right" or "Wrong", choose "Not Mentioned".
- You will hear the recording twice.

---

6 Mr. Button still suffers from pain when the doctor sees him.

A Right B Wrong C Not Mentioned

7 There is visible ulcer on the X-ray.

A Right B Wrong C Not Mentioned

8 The best way of treating ulcer is surgery.

A Right B Wrong C Not Mentioned

9 For young patients with ulcer, we prefer medical treatment to surgery.

A Right B Wrong C Not Mentioned

10 Ulcers tend to be passed from parents to children.

A Right B Wrong C Not Mentioned

11 The patient's mother is also suffering from ulcer.

A Right B Wrong C Not Mentioned

12 The patient is a heavy smoker and the doctor asks him to quit smoking.

A Right B Wrong C Not Mentioned

13 The patient will visit Mr. Oakes for further advice.

A Right B Wrong C Not Mentioned

# Part 3

**Questions 14—18**

- You will hear a conversation between the physician and the intern.
- For questions 14—18, choose the best answer.
- You will hear the conversation twice.

---

14 What disease is the patient suffering from?

A Gastric ulcer. B Duodenal ulcer. C Peptic ulcer.

15 What did the intern find on the physical exam?

A Abdominal distension and positive stool test.

B Muscle tension and abdominal distension.

C Epigastric tenderness and muscle guarding.

16 What are the complications of a duodenal ulcer?

A Irritability, perforation, distortion and penetration.

B Irregularity, obstruction, bleeding, erosion and perforation.

C Intractability to treatment, blockage, perforation, hemorrhage and penetration.

17 Which of the following descriptions about the history of the patient is NOT true?

A The bowel sounds were absent.

B There was no air under the diaphragm on abdominal film.

C There was no abdominal rigidity.

18 How can a doctor determine whether a patient has obstruction in the gastrointestinal tract?

A Nausea and vomiting occurs after meals.

B The patient vomits of overnight gastric residual and X-ray evidence confirms the diagnosis.

C The upper GI films reveal an ulcer crater present in the duodenal cap.

## Part 4

**Questions 19—25**

- You will hear a talk of the case history of Mrs. Jones, a patient.
- For questions 19—25, complete the notes. In each space write only one word.
- You will hear the talk twice.

THE ALEXANDRA HOSPITAL

**CASE NOTES**

| PATIENT DETAILS | |
|---|---|
| **Full Name**: Judy Jones **Age**: 26 | **Occupation**: driver |
| **Chief complaint** | (19)……… from nose and mouth since the previous night |
| **Present illness** | small, reddish spots on her lower (20)……… in the morning |
| **Past history** | upper(21)……… infection 2 weeks before admission |
| **Personal history** | denies fever, chills, nausea, (22)……… , abdominal pain, joint pain<br>Menses: (23)………<br>LMP: (24)……… weeks ago |
| **Family history** | no family history of abnormal bleeding |
| **Physical examination** | Consciousness: alert, oriented, anxious<br>Vital signs: BP 110/70 mmHg, P 90 bpm<br>Skin: multiple 1 mm flat reddish spots<br>Laboratory findings: CBC: normal<br>(25)……… count: 12000/mm³<br>PT & PTT: normal |

# Ⅱ Reading

## Part 1

**Questions 1—10**

- Read the following article about diabetes care.
- Choose the most suitable heading from the list A—K for each part (1—10) of the article. There is one extra heading which you do not need to use.
- Mark the correct letter A—K on your answer sheet.

## Diabetes care: 10 ways to avoid diabetes complications

Diabetes is a serious disease. Following your diabetes treatment plan takes round-the-clock commitment. But your efforts are worthwhile. Careful diabetes care can reduce your risk of serious—even life-threatening—complications.

Here are 10 ways to take an active role in diabetes care and enjoy a healthier future.

1 ________

Members of your diabetes care team—doctor, diabetes nurse educator and dietitian, for example—will help you learn the basics of diabetes care and offer support and encouragement along the way. But it's up to you to manage your condition. After all, no one has a greater stake in your health than you. Learn all you can about diabetes. Make healthy eating and physical activity part of your daily routine. Maintain a healthy weight. Monitor your blood sugar level, and follow your doctor's instructions for keeping your blood sugar level within your target range. Don't be afraid to ask your diabetes treatment team for help when you need it.

2 ________

If you smoke or use other types of tobacco, ask your doctor to help you quit. Smoking increases your risk of various diabetes complications, including heart attack, stroke, nerve damage and kidney disease. In fact, smokers who have diabetes are three times more likely to die of cardiovascular disease than are nonsmokers who have diabetes, according to the American Diabetes Association. Talk to your doctor about ways to stop smoking or to stop using other types of tobacco.

3 ________

Like diabetes, high blood pressure can damage your blood vessels. High cholesterol is a concern, too, since the damage is often worse and more rapid when you have diabetes. When these conditions team up, they can lead to a heart attack, stroke or other life-threatening conditions. Eating healthy foods and exercising regularly can go a long way toward controlling high blood pressure and cholesterol. Sometimes medication is needed, too.

4 ________

Your regular diabetes checkups aren't meant to replace yearly physicals or routine eye exams. During the physical, your doctor will look for any diabetes-related complications—including signs of kidney damage, nerve damage and heart disease—as well as screen for other medical problems. Your eye care specialist will check for signs of retinal damage, cataracts and glaucoma.

5 ________

High blood sugar can weaken your immune system, which makes routine vaccines more important than ever. Ask your doctor about: **Flu vaccine.** A yearly flu vaccine can help you stay healthy during flu season, as well as prevent serious complications from the flu.

**Pneumonia vaccine**. Sometimes the pneumonia vaccine requires only one shot. If you have diabetes complications or you're age 65 or older, you may need a five-year booster shot. **Other vaccines**. Stay up to date with your tetanus shot and its 10-year boosters, and ask your doctor about the hepatitis B vaccine. Depending on the circumstances, your doctor may recommend other vaccines as well.

6 ________

Diabetes may leave you prone to gum infections. Brush your teeth at least twice a day, floss your teeth once a day, and schedule dental exams at least twice a year. Consult your dentist right away if your gums bleed or look red or swollen.

7 ________

High blood sugar can damage the nerves in your feet and reduce blood flow to your feet. Left untreated, cuts and blisters can lead to serious infections. To prevent foot problems:

Wash your feet daily in lukewarm water. Dry your feet gently, especially between the toes.

Moisturize your feet and ankles with lotion. Check your feet every day for blisters, cuts, sores, redness or swelling. Consult your doctor if you have a sore or other foot problem that doesn't start to heal within a few days.

8 ________

Aspirin reduces your blood's ability to clot. Taking a daily aspirin can reduce your risk of heart attack and stroke—major concerns when you have diabetes. In fact, daily aspirin therapy is recommended for most people who have diabetes. Ask your doctor about daily aspirin therapy, including which strength of aspirin would be best.

9 ________

Alcohol can cause low blood sugar, depending on how much you drink and if you eat at the same time. If you choose to drink, do so only in moderation and always with a meal. Remember to include the calories from any alcohol you drink in your daily calorie count.

10 ________

If you're stressed, it's easy to neglect your usual diabetes care routine. The hormones your body may produce in response to prolonged stress may prevent insulin from working properly, which only makes matters worse. To take control, set limits. Prioritize your tasks. Learn relaxation techniques. Get plenty of sleep. Above all, stay positive. Diabetes care is within your control. If you're willing to do your part, diabetes won't stand in the way of an active, healthy life.

| | | |
|---|---|---|
| 1 ________ | A | Take stress seriously. |
| 2 ________ | B | Pay attention to your feet. |
| 3 ________ | C | If you drink alcohol, do so responsibly. |
| 4 ________ | D | Take daily aspirin. |
| 5 ________ | E | Don't smoke. |
| 6 ________ | F | Make a commitment to managing your diabetes. |
| 7 ________ | G | Keep your blood pressure and cholesterol under control. |
| 8 ________ | H | Schedule yearly physicals and regular eye exams. |
| 9 ________ | I | Stay active. |
| 10 ________ | J | Keep your vaccines up to date. |
| | K | Take care of your teeth. |

# Part 2

**Questions 11—15**

- Read the following passage.
- For questions 11—15, choose the answer (A, B, C or D) which you think fits best according to the text.
- Mark your answers on the answer sheet.

## Pain Relief in Labor

Most women require some method of pain relief in labor and some women later consider that the analgesia they had in labor was inadequate. The mental stress and tension which may accompany labor should never be underestimated. It is important to make a correct and safe choice of method in view of the needs of the patient and the facilities available. There is no doubt that knowledge of the process of labor and confidence in the doctors and midwives who attend her is of great value to the woman in labor and reduces the need for drugs. Patients should know that efficient methods of pain relief are available and, in general terms, what these are. Complex psychoprophylactic (心理预防的) and hypnotic methods may have their place but are not in general use. Any method which involves hyperventilation(通气过度) should be discouraged. Sedatives such as diazepam have no analgesic effect and their use during early labor is no substitute for adequate psychological preparation and support.

When uterine contractions become painful it is important that the first dose of an analgesic should be effective so that the woman's confidence is maintained. If the drug is given too little and too late, she becomes demoralized and analgesia is ineffective. Pethidine (哌替啶) 150 mg is generally a suitable first choice and subsequent injections of 100 mg can be given. A combination of pethidine and a phenothiazine (吩噻嗪) derivative may be indicated when anxiety is a prominent feature. When this combination is given, care must be taken not to produce hypotension, which is particularly liable to occur when the drugs are given intravenously.

Opiates(阿片类)can produce respiratory depression in the neonate but this is seldom severe with normal dosage. Morphine 15 mg causes more respiratory depression than pethidine but still has a valuable place because of its powerful analgesic effect. Papaveretum (阿片全碱) 20 mg is less liable to produce vomiting than morphine. Narcotic analgesics and sedatives have no effect on uterine contractions and do not alter the progress of labor.

11 Some women later think that the analgesia they were given in labor ________.

A was a method of pain relief

B was not strong enough to relieve the pain

C was considered to be adequate

D was effective in view of safety

12 There is no doubt that ________ is very valuable to the woman in labor.

A knowledge of the process of labor and confidence in the doctors

B knowledge of efficient methods of pain relief and drugs available

C confidence in the doctors and midwives who attend her

D confidence in the facilities available and the doctors' skill

13 All the following statements are true except that ________.

A the mental stress and tension often accompany the woman in labor

B the use of sedatives as diazepam has some analgesic effect in labor

C the woman in labor should know about the efficient methods of pain relief

D the hypnotic method has its place in labor but is seldom used

14 When uterine contractions become painful, ________.

A the first dose of an analgesic should be given as early as possible

B it is important for the woman in labor to cry for help

C it is important to make a correct and safe choice of method

D the first dose of an analgesic should be effective above all

15 Narcotic analgesics and sedatives ________.

A have no effect on uterine contractions but change the progress of labor

B have an effect on uterine contractions but do not alter the progress of labor

C have no effect on uterine contractions and do not alter the progress of labor

D have an effect on uterine contractions and change the progress of labor

# Part 3

**Questions 16—23**

• Read the following article on cardiopulmonary resuscitation.

• Are sentences 16—23 on the next page "Right" or "Wrong"? If there is not enough information to answer "Right" or "Wrong", choose "Not Mentioned".

- For each sentence 16—23 mark one letter A—C on your answer sheet.

## Cardiopulmonary Resuscitation

Cardiopulmonary resuscitation (CPR) is an emergency procedure used to resume breath and circulation by exerting artificial respiration and external cardiac massage. It is widely spread and taught among health care workers and the public.

The procedure of CPR follows an ABC rule, that is, A for airway, B for breathing and C for circulation. Assessment is the first step during the rescue and should be re-applied before and after each step. At the beginning of CPR, rescuer needs at first to gently shake the victim, shouting "Are you OK?" If the victim gives no response, emergency response system should be called at once for further help.

Before starting CPR, the victim should be carefully moved onto the back. Then open the airway by tilting the victim's head back with one hand and lifting the chin with the other hand. When head or neck injuries are suspected, choose the "jaw thrust" way. By holding the airway open, the rescuer needs to look at the victim's chest, listen for sounds of breathing and feel for air movement from the victim's noses and mouth.

If no regular breathing is detected, twice mouth-to-mouth or mouth-to-nose breathing rescue should be performed immediately. The artificial respiration should be delivered slowly. And also check for signs of effectiveness such as chest rise and air escape during exhalation.

Circulation assessment is followed after two breathing rescues. Index and middle fingers should be put between the trachea and muscle at the side of the neck for carotid pulse detection. When no normal pulse could be felt, chest compression needs to be initiated right away. The heel of one hand should be placed on the lower half of the sternum between the victim's nipples and the other on top of the first so as to keep the two hands parallel. 15 compressions should be performed continuously at a rate of 100 times per minute.

A one-minute rotation of 15 chest compressions and two rescue breaths should be performed before the second circulation assessment. If no sign of circulation is detected, the rotation needs to be replicated. If the victim resumes normal pulses, no more chest compressions are needed. Rescue breaths may be delivered if needed.

16 Cardiopulmonary resuscitation (CPR) is widely spread and taught among health care workers and the public.

A Right B Wrong C Not Mentioned

17 The significance of shouting "Are you OK?" to the victim is to ascertain the state of consciousness of the victim.

A Right B Wrong C Not Mentioned

18 Rescuer needs at first to quickly shake the victim to know whether he is in conscious at the beginning of CPR.

A Right B Wrong C Not Mentioned

19 The artificial respiration is the act of simulating respiration, which provides for the overall exchange of gases in the body by pulmonary ventilation, external respiration and internal respiration.

A Right B Wrong C Not Mentioned

20 Hematological system plays an important role in Cardiopulmonary resuscitation.

A Right B Wrong C Not Mentioned

21 The chest compression should be performed at a rate of 15.

A Right B Wrong C Not Mentioned

22 According to the passage, the "ABC" should be administered again for a victim under the condition of resumed consciousness.

A Right B Wrong C Not Mentioned

23 Tilting the head and lifting the chin should be performed when rescuing a victim with injured neck.

A Right B Wrong C Not Mentioned

# Part 4

**Questions 24—28**

- Read the following text about professional nurses. Seven sentences have been removed from the article.
- Choose from the sentences A—F the one which fits each space (24—28. There is one extra sentence which you do not need to use.
- For each space (24—28), mark one letter A—F on your answer sheet.

---

## Understanding Psychiatry

Psychiatry is undeniably a branch of Western medicine and our conception of psychiatric illness (and how best to treat it) is undoubtedly heavily influenced by Western social and cultural factors. (24) ________

Emil Kraepelin recognized this argument when he visited Java in 1896 and found that the clinical symptoms of "dementia praecox"(早发性痴呆症) could be seen in patients he met there, just as they were manifest in his own patients in Germany. It was not until the WHO International Pilot Study of Schizophrenia in 1973 that the incidence of schizophrenia (精神分裂症) (defined by narrow criteria) was found to be 0.7—1.4 per 10,000 aged 15—54 across all nine countries studied worldwide. (25) ________ These conclusions have been supported by a large number of epidemiological studies and similar results have been found for bipolar disorder.

(26) ________ The myth that these are predominantly Western diseases held sway for a long time, based on views of Western civilization articulated most eloquently by Freud in Civilization and its Discontents (1930).

Certain manifestations of emotional distress, termed "culture-bound syndromes" by PM Yap, a former professor of psychiatry in Hong Kong, are particular to different cultures. These present as mixed disorders of behaviour, emotions, and beliefs and may have local names. Some are clear symptom-correlates of disorders found in ICD-10 and DSM-Ⅳ; others have no Western equivalent but appear to be variations of somatoform, conversion, or dissociative disorders. (27) ________ However, as we move towards a more global society, "Western influences" appear to be making these types of disorder increasingly frequent in non-Western societies.

(28) ________ Understanding the biological underpinnings of the common disease entities (e. g. schizophrenia, bipolar affective disorder, depression, anxiety) and the development of treatments based upon our understanding of neurophysiological and neuropharmocological mechanisms will inform this debate. However, awareness of cultural issues as they impact upon an individual, their illness (and illness beliefs), and the relationship between psychiatry and patient, is critical if we are to successfully provide appropriate interventions.

A Despite the variations in the content of delusions and hallucinations (which were culturally derived) the form was found to be the same.

B If the patient with a mood disorder does not know how to contact a psychiatrist, he can begin by seeing his family practitioner or internist.

C Some Western disorders (e. g. deliberate self-harm) are rarely seen in non-Western countries.

D However, the scientific validity of these concepts can be readily tested if they can be shown to cross cultural boundaries.

E Debate continues as to whether Western diagnostic categories are universally valid.

F The manifestations of depressive, stress-related, and anxiety disorders show the greatest cultural variations.

# Part 5

**Questions 29—43**

- Read the following passage on wound care basis.
- Choose the best word (A, B, C or D) for each space.
- For each space 29—43, mark one letter A—D on your answer sheet.

## Wound Care Basis

Wound care is an important skill for everyone to (29)…… You never know when you or a loved one might get (30)……and knowing how to (31)……a wound properly is necessary. It is important that a wound (32)…… proper treatment in order to prevent infection from occurring.

Care must be taken to avoid infection, as infection not only will prolong the healing process but can also lead to life(33)……conditions if the infection becomes severe. Wounds must be cared for daily.

The first step in wound care treatment is to clean the wound thoroughly at (34) ……once a day, either with plain water or with a gentle skin cleanser. A good soaking in a bowl of sudsy (肥皂液的) water or with a nice warm damp cloth can help to loosen scabs and dry skin that surround the wound. Be sure not to scrub the wound or use abrasive (磨损的) cleansers that can (35)……the wound and prolong healing.

Applying antibiotic ointment(36)……the wound daily helps to expedite(促进) healing while helping to prevent infection and scarring. You may wish to consult (37) ……your physician for advice (38)……which topical ointment would be best for your specific wound. There are many over-the-counter(非处方的)ointments as well as prescription ones available.

Applying non-medicinal ointments, such as *petroleum* jelly, may also prove (39) …… Petroleum jelly helps to keep the skin moist and prevent any bandages or coverings from adhering to the wound and possibly injuring it further.

When selecting bandages, dry bandages and adhesive bandages should be (40) ……as they can stick to the wound. Silicon bandages work best, but it is important to know that they are the more expensive option. It is generally best to (41)……a wound covered while healing, but some scrapes may be left uncovered (42)…… antibiotic ointment is applied to help prevent infection from (43)……

| | A | | B | | C | | D | |
|---|---|---|---|---|---|---|---|---|
| 29 | A | hold | B | grasp | C | master | D | catch |
| 30 | A | hurt | B | damaged | C | injury | D | endure |
| 31 | A | attend to | B | tend to | C | prone to | D | predispose to |
| 32 | A | receives | B | receive | C | received | D | receiving |
| 33 | A | alarming | B | frightful | C | risky | D | threatening |
| 34 | A | least | B | most | C | best | D | better |
| 35 | A | impair | B | destroy | C | damage | D | injure |
| 36 | A | to | B | for | C | on | D | of |
| 37 | A | from | B | to | C | with | D | for |
| 38 | A | on | B | in | C | by | D | with |
| 39 | A | advantageous | B | beneficial | C | efficient | D | curable |

| | | | | |
|---|---|---|---|---|
| 40 | A avoided | B ignored | C resisted | D abandoned |
| 41 | A allow | B let | C leave | D permit |
| 42 | A even if | B as far as | C as soon as | D as long as |
| 43 | A exposure | B disclosure | C discovering | D revealing |

# Ⅲ Writing

**Question 44**
**Blood Donation Without Repayment**
**Outline:**
1. 无偿献血的人越来越多；
2. 无偿献血的意义；
3. 总结。

# Model Test 2 参考答案

## 听力部分录音稿

**This is METS listening test.**
**There are four parts in the test. Parts 1,2,3,and 4.**
**You will hear each part twice.**
**We will now stop for a moment before we start the test.**
**Please ask any questions now because you must not speak during the test.**

*Pause*(10 seconds)

**Now,look at the instructions for Part 1.**

*Pause*(3 seconds)

**You will hear five extracts from conversations on a ward.**
**For questions 1—5,choose from the list A—F which case each intern is talking about. Use the letter only once. There is one extra letter which you do not need to use.**
**You will hear each recording twice.**

*Pause*(3 seconds)

**Now we are ready to start.**

*Pause*(3 seconds)

**Conversation 1**

Mrs. Wilson is 50 years old and has had severe frontal headaches for the past five days. The headache comes on mostly when she gets nervous, lasting for one to two hours and not relieved by rest or aspirin. She has a history of headaches of five years' duration, but none as bad as the present ones. There is no nausea or vomiting accompanying the headaches. Over the past two weeks she has had blurred vision. There is no past history of convulsions or syncope. She does have dyspnea on exertion. There is no history of chest pain, paroxysmal, nocturnal dyspnea, orthopnea or ankle edema.

*Pause*(3 seconds)

**Conversation 2**

Mr. Roe is a 43-year-old office worker who apparently was in good health up to this morning. He tripped over an object, hit his head, and lapsed into unconsciousness lasting for a few hours. He seems to have been lucid for a few hours and was able to take a bus downtown. Then he was found slightly confused and after coming here lapsed into unconsciousness.

*Pause*(3 seconds)

**Conversation 3**

This is a five-year-old female who was apparently in good health until about four days prior to admission. At that time she began to sneeze and to complain of some nasal obstruction and a sore throat. Her cough was persistent and non-productive. The patient also has conjunctivitis with swelling and photophobia. She has had a fever for the past few days, and today it was 103 °F.

*Pause*(3 seconds)

**Conversation 4**

Mrs. Evans is well developed, well nourished, and appears to be her stated age. Physical examination shows a firm, fixed 2x2 cm painless mass in the upper outer quadrant of the left breast. There is slight skin retraction over this area. No nipple retraction, erosion, or discharge. There is no edema or injection over the site. The right breast is without masses. There is no adenopathy. The chest is clear. The rest of the physical exam is not remarkable.

*Pause*(3 seconds)

**Conversation 5**

I'll just explain to you what's happening with your husband's breathing. Mr. Sims has a fast respiratory rate at the moment, which is caused by the lung infection he's had for the past few weeks. He has very labored inspiration and expiration, which is why I've given him some oxygen.

*Pause*(3 seconds)

***Now you'll hear Part 1 again.***

**This is the end of Part 1.**

*Pause*(3 seconds)

**Now look at Part 2.**

**You will hear a conversation between the patient and the doctor.**

**Are the following statements "Right" or "Wrong"? If there is not enough information to answer "Right" or "Wrong", choose "Not Mentioned".**

**You will hear the recording twice.**

*Pause*(3 seconds)

**Doctor:** How are you, Mr. Button?

**Patient:** Not too good.

**Doctor:** Are you still getting the pain?

**Patient:** Yes.

**Doctor:** Well, the X-ray doctor found irritability and distortion of the duodenum although there was no actual ulcer visible on the X-ray.

**Patient:** Does that mean that I have no ulcer?

**Doctor:** Not necessarily. We have to decide the best way of treating it.

**Patient:** Like what?

**Doctor:** There are two ways: medical and surgical. In young people we try to avoid operations and we hope that medical means will help.

**Patient:** I'm glad to hear that.

**Doctor**: There is no risk attached to the operation, but we can't give a hundred per cent guarantee that it would relieve all your symptoms. Most patients get better after it and have no side effects. But with young people we usually persist with medical treatment. Has anyone in your family had an ulcer?

**Patient**: Yes, my father had one but it cleared up.

**Doctor**: Well, this could be relevant as ulcers may run in families. But there isn't much you can do about that as you can't choose your parents. The other factors, of course, are smoking, worry, anxiety, irregular meals, over-tiredness, overwork and stress. These all affect an ulcer. I'd like you to see Mr. Oakes. He has a great deal of experience with ulcer and I think we should take his advice. Now, have you managed to do anything about your smoking?

**Patient**: I smoke about 50 a day.

**Doctor**: I really think you should stop it right now.

**Patient**: I'll try, Doctor.

**Doctor**: Well, make an appointment to see Mr. Oakes and I'll write to him.

**Patient**: Thank you, Doctor.

*Pause*(3 seconds)

*Repeat*

*Pause*(3 seconds)

**This is the end of Part 2.**

**Now look at Part 3.**

**You will hear a conversation between the physician and the intern.**

**For questions 14—18, choose the best answer.**

**You will hear the conversation twice.**

*Pause*(3 seconds)

**Physician**: Have you had a chance to look over Mr. Morgan yet?

**Intern**: Yes, I just finished.

**Physician**: Why don't we sit down and talk about him for a few minutes?

**Intern**: Fine.

**Physician**: What do you think he has?

**Intern**: A duodenal ulcer.

**Physician**: Yes, I think I agree with that. What did you find on the physical exam?

**Intern**: The only positive signs were tenderness in the epigastrium, to both deep and superficial palpation, and voluntary epigastric muscle guarding. The stool was positive, and there were no gross findings that would lead me to believe that the patient was in shock.

**Physician**: These are the only things I found when I examined him this afternoon. What are the five complications of a duodenal ulcer?

**Intern**: Intractability to treatment, obstruction, perforation, hemorrhage, and penetration.

**Physician**: That's correct. We wouldn't say that he was intractable at the present time, because this should be reserved for those patients who have already received supervised therapy. Would you say that he had perforated?

**Intern**: No, not by the history. There was also no board-like rigidity of the abdomen. The bowel sounds were present, and the abdominal film revealed no air under the diaphragm.

**Physician**: Do you think he's obstructed?

**Intern**: I didn't get any history of vomiting after meals.

**Physician**: We would confirm this by the presence of an overnight gastric residual of greater than 50 ml, containing undigested food, and X-ray evidence. Did you ask him about alcoholic intake?

**Intern**: No, I forgot that.

**Physician**: He's been drinking about three to four cans of beer each night, and this certainly hasn't helped his status.

*Pause*(3 seconds)
*Repeat*
*Pause*(3 seconds)

**This is the end of Part 3.**
**Now look at Part 4.**
**You will hear a talk of the case history of Mrs. Jones, a patient.**
**For questions 19—25, complete the notes. In each space write only one word.**
**You will hear the talk twice.**

**Female**: Mrs. Jones, a 26-year-old driver presents herself to the emergency department on a Saturday afternoon with complaints of bleeding from her nose and mouth since the previous night. She has also noticed small, reddish spots on her lower extremities when she got out of the bed in the morning. She denies fever, chills, nausea, vomiting, abdominal pain, or joint pain. The patient reports developing an upper respiratory infection 2 weeks prior to the emergency room visit, which has now resolved. She denies significant medical problems. Her menses have been normal, and her last menstrual period was about 2 weeks ago. She denies excessive bleeding in the past, even after delivering her baby. She never had nose bleeding or bleeding into her joints prior to this episode. There is no family history of abnormal bleeding. The patient does not take any medication.

On examination, she is alert, oriented, somewhat anxious. Her blood pressure is 110/70 mmHg, her heart rate is 90 bpm, and her temperature is normal. No pallor or jaundice is noted. There is bright red oozing from the nose and the gingiva(齿槽). Skin exam reveals multiple 1 mm flat reddish spots in her lower extremities. The rest of the exam is normal. There is no enlargement of the liver or the spleen. Her CBC is normal except for a platelet count of 12000/$mm^3$. The PT and PTT are normal.

*Pause* (3 seconds)

*Repeat*

*Pause*(3 seconds)

**This is the end of Part 4.**

**You now have five minutes to write your answers on the answer sheet.**

*Pause*(4 minutes)

**You have one more minute.**

**This is the end of the test.**

## 参考答案

## Ⅰ Listening

**Part 1** 1. D 2. F 3. A 4. E 5. B

**Part 2** 6. A 7. B 8. C 9. A 10. A 11. B 12. A 13. A

**Part 3** 14. B 15. C 16. C 17. A 18. B

**Part 4** 19. bleeding 20. extremities 21. respiratory 22. vomiting 23. normal 24. two 25. Platelet

## Ⅱ Reading

**Part 1** 1. F 2. E 3. G 4. H 5. J 6. K 7. B 8. D 9. C 10. A

**Part 2** 11. B 12. A 13. B 14. D 15. C

**Part 3** 16. A 17. A 18. B 19. C 20. C 21. B 22. A 23. B

**Part 4** 24. D 25. A 26. F 27. C 28. E

**Part 5** 29. C 30. A 31. B 32. B 33. D 34. A 35. C 36. A 37. C 38. A 39. B 40. A 41. C 42. D 43. A

## Ⅲ Writing

44.

At present, blood donation has aroused considerable concern. In other words, blood donation is widely advocated in many countries including China. More and more people gather together in different areas to donate their blood without repayment.

It is a noble action for a person to donate blood without repayment. The action shows his love to his country and people, because the blood transfusion is saving thousands dying men every day. We firmly believe that it won't be the problem to keep adequate store of blood if more people join in as voluntary donators. On the other hand, blood donation does no harm to the donator's health. As we know, only health people are allowed to donate blood. After blood donation, his body will make a quick adjustment to let mechanism operate in its normal way.

Generally speaking, blood donation is a meaningful and selfless deed; it's unnecessary for people to be afraid of blood donation and blood donation should be encouraged.

# 医护英语水平考试
# Medical English Test System（METS）
# Model Test 3

姓名________　准考证号________　时间:120 分钟

## 考生须知

1. 严格遵守考场规则,考生得到监考人员指令后方可开始答题。

2. 答题前考生须将自己的姓名和准考证号写在试卷和答题卡上。

3. 答客观题时,一律用 2B 铅笔,按照答题卡上的要求答题。如要改动答案,必须用橡皮擦干净。

4. 答写作题时,必须用黑色签字笔在答题卡上答题。

5. 注意字迹清楚,保持卷面整洁。

6. 考试结束时将试卷和答题卡放在桌上,不得带走。待监考人员收毕清点后,考生方可离场。

※ 未经批准,本试卷任何单位或个人不得保留、复制和出版,违者必究。

# Ⅰ Listening

## Part 1

**Questions 1—5**

- You will hear five short conversations. Each conversation is followed by a statement.
- Are the statements "Right"(A) or "Wrong"(B)?
- For questions 1—5, tick (√) A or B.
- You will hear each conversation and statement twice.

**Example:**

| | | | | | | |
|---|---|---|---|---|---|---|
| 0 | A | Right | √ | B | Wrong | ☐ |
| 1 | A | Right | ☐ | B | Wrong | ☐ |
| 2 | A | Right | ☐ | B | Wrong | ☐ |
| 3 | A | Right | ☐ | B | Wrong | ☐ |
| 4 | A | Right | ☐ | B | Wrong | ☐ |
| 5 | A | Right | ☐ | B | Wrong | ☐ |

## Part 2

**Questions 6—10**

- Listen to Dr. Smith talking to a patient in the ward.
- Are the sentences (6—10) "Right" (A) or "Wrong" (B)?
- For questions 6—10, tick (√) A or B.
- You will hear the conversation twice.

**Example:**

0 The patient has pain all over. A Right ☐ B Wrong √

---

6 The patient vomits sometimes. A Right ☐ B Wrong ☐

7 The patient's pain in the abdomen started yesterday. A Right ☐ B Wrong ☐

8 The patient has a slight fever. A Right ☐

B Wrong ☐

9 The patient doesn't have pain in the stomach. A Right ☐

B Wrong ☐

10 The patient has to be checked in the abdomen. A Right ☐

B Wrong ☐

# Part 3

**Questions 11—15**

- Listen to a husband's description of his wife's disease to a doctor.
- For questions 11—15, tick (√) A,B or C.
- You will hear the talk twice.

**Example**:

0 The wife is A 25. ☐

B 30. ☑

C 48. ☐

---

11 The wife is sick in A the stomach. ☐

B brain. ☐

C heart. ☐

12 She has taken A x-ray examination. ☐

B neurological examination. ☐

C blood examination. ☐

13 Her state is getting A better. ☐

B unchanged. ☐

C worse. ☐

14 The child of the couple is A very little. ☐

B a boy. ☐

C a girl ☐

15 The husband wants A a psychiatric hospital treatment. ☐

B Doctor White's treatment. ☐

C Doctor Yang's treatment. ☐

## Part 4

**Questions 16—20**

- You will hear a nurse getting personal details from a patient.
- Listen and complete questions 16—20.
- You will hear the conversation twice.

| **Friendship Hospital**<br>**Admission Card** | **Date& Time**<br>9:00<br>15/4/2011 |
|---|---|
| **Surname** (16) ·············· | **First name** Bree |
| **DOB** (17) ·············· | **Gender** **F** |
| **Occupation** | **teacher** |
| **Marital status** | (18) ·············· |
| **Next of kin** | **Husband, John...** |
| **Contact No.** | (19) ·············· |
| Address | (20) ·············· |
| Family doctor | Dr. Zhang |

# Ⅱ Reading

## Part 1

**Questions 1—5**

- Read the following text and the list of headings.
- Choose a heading from the list A—F that best fits the meaning of each numbered part of the text (1—5).
- The first paragraph is not numbered.
- Mark the correct letter A—F on your answer sheet.

**Example:**

0 Improve the results of the medical experiment

| 0 | A ■ | B □ | C □ | D □ | E □ | F □ | G □ | H □ |
|---|---|---|---|---|---|---|---|---|

**Answer:**

**A. Ounces of water needed per day**

**B. Importance of water**

**C. Careful use of flavored water**

**D. Signs of dehydration**

**E. Supply of water**

**F. Necessity for bringing a bottle for water with you**

## The Drink Your Body Needs Most

The human body is estimated to be approximately 60% to 70% water. Blood is, of course, mostly water; our muscles contain a lot of water; many organs, such as lungs, liver, and brain all contain a lot of water.

1. ________

Water is needed to regulate body temperature and to provide the means for nutrients to travel to all our organs. Water also transports oxygen to our cells, removes waste, and protects our joints and organs.

2. ________

We lose water through urination, respiration, and by sweating. If you are physically very active, you lose more water than if you do not take much exercise. Symptoms of mild dehydration include chronic pains in joints and muscles, lower back pain, headaches, and constipation. A strong smell to your urine, along with a yellow color indicates that you are not getting enough water. Thirst is an obvious sign of dehydration and in fact, you need water long before you feel thirsty.

3. ________

A good way is to take your body weight in pounds and divide that number in half. That gives you the number of ounces of water per day that you need. For example, if you weigh 160 pounds, you should drink at least 80 ounces of water per day. If you exercise you should drink another 8-ounce glass of water for every 20 minutes you are active. If you drink coffee or alcohol, you should add at least an equal amount of water. When you are traveling on an airplane, it is good to have 8 ounces of water for every hour you are on board the plane.

4. ________

It may be difficult to drink enough water on a busy day. Therefore, be sure you have water handy at all times by keeping a bottle for water with you when you are working, traveling, or exercising. In this way, you can maintain enough water in your body and effectively avoid dehydration.

5. ________

If you get bored with plain water, you can add a bit of lemon in your water for a touch of flavor. There are, in the meantime, a lot of brands of flavored water available on the market, but you have to be very careful when you drink them as some of them have sugar or artificial sweeteners that you don't need or that might even do harm to you.

## Part 2

**Questions 6 —10**

- There are 5 short paragraphs below.
- For each paragraph put the italicized sentence into one of the three positions marked (A),(B),and (C).
- Mark the correct letter on your answer sheet.

**Example:**

0 ___C___ *The Red Cross is an international organization.*

---

6 ________ *They knew little about the process of pain itself.*

Pain is the most common reason we go to a doctor. It is the most common reason we take medicines. Until recently, however, most doctors knew of only a few drugs that stopped some pains. (A) But new knowledge about the process of pain is helping them to control pain better. Scientists have learned that the sense of pain is made up of both chemical and electrical signals. (B) Scientists also have learned that the nervous system sends two different kinds of pain messages to the brain: one very fast, the other slow. (C) The first message is the warning signal. It moves at a speed of 30 meters a second. In less than a second, the brain understands that part of the body is hurt and how badly it is injured.

7 ________ *Some have achieved even greater recognition and responsibility.*

The term "multidisciplinary" refers not only to the physicians who may participate as consultants in the ICU, but also to the other health care professionals who work side by side, around the clock in the ICU. (A) The most numerous of these are the critical care nurses, many of whom also have advanced training and certification in critical care and are recognized as CCRNs. (B) They are the acute care nurse practitioners and clinical nurse specialists who complement the physician staff in establishing plans, writing orders, and directing management. (C) Physician assistants also provide care in the ICU.

8 ________ *A case in point is the coal miners.*

People work or live in a specific environment. The environment may do harm to people's health. (A) In the past several decades, a lot of study has been made. (B) It makes people keenly aware of the relationship between environment and health. Studies have shown, for example, that industrial workers are more likely to have some kinds of cancer and other diseases if they are exposed to certain chemicals. (C) They once suffered from black lung disease when they were poorly protected from coal dust. The workplace may include other kinds of risk factors as well, such as high noise levels or increased emotional stress.

9 ________ *But it cannot reduce this output to zero, and some salt is always escaping.*

The human body demands that the amount of salt in the blood always stay the same. When the body does not get enough salt, it protects itself by letting less salt leave the body in urine and sweat. (A) On a completely saltless diet, like that of some people in Africa, the body steadily loses small amounts of salt through the kidneys and sweat glands. (B) It then tries to adjust to this loss by speeding up its secretion of water. In this way, the body attempts to keep the amount of salt in the blood at the necessary level. (C) The result is a slow drying up of the body and, finally, death. The person dies of thirst.

10 ________ *In addition, the nutritionist looks at the patient's mouth.*

In the physical exam, the nutritionist looks for external signs of malnutrition. (A) For one thing, the nutritionist looks at the patient's skin. Rough, dry skin, for example, may mean that the patient does not have enough vitamin A. (B) Cracks at the corner of the mouth, a purplish or bright red tongue, and bleeding gums can all be signs of vitamin deficiencies. (C) The nutritionist also notices the patient's hair. If a patient does not have enough protein, the hair may be thinner and duller than normal.

## Part 3

**Questions 11—15**

- The following paragraphs are given in a wrong order.
- For questions 11—15, you are required to reorganize these paragraphs into a coherent article by choosing from the list A—G to fill in each numbered blank.
- The first and the last paragraphs have been placed for you.
- Mark the correct letter A—G on your answer sheet.

**Example**

0 Order: G→11 __B__ →12 __A__ →13 __D__ →14 __C__ →15 __E__ →F

---

[A] In fact, more than a third of patients who had an operation in the last five years never reviewed the qualifications of the surgeon who operated. Patients are more likely to spend time researching a job change (on average, about 10 hours) or a new car (8 hours) than the operation they are about to receive or the surgeon who wields (使用，挥舞) the knife. And many patients are satisfied with the answers they receive from their surgeon or primary care doctor, whoever those individuals happen to be.

[B] There are consequences to that kind of "blind trust". "Today, medicine and surgery are really team sports," Dr. Russell continued, " and the patient, as the ultimate decision maker, is the most important member of the team. Mistakes can happen, and parents have to be educated and must understand what is going on."

[C] I felt curious about the survey, so I called Dr. Thomas Russell, executive director of the American College of Surgeons. "There is a tendency for patients not to get involved and not to feel forced to look into their surgery or surgeons," he told me.

[D] In other words, a healthy doctor-patient relation does not simply require good bedside manners and responsible office management on the part of the doctor. It also requires that patients should be educated about their doctors, their illness and their treatment.

[E] Trust is important. But as Sir Francis Bacon, who was among the first to understand the importance of gathering data in science, once said, knowledge is power.

[F] "If we are truly going to reform the health care system in the U. S.," Dr. Russell said, "everybody must participate actively and must educate themselves. That means doctors, nurses, other health care professionals, lawyers, pharmaceutical companies, and insurance companies. But most of all, it means the patient."

[G] Earlier this year, the American College of Surgeons, the national scientific and educational organization of surgeons, conducted a nationwide survey that found that the average patient devotes an hour or less to researching his or her surgery or surgeon. While prospective patients worry about the costs or complications of an operation, they don't necessarily look for information about their concerns.

Order: G→11 ____→12 ____→13 ____→14 ____→15 ____→E

---

## Part 4

**Questions 16—20**

- Complete the conversation between the doctor and the patient.
- Mark the correct letter A—H on your answer sheet.

**Example:**

Jenny: Good afternoon, Mr Paul, come in and have a seat.

Tim: 0 ··············

| 0 | A | B | C | D | E | F | G | H |
|---|---|---|---|---|---|---|---|---|
|  | □ | □ | □ | □ | □ | □ | □ | ■ |

Doctor: Where is your injury?

Patient: Here, my ankle.

Doctor: 16 ··············

Patient: I tripped over on the pavement and twisted it and it is swollen and very painful.

Doctor: When did it happen?

Patient: 17 ··············

Doctor: I'd like you to have an X Ray and after you have had it, come back to me.

Doctor: 18 ··············

Patient: Will I be able to walk soon?

Doctor: 19 ··············

Patient: What's that?

Doctor: Put your foot in hot and cold water in turn, three or four times a day. The pain and swelling should go, but if the pain is not eased, come and see me again.

Patient: 20 ··············

A Yes, in fact, I want you to do exercises and have walking sticks.

B How did it happen?

C Yes, that's right, doctor.

D This morning.

E If I'm out in a cold wind my eyes start running.

F OK. Thank you very much.

G Well, as nothing is broken, it is just a sprain. The nurse will put on some supporting bandage for you.

H Good afternoon, Dr. Green.

# Part 5

**Questions 21—27**

- Read the following sentences about how to instruct a patient to have a chest X-Ray check.
- Choose the best word marked A, B or C for each space (21-27)?
- Mark the correct letter A, B or C on your answer sheet.

**Example:**

21 ________ me your slip for fluoroscopic(荧光镜的,荧光检查法的) examination.

A Give B Bring C Take

22 Take off your clothes to the ________.

A head B waist C hip

23 Go and stand ________ the X-ray apparatus.

A behind B back C in front of

24 Keep your chest ________ the plate.

A against B on C in front of

25 Place your hands on the ________ and put the elbows ________.

A hips, up B waist, high C hips, forward

26 Now, breathe ________. Breathe out. Left turn slightly, please.

A slightly B heavily C usually

27 Please take this form to your ________ doctor.

A healing B treating C consulting

# Part 6

**Questions 28—35**

- Read the following passage about Mr. Anderson, an inpatient.
- Are sentences 28—35 "Right" or "Wrong"? If there is not enough information to answer "Right" or "Wrong", choose "Doesn't Say".
- For each sentence 28—35, mark one letter A—C on your answer sheet.

---

## Mr. Anderson

Mr. Anderson is not quite an active old man. He has been in hospital for three days, but it seems that he's quite unhappy here. He spends each day watching and observing, sometimes chatting a little with the nurses. Living in hospital is a great challenge to him.

Today he looks better. He is standing at the door of the ward alone, although both the reading room and the TV room are open. He is not interested at all. He said that he had read too much all his life and got tired of reading. And he doesn't like television, either. It's too noisy. Some nurses come and go in a hurry, and some talk to him a little.

Two patients are talking loudly at the window with great laughter. Mr. Anderson seems a little annoyed but he says nothing. He is still standing at the door, motionless. One of the two patients remarks to him, "Mr. Anderson, why not join us? We know you've read a lot, and we have a lot of questions to ask." Mr. Anderson smiles a little, and walks to them with quick steps. It seems living in the hospital is not so hard.

**Example**

0 Mr. Anderson is an inactive man.

A Right B Wrong C Doesn't Say

*Answer*:

| 0 | A ■ B □ C □ |
|---|---|

---

28 Mr. Anderson is a nurse in the hospital.

A Right B Wrong C Doesn't Say

29 Mr. Anderson has been in the hospital for a long time.

A Right B Wrong C Doesn't Say

30 Mr. Anderson read a lot when he was young.

A Right B Wrong C Doesn't Say

31 Mr. Anderson loves watching TV when he feels bored.

A Right B Wrong C Doesn't Say

32 Books and TV programs in the hospital are very interesting.

A Right B Wrong C Doesn't Say

33 The two patients are in the same ward with Mr. Anderson.

A Right B Wrong C Doesn't Say

34 Mr. Anderson doesn't want to talk with those patients.

A Right B Wrong C Doesn't Say

35 Living in hospital is hard for Mr. Anderson because he is very lonely.

A Right B Wrong C Doesn't Say

# Part 7

**Questions 36—45**

- Read the following passage.
- Choose the best word marked A, B or C for each space.
- For each space 36—45, mark one letter A—C on your answer sheet.

Anatomy and physiology are two important areas in the study of (0) ············ organisms. Anatomy is the study of an organism's form—(36) ············ is, its morphology. In animals and human anatomy, it (37) ············ the structure of organs. Physiology, on the (38) ············ hand, is the study of the function of organs and the body as a whole.

The word, anatomy, is derived(39)…………… the Greek word "anatomy". It means dissection. It is an old science where centuries ago, anatomical knowledge (40)…………… largely of observations of dissected plants and animals. In modern anatomy, it is (41)……………… important to identify areas of the body accurately. To do (42)……………, anatomical terms are used to (43)…………… to the body in certain position. For example, the term "superior" means above another structure and (44)……………such, one would say the heart is superior(45)……………the stomach.

**Example**

0 A live B living C alive

| *Answer*: | 0 | A ☐ B ■ C ☐ |
|---|---|---|

| | | | |
|---|---|---|---|
| 36 | A that | B it | C this |
| 37 | A meaning | B means | C meant |
| 38 | A one | B another | C other |
| 39 | A from | B by | C with |
| 40 | A consist | B consisted | C consists |
| 41 | A too | B also | C either |
| 42 | A it | B that | C so |
| 43 | A mean | B point | C refer |
| 44 | A so | B as | C in |
| 45 | A to | B above | C over |

# Ⅲ Writing

• Read the brief case note.

| | | |
|---|---|---|
| Surname: Pritt | | First Name: Grace |
| DOB: 3/7/86 | Sex: F | Marital Status: S |
| Occupation: waitress | | Contact No.: 88850031 |
| Family history: heart disease (mother's side) | | |
| Present complaint:<br>Agitation, difficulty in sleeping, appetite, ↑ wt ↓ | | |

| O/E |
|---|
| General Condition: |
| Sweaty skin, tachycardia, soft goiter with bruit |

- Write a summary about the patient on your answer sheet.
- You should write approximately 100 words.

# Model Test 3 参考答案

## 听力部分录音稿

**This is METS listening test.**
**There are four parts to the test. Part 1, 2, 3, and 4.**
**You will hear each part twice.**
**We will now stop for a moment before we start the test.**
**Please ask any questions now because you must not speak during the test.**

*Pause*(10 seconds)

**Now, look at the instructions for Part 1.**

*Pause*(5 seconds)

- **You will hear five short conversations. Each conversation is followed by a statement.**
- **Are the statements "Right" A or "Wrong" B?**
- **For questions 1—5, tick (√) A or B.**
- **You will hear each conversation and statement twice.**

**Here is an example:**
**Man:** Are you going to see Dr. Smith this afternoon?
**Woman:** Not until Friday morning.
**Statement:** The woman will go to see Dr. Smith Friday morning.

*Pause*(5 seconds)

**The answer is Right, so tick A in the box.**
**Now we are ready to start.**

*Pause*(5 seconds)

**Conversation 1**

**Man**: Welcome to my clinic. I'm Dr. Meats. Can I help you?

**Woman**: Yes, please. I'm Mr. Jones, and this is my son Daniel, who needs an operation in a few days.

**Statement**: The woman's operation is scheduled in a few days.

*Pause*(5 seconds)

*Repeat*

*Pause*(5 seconds)

**Conversation 2**

**Man**: You clearly know the therapy will not work; why do you still want to try it tomorrow?

**Woman**: How can I know without a try?

**Statement**: The woman will not try the therapy.

*Pause*(5 seconds)

*Repeat*

*Pause*(5 seconds)

**Conversation 3**

**Man**: The doctor gave me a prescription for some antibiotics.

**Woman**: Why don't we stop at the pharmacy on the way to work?

**Statement**: The woman suggests going to the drug store.

*Pause*(5 seconds)

*Repeat*

*Pause*(5 seconds)

**Conversation 4**

**Man**: Something went wrong with my teeth.

**Woman**: You'd better go and see a doctor.

**Statement**: The man is probably going to see a dermatologist.

*Pause*(5 seconds)
*Repeat*
*Pause*(5 seconds)

**Conversation 5**

**Man**: I pointed out a wrong diagnosis—that's all. Do you suggest we keep quiet about such things?
**Woman**: You know better than to ask that.
**Statement**: The woman means that the man should not ask such a question.

*Pause*(5 seconds)
*Repeat*
*Pause*(5 seconds)

**This is the end of Part 1.**

*Pause*(5 seconds)

**Now look at Part 2.**

*Pause*(5 seconds)

**Listen to Peter Long talking to a patient in the ward.**
**Are the sentences (6—10) "Right" (A) or "Wrong" (B)?**
**For questions 6—10, tick (√) A or B.**
**You will hear the conversation twice.**
**Patient (Woman)**: I have a pain in my abdomen.
**Doctor (Man)**: How long have you had it?
**Patient (Woman)**: It started in the morning. At the beginning I have a stomachache.
**Doctor (Man)**: How long did it last?
**Patient (Woman)**: About 3 hours, but this afternoon it moved to the lower right part of the abdomen for 5 hours.
**Doctor(Man)**: Have you had any vomiting?
**Patient (Woman)**: I have only nausea.
**Doctor(Man)**: Have you any diarrhea?
**Patient (Woman)**: No.
**Doctor (Man)**: Any fever?
**Patient (Woman)**: I don't know.

**Doctor (Man):** Let me take your temperature. All right, you have a slight fever.

**Doctor (Man):** Please lie down on the bed, loosen your belt, please. Let me examine your abdomen.

**Patient (Woman):** Thank you.

*Pause* (5 seconds)
*Repeat*
*Pause*(5 seconds)

**This is the end of Part 2.**

*Pause*(5 seconds)

**Now look at Part 3.**
**Listen to a husband's description of his wife's disease to a doctor.**
**For questions 11—15, tick (√) A, B or C.**
**You will hear the talk twice.**

*Pause*(5 seconds)

**Husband:** Doctor Yang, would you please help my wife? She sings and dances round the clock, sometimes just like an actress. And sometimes she laughs loudly as well as cries. Maybe she is mad. In very severe cases, she beat some persons and wanted to kill someone. She's been like this over one week, but her condition has been getting from bad to worse for a few days. We have taken a neurological examination. The result is not quite good. Doctor White said some further examinations should be done, including an electroencephalogram and a brain scan and so on because her condition was very serious. And he even suggested that she should go to a psychiatric hospital to be treated. I really don't want her to be in there. You know, she's so young, only 30 years old. And we have a 3 year-old child to take care of. Doctor, please help us. The child is waiting her at home and crying all day long.

*Pause*(5 seconds)
*Repeat*
**This is the end of Part 3.**

*Pause*(5 seconds)

**Now look at Part 4.**

**You will hear a nurse getting personal details from a patient.**

**Listen and complete questions 16—20.**

**You will hear the conversation twice.**

**P**: Excuse me, nurse. Is this the General Surgical Ward?

**N**: Yes, it is.

**P**: I'm Bree Sharp. I was notified to be here at half past 3.

**N**: Mrs. Sharp, please come in and take a seat. Let's fill in an admission card.

**N**: Your surname is Sharp. Would you mind spelling it, please?

**P**: S-H-A-R-P.

**N**: Thank you. And your first name?

**P**: Bree.

**N**: Your address?

**P**: 331 Chang'an Street, Beijing.

**N**: And your telephone number?

**P**: 88850011, Extention 202.

**N**: The date of your birth?

**P**: 1st June, 1983.

**N**: And what's your occupation?

**P**: I'm a teacher.

**N**: It says here, "Name and address of next of kin." Who is your nearest relation?

**P**: My husband, John Sharp.

**N**: And you live at the same address.

**P**: Yes.

**N**: Now, who is your family doctor?

**P**: Dr. Zhang.

**N**: And his address?

**P**: 70 Fuxing Road.

**N**: Do you know which doctor is in charge of your case?

**P**: I don't know.

**N**: It's Dr. Liu.

**P**: I see. Thank you.

**N**: If you would just wait here for a few minutes. I'll get a nurse to take care of you.

*Pause* (5 seconds)

*Repeat*

*Pause*(5 seconds)

**This is the end of Part 4.**

**You now have four minutes to write your answers on the answer sheet.**

*Pause*(4 minutes)

**You have one more minute.**

*Pause*(60 seconds)

**This is the end of the listening test.**

# 参考答案

## Ⅰ Listening

**Part 1** 1. B 2. B 3. A 4. B 5. A

**Part 2** 6. B 7. B 8. A 9. B 10. A

**Part 3** 11. B 12. B 13. C 14. A 15. C

**Part 4** 16. Sharp 17. 1st June, 1983 18. married 19. 88850011, Extention 202
20. 331 Changan Street, Beijing

## Ⅱ Reading

**Part 1** 1. B 2. D 3. A 4. F 5. C

**Part 2** 6. A 7. B 8. C 9. A 10. B

**Part 3** 11. A 12. C 13. B 14. D 15. F

**Part 4** 16. B 17. D 18. G 19. A 20. F

**Part 5** 21. A 22. B 23. C 24. A 25. C 26. B 27. C

**Part 6** 28. B 29. B 30. A′ 31. B 32. C 33. C 34. B 35. A

**Part 7** 36. A 37. B 38. C 39. A 40. B 41. B 42. C 43. C 44. B 45. A

## Ⅲ Writing

Miss Grace Pritt is a 25 year-old single woman. She serves as an actress. When asked about family history, she declared that her mother had heart disease. She complained that she felt easily angered. And she had difficulty in sleeping. What's worse, although she had great appetite these days, she was losing weight. After her primary diagnosis, the doctor found that she had sweaty skin, and some other problems such as tachycardia and soft goiter with bruit. These may be the cause of her problems. The hospital may contact her by calling 88850031 if she got more serious problems.

# References


[1] 邱懋如.护士常用英语会话[M].上海:上海外语教育出版社,1990.

[2] 刘慎军.医学英语 900 句[M].北京:中国书籍出版社,2002.

[3] 史学敏.涉外护理英语阅读与写作[M].北京:外语教学与研究出版社,2007.

[4] 何祖佳.现代护理英语教程[M].北京:科学出版社,2005.

[5] 邵循道,周璐玲.英语[M].北京:人民卫生出版社,1978.

[6] Jimmy Lin.涉外护理英语情景对话[M].北京:外语教学与研究出版社,2006.

[7] 彭丽.现代医护英语[M].重庆:重庆大学出版社,1998.

[8] 李敏.专业英语[M].北京:高等教育出版社,2005.

[9] 曹红.护理英语[M].北京:高等教育出版社,2005.

[10] 雷慧.护理英语[M].北京:中国医药科技出版社,1993.

[11] 陈迎.新职业英语医护英语[M].北京:外语教学与研究出版社,2009.

[12] 田祥斌.医用拉丁文[M].北京:中国医药科技出版社,1993.

[13] 章国斌.药学英语[M].上海:复旦大学出版社,2007.

[14] 华仲乐.医院情景英语口语[M].北京:高等教育出版社,2005.

[15] 冯桂冰.中医英语[M].北京:高等教育出版社,2007.

[16] 张燕,章国英.医学英语视听说教程[M].北京:高等教育出版社,2008.

[17] 刘航.护理英语[M].北京:高等教育出版社,2004.

[18] 江晓东.实用护理英语[M].重庆:重庆大学出版社,2008.

[19] 何萍.医学基础英语[M].重庆:重庆大学出版社,2008.

[20] Coco C D. Intravenous Therapy[M]. London: The C. V. Mosby Company, 1908.

[21] Richards P. Clinical Medicine and Therapeutics[M]. London: Blackwell, 1979.

[22] Brasnett C. English for Medical Students[M]. London: Methuen Educational, 1976.

[23] Charles J. Medicine [M]. Washington, D. C.: English Language Services, INC., 1973.

[24] Maclean J. English in Basic Medical Science[M]. London: Oxford University Press, 1975.

[25] http://www. naturalnews. com/027981_doctors_hand_washing. html

[26] http://www. floridahospital. com/AboutUs/Mission/OurStories/2009Archive/12212009. aspx

[27] http://stopstigma. samhsa. gov/publications/collegelife. aspx

[28] http://www. njha. com/myhospstory/fullstory. aspx? id=22

[29] http://www. cdc. gov/flu

[30] http://abcnews. go. com/Nightline/SwineFluNews/swine flu-stories-young-victims-h1n1

[31] http://abclocal. go. com/wabc/story? section=news/health&id=7452793

[32] http://www. 51voa. com/VOA _ Standard _ English/VOA _ Standard _ English _ 36856. html

[33] http://www1.voanews.com/english/news/Antibiotic-Resistance
[34] http://www.njha.com/myhospstory/fullstory.aspx? id=12
[35] China Daily 2011-01-14 07:59 By Shan Juan
[36] http://www.doctorswithoutborders.org/news/article
[37] China Daily 2011-01-11 14:25 By Lian Mo
[38] http://hubpages.com/hub/My-Visit-to-a-TCM-Doctor-in-Beijing By BkCreative
[39] http://www.wwenglish.com/en/voa/spec/2010/01/2010010635496.htm
[40] http://www.njha.com/myhospstory/archive.aspx
[41] http://www.wwenglish.com/en/voa/spec/2010/03/2010030336086.htm
[42] http://funlok.com/index.php/inspiration/hospital-window-story.html
[43] http://www.headacheaustralia.org.au/management_of_headache